CORRECTIVE FEEDBACK IN SECOND LANGUAGE TEACHING AND LEARNING

Bringing together current research, analysis, and discussion of the role of corrective feedback in second language teaching and learning, this volume bridges the gap between research and pedagogy by identifying principles of effective feedback strategies and how to use them successfully in classroom instruction. By synthesizing recent works on a range of related themes and topics in this area and integrating them into a single volume, it provides a valuable resource for researchers, graduate students, teachers, and teacher educators in various contexts who seek to enhance their skills and to further their understanding in this key area of second language education.

Hossein Nassaji is Professor of Applied Linguistics in the Department of Linguistics at the University of Victoria, Canada.

Eva Kartchava is Assistant Professor of Applied Linguistics and TESL in the School of Linguistics and Language Studies at Carleton University, Canada.

ESL & Applied Linguistics Professional Series
Eli Hinkel, Series Editor

Nassaji/Kartchava, Eds.
Corrective Feedback in Second Language Teaching and Learning: Research, Theory, Applications, Implications

Bitchener/Storch/Wette, Eds.
Teaching Writing for Academic Purposes to Multilingual Students: Instructional Approaches

Macalister/Mirvahedi, Eds.
Family Language Policies in a Multilingual World: Opportunities, Challenges, and Consequences

Hinkel, Ed.
Handbook of Research in Second Language Teaching and Learning, Volume III

Ortmeier-Hooper/Ruecker
Linguistically Diverse Immigrant and Resident Writers: Transitions from High School to College

Johnson/Golombek
Mindful L2 Teacher Education: A Sociocultural Perspective on Cultivating Teachers' Professional Development

Hinkel
Teaching English Grammar to Speakers of Other Languages

Visit www.routledge.com/education for additional information on titles in the ESL & Applied Linguistics Professional Series

CORRECTIVE FEEDBACK IN SECOND LANGUAGE TEACHING AND LEARNING

Research, Theory, Applications, Implications

Edited by Hossein Nassaji and Eva Kartchava

Routledge
Taylor & Francis Group

NEW YORK AND LONDON

First published 2017
by Routledge
711 Third Avenue, New York, NY 10017

and by Routledge
2 Park Square, Milton Park, Abingdon, Oxon, OX14 4RN

Routledge is an imprint of the Taylor & Francis Group, an informa business

Library of Congress Cataloguing in Publication Data
A catalog record for this book has been requested.

ISBN: 978-1-138-65728-1 (hbk)
ISBN: 978-1-138-65729-8 (pbk)
ISBN: 978-1-315-62143-2 (ebk)

Typeset in Bembo
by Deanta Global Publishing Services, Chennai, India

CONTENTS

ACKNOWLEDGMENTS

We would like to offer our sincere thanks and gratitude to the contributors of this collection. Without their belief in the project and willingness to work tirelessly to deliver state-of-the-art chapters, this volume would not have been possible. We would also like to express our gratitude to the editorial team at Routledge, in particular Eli Hinkel and Naomi Silverman, for recognizing the need for such a collection and their unwavering support in making sure that the book gets off to a good start and was published in time. We appreciate all their guidance throughout the process. In addition, we are grateful to the anonymous reviewers of the book proposal forwarded to Routledge for their helpful and supportive comments and suggestions.

The collection before you is a joint effort to produce a volume on corrective feedback that speaks to both researchers and language teachers alike. While the ideas presented here are varied and many require further investigation, we hope that this collection may represent a point from which additional discussions, considerations, and questions about corrective feedback originate.

INTRODUCTION

Hossein Nassaji and Eva Kartchava

The Role of Corrective Feedback: Theoretical and Pedagogical Perspectives

The issue of how to correct learner errors has long been of interest not only to teachers but also to researchers. Corrective feedback refers to utterances that indicate to the learner that his or her output is erroneous in some way. Chaudron (1988) defined corrective feedback as "any teacher behavior following an error that minimally attempts to inform the learner of the fact of error" (p. 150). This behavior may overtly elicit a response from the learner and hence may result in self-correction or may correct the error in ways that the learner may not realize that a response is needed. Corrective feedback can be provided both orally and in written form and in response to a range of errors, including linguistic, content, organization, and even discourse and pragmatic errors.

Although corrective feedback is considered an important aspect of second language (L2) pedagogy, there has been considerable controversy over its role and usefulness in both L2 acquisition and instruction. Theoretically, the argument for the role of corrective feedback relates closely with the notion of whether or not there is a need for negative evidence in language acquisition (Nassaji, 2015). Negative evidence is defined as information that tells the learner what is not possible in a given language. This has been contrasted with positive evidence, which refers to the information that tells the learner what is possible in a given language. Positive evidence is received mainly through naturalistic exposure to language input or input that has been modified or simplified for the purpose of comprehension (e.g., Gass, 2003; Long, 1996). Negative evidence can be obtained in various ways. It can be obtained through explanation or presentation of grammatical rules and can also be obtained in the form of corrective feedback on learner errors (Long, 1996). Such feedback can be provided both directly through overt correction or indirectly through strategies that signal to the learner that his or her utterance may contain an error, such as repetition of the learner error or clarification requests, confirmation checks, and other indications of failure to understand the message by the interlocutor (Nassaji, 2015).

While many researchers have argued that corrective feedback is needed and plays a crucial role in the development of linguistic knowledge, there are others who have contended that there is no need for it and that it has little impact on the acquisition of L2 knowledge. One such position, for example, is the nativist position, which posits that what drives language learning are some biologically innate linguistic principles called Universal Grammar (UG). In this view, learning becomes possible when the UG principles are triggered by exposure to instances of natural language use or positive evidence only. The role of negative evidence is downplayed because if learners have access to UG, corrective feedback hardly plays a role (e.g., Flynn, 1988, 1996; Schwartz, 1993; White, 1991). Other researchers, however, who have taken a cognitive or an interactionist perspective, have argued that corrective feedback is not only available in the L2 environment but is also necessary for successful L2 acquisition (e.g., Doughty & Long, 2003; Doughty & Williams, 1998a; Gass, 2003; Gass & Mackey, 2006; Long, 1991, 1996; Long & Robinson, 1998; Schachter, 1991). Doughty and Williams (1998b), for example, argued that "second language learning is not identical to first language learning, and so we do not consider leaving learners to their own devices to be the best plan" (p. 197).

Error correction has not only been a debatable topic theoretically; language teaching methodologies have also varied considerably regarding their stance on the role and usefulness of error correction (Nassaji, 2015). For example, Communicative Language Teaching (CLT), particularly in its strong version, has emphasized that teaching must be primarily meaning-focused with no explicit correction. This approach defines the aim of language learning as acquiring communicative ability, that is, the ability to use and interpret meaning in real-life communication. Thus, it emphasizes that teaching should also be primarily meaning-focused and based on communicative language use. The assumption is that if learners have sufficient opportunities to use the language for communicative purposes, they will be able to master the language successfully without any explicit instruction. As a result, corrective feedback is deemed unnecessary.

On the other hand, some other teaching approaches such as the cognitive code method and the focus on form approaches have emphasized the importance of error correction. From a cognitive perspective, learning is a process of creating a mental representation of the language through cognitive processes such as association, or discovering regular patterns from exemplars, and abstracting generalizations (e.g., Ellis, 1994). In this view, corrective feedback is crucial because it helps learners to construct a correct mental representation of the target language. Also, since learning takes place through problem-solving and making and trying out hypotheses, feedback is essential as it helps learners to refine their hypothesis (Celce-Murcia, 2001; 1991). From a focus on form perspective, noticing and attention to form is required for effective language learning. In this view, corrective feedback is beneficial because it not only provides learners with negative evidence but also helps learners notice the gap between their non-targetlike L2 production and the targetlike form (Long, 1996). Since corrective feedback occurs in response to learners' errors, attention to form occurs at the time when needed. Thus, the feedback provides learners with opportunities for form-meaning mapping, required for L2 learning (e.g., Doughty & Varela, 1998; Long & Robinson, 1998).

Due to varying theoretical and pedagogical viewpoints, a considerable amount of research in both past and present has focused on examining the effects of corrective feedback on L2 learning. Empirical research in this area has been both descriptive and experimental and has been conducted in various contexts, with various learners and on various types of feedback. This research has examined a variety of issues including not only those related to whether corrective feedback assists language acquisition but also the differential effects of different types of feedback and the mechanisms underlying their effectiveness. It has also addressed a number of other key issues such as the role of peer feedback, learners' and teachers' perspectives, and the various individual learner differences. Current research has even extended this line of research by examining the effects of feedback in various technology-mediated settings and comparing these effects with those in traditional face-to-face interactions. Although there are still many questions about how and when to provide effective feedback, research has provided increasing evidence that corrective feedback plays a crucial role in second language learning and teaching. In particular, considerable research suggests that L2 learners, particularly adults, can not develop native-like accuracy based on mere exposure to models of grammatical input and that they need corrective feedback in order to acquire an L2 successfully.

The Aim of this Book

The aim of this edited volume is twofold. One aim is to synthesize recent works on a range of corrective feedback topics that have been the focus of current research, and integrate them into a single volume that can serve as a resource for those interested in error correction and feedback in various contexts. Although there are many studies on corrective feedback and their results have been published in numerous individual journal articles and book chapters, there is not yet a collection that brings together the findings of these investigations and/or discusses their implications for theory and research. This edited volume intends to fill this gap by contributing to the knowledge accumulated over the years in the various areas of corrective feedback. Another major aim is to connect theory, research, and practice. Although many studies have investigated corrective feedback, there is clearly a missing link between the findings of this research and what is actually practiced in many L2 classrooms. Thus, this books aims to address this gap too, by identifying the principles of effective feedback and discussing how to use it successfully in classroom instruction.

To meet its goals, the book brings together cutting-edge research and state-of-the-art articles that address recent developments in theory and research on a range of core corrective feedback areas, including oral, written, and computer-assisted feedback, as well as studies of learner and teacher perceptions, the timing of feedback, and the role of non-verbal feedback. The contributors include expert researchers who have conducted research in each of the specific areas covered as well as those who have applied and tested their implications in practice. They each explore their own topic and identify the implications of their examination for classroom instruction.

The Organization of the Book

The book consists of four parts and eleven chapters. Part 1 focuses on oral feedback. Chapter 1, "Oral corrective feedback in L2 classrooms: What we know so far," by Ellis sets the tone for the book by discussing and reviewing current research related to the five key questions posed by Hendrickson (1978): (1) Should learner errors be corrected? (2) When should learners' errors be corrected? (3) Which errors should be corrected? (4) How should errors be corrected? and (5) Who should do the correction? The chapter concludes by examining the advice often given to teachers in light of current research. In Chapter 2, Sato examines the role of peer feedback. It explores various aspects of peer feedback including its affective, social and cognitive dimensions and how they affect the usefulness of such feedback. Among the factors, the author argues that learners' mindset and the social dynamics of peer interaction are the two most important factors affecting the impact of peer feedback. The chapter concludes with suggestions for how to increase the efficacy of peer feedback in L2 instruction. Quinn and Nakata (Chapter 3) examine the timing of oral feedback. Feedback timing is both a pedagogically and theoretically important issue in the field of L2 corrective feedback and concerns at what time feedback should be provided to be optimally effective, for example, whether it should be provided immediately after an error is made or whether it should be provided with some delay. The chapter begins by examining the theoretical and empirical research related to feedback timing and ends with suggestions for further research and classroom teaching.

Due to the increasing use of technology in language teaching, an examination of the role of the computer in facilitating and providing feedback has recently received considerable attention. Thus, Part 2 deals with computer-mediated feedback. Chapter 4, by Heift and Hegelheimer, addresses the role of feedback in Computer-Assisted Learning (CALL). The focus is on feedback in two contexts: in tutorial CALL programs and in various Automatic Writing Evaluation

(AWE) systems. The chapter reviews research and its findings and examines their implications for classroom teaching. In Chapter 5, Storch also explores the role of feedback in computer-mediated settings, but the focus is on peer feedback when provided in computer-mediated collaborative writing tasks through online tools such as wikis or Google Docs. The chapter reviews research in these areas and discusses how such platforms could be used most effectively to promote opportunities for peer feedback. Ziegler and Mackey (Chapter 6) address the use of interactional feedback in synchronous computer-mediated communication (SCMC). The chapter provides a review of the current research in a variety of such contexts, including Web 2.0 and multi-media learning. It also discusses the similarities and differences between feedback in such settings and in face-to-face interaction. Finally, the chapter draws out the implications of such research for classroom teaching.

Part 3 deals with the role of written feedback. In Chapter 7, Tigchelaar and Polio focus on the role of peer feedback in writing. They begin by examining the existing beliefs in the literature regarding the use and effectiveness of peer feedback and then review research and its implications for classroom instruction and future research. Chapter 8 by Nassaji discusses the role of negotiated feedback in response to written errors. Being framed within an interactionist and a socio-cultural perspective, the chapter argues that in addition to written feedback oral feedback can also be used as an option to address written errors. The chapter reviews current research in this area and concludes with a discussion of its implications for classroom teaching and learning. In Chapter 9, Bitchener addresses when and how written feedback can facilitate L2 development. To this end, the author reviews various conditions that have been considered necessary for effective feedback and also the factors that can account for feedback failure. He then concludes with recommendations of this discussion for future research and classroom pedagogy.

Part 4 deals with other important issues in corrective feedback: teacher beliefs and perspectives and the role of non-verbal feedback. Li (Chapter 10) provides a combination of a meta-analysis and narrative review of research on teachers' and learners' beliefs and opinions about corrective feedback. The data were analyzed with respect to the five key questions posed by Hendrickson (1978) mentioned earlier and a number of other important feedback dimensions such as the effects of training, the relationship between teachers' beliefs and their practice, and the role of learners' attitudes on the effectiveness of feedback. Research findings related to these issues are discussed and their implications for classroom teaching are considered. The final chapter (Chapter 11) deals with non-verbal feedback. Loewen and Nakatsukasa begin by discussing how non-verbal cues can be used in classroom interaction in ways that can provide corrective feedback. With a focus on gestures, they review a number of both descriptive and experimental studies in this area and examine their implications for how teachers can incorporate non-verbal feedback into their classroom teaching. The authors argue that since non-verbal feedback does not necessitate verbal explanation, it can be used as a time-saving strategy in L2 classrooms.

The Audience

The book provides a key resource for all those interested in gaining insight into the role of corrective feedback in L2 learning and how it can be used to enhance L2 teaching. The role of corrective feedback and how it assists language acquisition is an issue of considerable theoretical and empirical importance in the field of second language acquisition (SLA). Thus, one major audience of the book is SLA students and researchers. The book helps these readers to be informed of current theoretical and empirical advances in this vibrant area of SLA research. It also provides them with a framework that can stimulate further research in this area. Since the volume provides theme-based chapters in different areas of feedback, it can be used as a stand-alone text or each chapter can be used as an independent resource. Since the treatment of learner error is also an important aspect of any second language class-room, another major audience is teachers and teacher educators as well as those in teacher preparatory or in-service professional development programs. Because the book provides a comprehensive survey of the state of knowledge in corrective feedback areas and their implications for pedagogy, it helps these readers to develop not only an understanding of the different ways in which and the means by which errors can be corrected, but also how to integrate them into classroom teaching. Finally, the chapters are written in a very accessible way and do not assume a great deal of prior knowledge. Therefore, the book will also appeal to undergraduate students in applied linguistics who do not have a strong background in SLA. By drawing on recent developments in theory and research, the book helps these read-ers to develop a good understanding of the nature of corrective feedback and the implications of the research in this area for second language learning and teaching.

References

Celce-Murcia, M. (2001). Language teaching approaches: An overview. In M. Celce-Murcia (Ed.), *Teaching English as a second or foreign language* (pp. 3–11). Boston, MA: Heinle & Heinle.

Celce Murcia, M. (1991). Grammar pedagogy in second and foreign language teaching. *TESOL Quarterly*, 25, 459–480.

Chaudron, C. (1988). *Second language classrooms*. Cambridge: Cambridge University Press.

Doughty, C., & Long, M. (2003). Optimal psycholinguistic environments for distance for-eign language learning. *Language Learning & Technology*, 7, 50–80.

Doughty, C., & Varela, E. (1998). Communicative focus on form. In C. Doughty & J. Williams (Eds.), *Focus on form in classroom second language acquisition* (pp. 114–138). Cambridge: Cambridge University Press.

Doughty, C., & Williams, J. (1998a). Issues and terminology. In C. Doughty & J. Williams (Eds.), *Focus on form in classroom second language acquisition* (pp. 1–10). Cambridge: Cambridge University Press.

Doughty, C., & Williams, J. (1998b). Pedagogical choices in focus on form. In C. Doughty & J. Williams (Eds.), *Focus on form in classroom second language acquisition* (pp. 197–261). Cambridge: Cambridge University Press.

Ellis, N. (1994). *Implicit and explicit learning of languages*. London, San Diego, CA: Academic Press.

Flynn, S. (1988). Nature of development in L2 acquisition and implications for theories of language acquisition in general. In S. Flynn & W. O'Neill (Eds.), *Linguistic theory in second language acquisition* (pp. 277–294). Dordrecht: Kluwer.

Flynn, S. (1996). A parameter-setting approach to second language acquisition. In W. Ritchie & T. Bhatia (Eds.), *Handbook of second language acquisition* (pp. 121–158). San Diego, CA: Academic Press.

Gass, S. (2003). Input and interaction. In C. Doughty & M. Long (Eds.), *The handbook of second language acquisition* (pp. 224–255). Oxford: Blackwell.

Gass, S., & Mackey, A. (2006). Input, interaction and output: An overview. *AILA Review*, 19, 3–17.

Hendrickson, J. (1978). Error correction in foreign language teaching: Recent theory, research, and practice. *Modern Language Journal*, 62, 387–398.

Long, M. (1991). Focus on form: A design feature in language teaching methodology. In K. DeBot, R. Ginsberge & C. Kramsch (Eds.), *Foreign language research in cross-cultural perspective* (pp. 39–52). Amsterdam: John Benjamins.

Long, M. (1996). The role of the linguistic environment in second language acquisition. In W. Ritchie & T. Bhatia (Eds.), *Handbook of second language acquisition* (pp. 413–468). San Diego, CA: Academic Press.

Long, M., & Robinson, P. (1998). Focus on form: Theory, research and practice. In C. Doughty & J. Williams (Eds.), *Focus on form in classroom language acquisition* (pp. 15–41). Cambridge: Cambridge University Press.

Nassaji, H. (2015). *Interactional feedback dimension in instructed second language learning*. London: Bloomsbury Publishing.

Schachter, J. (1991). Corrective feedback in historical perspective. *Second Language Research*, 7, 89–102.

Schwartz, B. (1993). On explicit and negative data effecting and affecting competence and linguistic behavior. *Studies in Second Language Acquisition*, 15, 147–163.

White, L. (1991). Adverb placement in second language acquistion: Some effects of positive and negative evidence in the classroom. *Second Language Research*, 7, 133–161.

PART I

Oral Corrective Feedback

1

ORAL CORRECTIVE FEEDBACK IN L2 CLASSROOMS

What We Know so Far

Rod Ellis

Introduction

Corrective feedback (CF) is an aspect of language pedagogy that is important for both teachers and second language acquisition (SLA) researchers. Teachers are concerned with whether they should correct learners' errors and, if so, when and how. SLA researchers are interested in testing theories of second language (L2) acquisition which make differing claims about the effect that CF has on acquisition and which type is the most effective. CF, then, constitutes an 'interface issue' by bringing together the concerns of teachers and researchers. It is perhaps for this reason that CF has attracted enormous interest over the years, as reflected both in teacher guides such as Hedge (2000) and Scrivener (2005) and in the plethora of research articles in both theoretically oriented journals such as *Studies in Second Language Acquisition* and *Language Learning* and more teaching-oriented journals such as *TESOL Quarterly* and *Language Teaching Research*. Potentially, then, CF constitutes an issue where the insights of teachers and researchers can be mutually informing. What we know about CF requires considering both what experienced teachers have to say about it and what researchers have found out through their research.

There are some notable differences in the perspectives of teachers and researchers. One key difference is that teacher-oriented discussions of feedback consider both positive and negative (corrective) feedback, whereas researchers have focused exclusively on CF. Positive feedback is feedback that provides "an affirmation of the content or correctness of a learner utterance" (Nassaji, 2015, p. 11) and is intended to provide the learner with affective support. Teacher guides often emphasize the importance of positive feedback. Nunan (1991), for example, devotes more attention to positive than corrective feedback, noting that it serves the dual function of letting students know that they have performed correctly and increasing motivation through praise. Teachers and teacher educators see CF as potentially damaging because it can lead to defensiveness in the learner. Thus, they propose it should occur in "an atmosphere of support and warm solidarity" (Ur, 1996, p. 255). In contrast, SLA researchers are concerned only with the cognitive dimension of CF, as they are interested in whether it facilitates acquisition.[1]

In the following sections of this chapter, I will draw on an early article by Hendrickson (1978) to examine what teachers and researchers 'know' about five key aspects of CF.

1. Should learners' errors be corrected?
2. When should learners' errors be corrected?
3. Which errors should be corrected?
4. How should errors be corrected?
5. Who should do the correcting?

I will draw on some popular teacher guides as evidence of what experienced teacher educators have to say about these issues and on published articles that have investigated CF. As I address each issue, I will not try to resolve potential conflicts in the 'knowledge' that these two sources of evidence provide, but in the conclusion to the chapter I will venture some general statements about what we know about CF.

Should Learners' Errors be Corrected?

CF has always been viewed with some suspicion in language pedagogy. Some language teaching methods reject it. According to the Audiolingual Method, errors should be prevented through strict control of learner output, thus removing the need for CF, which was viewed as a form of punishment that can inhibit learning. The humanistic approaches that appeared in the 1970s also advocated against correction on the grounds that it was judgmental and would have a negative impact on the positive self-image that these approaches aimed to foster in learners. Gattegno (1972, p. 31), who developed the Silent Way, for example, proposed that students be allowed "to try their hand and to make mistakes in order to develop their own criteria of rightness, correctness, and adequacy" and that therefore "correction is seldom part of the teacher's work." Caring and sharing was the order of the day (Moskowitz, 1978). In Krashen and Terrell's (1983) Natural Approach error correction is also viewed negatively, as "even in the best of circumstances (it) is likely to have a negative effect on the students' willingness to express themselves" (p. 177). In early versions of Communicative Language Teaching, where there was an exclusive focus on meaning in order to develop fluency, there was little room for error correction. In later versions of Communicative Language Teaching and in Task-Based Language Teaching, however, CF was reinstated as important for helping learners to develop accuracy, especially if it occurred while learners were struggling to communicate.

The teacher guides, written by authors who had grown up with and experienced the use of these different methods, not surprisingly manifest some uncertainty about CF. Written in the era of post-method pedagogy (Kumaradivelu, 1994), they acknowledge the need for correction but also show concern for its dangers. Ur (1996), for example, recognized that "there is certainly a place for correction" but "we should not over-estimate this contribution" and argued that it would be better to invest time in avoiding errors rather than in correcting them. In other words, Ur favored what Lightbown (1998) called "preventive pedagogy" (p. 139).

CF is often discussed in relation to 'accuracy' and 'fluency.' Scrivener (2005), for example, proposed that error correction was necessary in accuracy work, but should be largely avoided in fluency work or delayed until the fluency activity had been completed. Bohlke (2014) also advised against correction during fluency activities, commenting that "during fluency activity, it is generally accepted that the teacher should not interrupt students to point out a grammar or vocabulary error, or to correct pronunciation" (p. 127) and going on to claim that "many teachers feel that the only appropriate time to focus on error correction is after the activity is completed" (p. 128). This view reflects the belief that in Communicative Language Teaching, communication should be unfettered. However, the authors of the guides hedge their advice. Scrivener did allow for "brief, unobtrusive, immediate correction" (p. 299) during fluency work, as did Ur (1996), who saw merit in "gentle, supportive intervention" to help the "floundering" student. These views reflect an attempt to achieve a balance among the positions adopted in the different methods. They are apparently based on the authors' experiences of teaching and observing teachers teach and not on research, which is never mentioned.

Research suggests, however, that while Bohlke (2014) is right that teachers resist correcting during fluency work, in fact they do correct. Basturkmen, Lowen and Ellis (2004) investigated experienced teachers' beliefs about focusing on form by means of CF during communicative lessons and their actual practice. They reported inconsistencies in the teachers' beliefs and a tenuous relationship between their beliefs and actual practice. Even though all of the teachers believed that correction in general should be avoided during fluency work, they frequently engaged in it.

The key issue, however, is whether CF 'works' (i.e., assists acquisition). There has been a wealth of classroom- and laboratory-based research that has addressed this issue. The research has been synthesized in a number of meta-analyses (e.g., Russell & Spada, 2006; Mackey & Goo, 2007; Li, 2010; Lyster & Saito, 2010), which show that CF is indeed effective in assisting acquisition. Li (2010), for example, reviewed a total of 33 oral CF studies, involving 1,773 learners, concluding that "corrective feedback had a medium effect on acquisition" (p. 335), which was evident in tests that immediately followed the treatment involving CF and over time. However, he also reported that the effect was much stronger in studies carried out in a laboratory than in a classroom, perhaps because learners are more likely to pay attention to the feedback they receive in the one-on-one interactions in a laboratory context than in the teacher–class interactions typical of the classroom studies. Li also found that the effect of CF was greater in foreign language than in second language settings and suggested that this might be because learners in the former are more predisposed to pay attention to the corrections that they receive. Another finding was that CF was more effective in treatments that involved discrete item practice of grammatical structures (i.e., in accuracy work), where the feedback is intensive, than in communicative activities (i.e., in fluency work), where it is not focused on a single linguistic feature. A key issue in determining whether CF has any effect is the nature of the tests used to measure learning. Li also investigated this, reporting that the effects of CF were evident in both tests that measured controlled language use and free production. Two general conclusions can be drawn from Li's meta-analysis: (1) CF does assist L2 acquisition and (2) it is more likely to be effective in contexts where it is salient to learners.

Sociocultural theory points to the need for the 'graduated' correction of errors and proposes that CF can also be examined in terms of the level of support that teachers provide when they correct learners' errors. Aljaafreh and Lantolf (1994) and Nassaji and Swain (2000) showed that the level of correction that a teacher used to correct a specific type of error diminished over time. That is, whereas quite explicit correction was needed to enable a learner to self-correct at one point in time, more implicit correction sufficed at a later time. They suggested that this constituted evidence of acquisition taking place.[2] Nassaji (2011a) also reported that negotiated feedback is more effective than non-negotiated feedback or feedback with limited negotiation.

When Should Learners' Errors be Corrected?

Oral errors can be corrected immediately or shortly after they are committed. Alternatively, correction can be delayed until the pedagogic activity has been completed. We have seen that the teacher guides favor immediate correction in accuracy work but recommend delaying it in fluency work. However, Gattegno (1972) advised against interfering immediately even in accuracy-oriented work, so as to "give time to a student to make sense of 'mistakes'" (p. 31). Discussing computer-mediated communication, where both immediate and delayed correction are possible, Bowyer and Kawaguchi (2011) argued that delayed, asynchronous correction is preferable to synchronous correction because it gives teachers time to identify and explain errors and also because learners have plenty of time to consider the corrections to their output.

To date, there has been very little research that has investigated the timing of CF. Research so far has focused on describing and investigating the effects of immediate CF. Rolin-Ianziti (2010), however, reported a descriptive study of delayed oral CF carried out by teachers of L2 French. The teachers noted the errors that learners made as they performed a role-play activity and then reviewed them later. One teacher simply provided the corrections, while another attempted to elicit corrections from the students and only provided the correction if the students failed to self-correct. Rolin-Ianzati drew on sociocultural theory to argue that the second approach was likely to be more effective. In an experimental study, Li, Zhu and Ellis (2016) investigated the comparative effects of immediate and delayed CF on the learning of the English past passive construction by Chinese junior high school students. In this study there were two feedback groups, one of which received immediate feedback and the other delayed feedback (i.e., after the learners had completed two tasks). Both immediate and delayed feedback led to gains in scores on a grammaticality judgment test, with immediate feedback also showing some advantage over delayed feedback. However, neither type of feedback had any effect on scores from an oral elicitation test. The limited effect of the CF in this study may have been because the learners were not developmentally ready to acquire the target feature (the English past passive construction).

There are theoretical grounds for preferring immediate feedback. Doughty (2001) argued that immediate feedback enables learners to map a specific form onto the meaning it conveys in a 'window of opportunity' (i.e., at that moment when the learner is struggling to express him/herself). The Transfer Appropriate Processing Hypothesis (Lightbown, 1998) also lends support to immediate feedback. This hypothesis posits that learning is context dependent and that learners will be better able to recall rules and forms in a communicative context if they had acquired them in such a context. In other words, immediate feedback occurring while learners communicate is more likely to result in the kind of L2 knowledge that can be accessed later for communication. From this perspective, immediate feedback is preferred because it integrates a focus on form continuously into learners' attempts to communicate.

Which Errors Should be Corrected?

Both Ur (1996) and Edge (1989) warn against overcorrection. But if teachers are to correct some errors and ignore others, ideally they need to do so in a principled manner. Various proposals have been advanced regarding which errors to correct. Corder (1967) distinguished "errors" and "mistakes." An error takes place as a result of lack of knowledge (i.e., it represents a gap in competence). A mistake is a performance phenomenon, reflecting processing failures that arise as a result of competing plans, memory limitations, and a lack of automaticity. Brinton (2014) suggested that this is a useful distinction and that feedback was appropriate for competence errors but probably not for performance mistakes. Burt (1975) suggested that teachers should focus on "global" rather than "local errors." Global errors are errors that affect overall sentence organization and are likely to lead to communication breakdown. Local errors are errors that affect single elements in a sentence (for example, errors in morphology) but do not impact on the comprehensibility of an utterance. Brinton thought that this was also a useful distinction and that teachers should focus on correcting global errors. However, it is not clear how teachers are to distinguish between errors and mistakes, especially during fluency work. Nor can it be assumed that only global-type errors lead to communication problems; local errors in certain contexts can also do so.

Turning to the research that has investigated the question of which errors should be corrected, a number of studies (e.g., Schulz, 2001) reported that learners welcomed correction in general. Loewen et al. (2009), however, found that error correction was viewed "somewhat negatively" (p. 101) by both ESL learners and learners of foreign languages, but also that marked differences were evident in subgroups of each type of learner.

Descriptive studies indicate that teachers are likely to address a high percentage of the errors that learners make. Lyster and Ranta (1997) analyzed 100 hours of French immersion classes, where the primary focus was on content and meaning. They reported that 62% of the errors they identified were corrected. Presumably, then, the teachers engaged in some kind of selection of what errors to correct, but Lyster and Ranta did not record this. Lochtman (2002) carried out a similar study in a foreign language teaching context (i.e., in German classrooms in Dutch-speaking secondary schools in Belgium). He reported that 90% of the turns that contained an error received CF. These studies suggest that CF is more prevalent in an accuracy context than in a fluency context, reflecting the general position of the teacher guides.

Experimental studies have investigated focused, intensive CF in task-based lessons—that is, feedback directed at a specific linguistic (usually grammatical) feature in a context where the learners' primary focus is on meaning. In general, the target features of these studies were 'local' in nature—for example, grammatical gender in the choice of French articles (Lyster, 2004), English past tense (Ellis, Loewen & Erlam, 2006; Yang & Lyster, 2010), French verb forms (Mifka Provozic, 2013), and possessive determiners (Ammar & Spada, 2006). Thus there is a clear discrepancy between the recommendation in the guides that teachers should focus on global errors and the kind of target features that researchers have chosen to investigate. The choice of these target forms, however, is well motivated by research that indicates that they are 'fragile' and difficult to acquire, either because they are non-salient, redundant in many contexts, or blocked by the influence of the learners' first language (L1). These studies all report that learners' accuracy in the use of these grammatical features improved as a result of the CF.

How Should Errors be Corrected?

The teacher guides propose various strategies for correcting oral errors. Bohlke (2014, p. 127) suggested that correction should involve two stages; first "the teacher alerts the student to the fact that an error has been made" and second "the teacher moves to the correction stage." He then drew on Harmer (2007) to list a set of techniques that the teacher can use to show the learner that an error has been committed (see Table 1.1). In fact, though, the last of these techniques (i.e., 'reformulation') does more than just indicate an error; it also corrects it. Other guides list other correction techniques. Scrivener (2005) included 'direct correction' (i.e., the teacher tells the student an error has been committed) and also 'discuss the error' (i.e., "Write the problem sentence on the board for discussion", p. 301). Hedge (2000) mentioned 'requesting clarification' (i.e., "the teacher looks puzzled and requests clarification", p. 291). These techniques are seen as applicable to both accuracy and fluency work. Interestingly, though, the guides do not provide any examples of the application of these techniques in classroom interaction. Ur (1996), however, proposed that teachers should use the list of techniques she provided to carry out observations of actual lessons.

In general the guides are content to simply list the different techniques and fight shy of recommending which ones teachers should use. Hedge (2000), for example, simply suggested that teachers should use a variety of strategies. The guides do, however, express a general preference for those techniques that require learners to correct their own errors over those techniques (such as 'reformulation') that provide learners with the correction, reflecting a general principle that underlies their thinking about CF, namely that "people learn more by doing things themselves rather than being told about them" (Scrivener, 2005, p. 3). The guides also emphasize the need to ensure that correction is carried out gently and tactfully, pointing once again to the emphasis the guides place on the affective as opposed to the cognitive aspect of correcting errors.

There is no mention in the guides of the research that has investigated the relative effectiveness of the different ways of correcting errors. In fact, this has been a major focus of the CF research to date. Descriptive studies aimed to identifying the corrective strategies that teachers actually use. There is a long history of such studies, including early ones such as Allwright (1975), Chaudron (1977) and

TABLE 1.1 Techniques for Correcting Errors in Bohlke (2014)

Technique	Description
Repeating	The teacher asks the students to repeat what he/she has just said.
Expressions or gestures	The teacher uses facial expressions or hand gestures to show an error has been made.
Hinting	The teacher uses metalanguage (e.g., 'article' or 'preposition').
Echoing	The teacher repeats what the student said, emphasizing the erroneous element.
Reformulation	The teacher unobtrusively repeats the student's utterance, correcting the error.

TABLE 1.2 A Classification of CF Strategies (Based on Sheen & Ellis (2011) and Lyster, Saito, & Sato (2012))

	Implicit	*Explicit*
Input providing	1. Conversational recasts	2. Didactic recasts
		3. Explicit corrections
Output prompting	4. Repetitions	6. Metalinguistic comments
	5. Clarification requests	7. Elicitations
		8. Paralinguistic signals

Long (1977) and more recent ones such as Lyster and Ranta (1977) and Lochtman (2002). These studies developed complex typologies of feedback strategies, but over time researchers settled on the simpler typology shown in Table 1.2. This is based on two key dimensions—whether a strategy is input providing (i.e., provides learners with the correct linguistic form) or output prompting (i.e., pushes the learners to self-correct) and whether a strategy is implicit (i.e., the corrective force remains covert) or explicit (i.e., the corrective force is made clear to the learners). Descriptions of the different strategies in Table 1.2 can be found in Appendix A.

These two dimensions of CF are theoretically motivated. If L2 acquisition is seen as input driven, then clearly input-providing strategies are to be preferred. However, if actually producing the correct form is seen as assisting acquisition, then output-prompting feedback is desirable. The choice of implicit or explicit strategies depends on the importance attached to conscious noticing of the correction; implicit feedback caters to implicit/incidental acquisition, whereas explicit feedback is more likely to lead to conscious noticing and explicit/intentional learning. Numerous experimental studies have investigated the differential effects of these strategies on whether they are successful in (1) enabling learners to notice the correction, (2) assisting learners to self-correct their errors, and (3) facilitating acquisition in the sense that they result in increased accuracy in the use of a target feature.

A comprehensive review of this research is not possible in this chapter, but see Sheen and Ellis (2011), Lyster, Saito and Sato (2010), and Nassaji (2016). Instead, I will summarize some of the key findings:

1. Learners are more likely to notice a correction if the strategy is explicit in nature (Egi, 2007). However, learners have also been found to notice corrections even if the feedback is implicit. Mackey (2006), for example, reported a higher level of noticing in a group that performed communicative tasks and received CF consisting of conversational recasts and clarification requests, both implicit CF strategies, than a group that performed the communicative task without any CF.

2. Learners are more likely to uptake a correction by self-repairing their errors following prompts, in particular if the prompts are of the explicit kind.

Conversational recasts, in particular, are less likely to result in uptake with repair (Lyster & Ranta, 1997). Nassaji (2011b) showed that repair was more likely to occur when the repair involved incorporation of the target form into new utterance than when it involved simple repetition of the feedback. The instructional context mediates whether learner self-repair is likely to occur. Lyster and Mori (2006) reported that the learners in a Japanese immersion program in the United States were more likely to repair their errors following recasts than learners in a French immersion program in Canada and suggested that this was because there was a greater emphasis on accurate oral production and repetition in the former. Repair is more prevalent in accuracy-oriented instruction (Sheen, 2004). The importance of uptake with repair for acquisition, however, remains a matter of some dispute. Researchers differ in whether they see it as contributing to acquisition depending on the importance they attach to input or output as the driving force of acquisition. See, for example, the different views expressed in Lyster (2004) and Long (2006).

3. There is evidence to show that input-providing and output-prompting strategies and also implicit and explicit strategies all facilitate acquisition. Lyster (2004) reported a study that pointed to the greater effectiveness of output-prompting strategies over input-providing strategies (i.e., recasts). Other studies (Ammar & Spada, 2006; Yang & Lyster, 2010) have reported similar results. Ellis et al. (2006) reviewed studies that compared the effects of implicit and explicit feedback. These showed that explicit was more effective, as did Ellis et al.'s own study.

As the body of research has accumulated, however, it has become clear that CF is a very complex phenomenon, influenced by a host of factors that can determine the relative effect of different strategies on noticing, uptake with repair, and acquisition. These factors include the instructional context (e.g., whether it is meaning or form centered), the nature of the target feature (e.g., whether it entails item learning as, for example, in the case of uncountable nouns and irregular past tense, or system learning, as in the case of rule-based features such as regular past tense), whether the target feature(s) is explicitly presented prior to the practice activities where correction takes place, and learner factors such as learners' proficiency level and differences in their working memory capacity and language aptitude. While in the long term it might be possible to determine how these factors determine the relative effectiveness of different strategies and arrive at some general conclusions, we are a long way from being able to do so. Lyster and Ranta (2013) came to the conclusion that the best advice they could give to teachers was to use a variety of strategies rather than rely on just one particular strategy.

Such a view also accords with sociocultural theory. Aljaafreh and Lantolf (1994) argued that teachers have at their disposal a variety of strategies that can be ordered in terms of how implicit/explicit they are. They proposed that teachers should work through such strategies with a view to using the most implicit strategy that helps a learner to self-correct an error. In other words, CF is a seen as process rather than the one-off application of a strategy and teachers should not just select randomly from the array of strategies available to them but should apply them systematically. Nassaji and Swain's (2000) study showed that when a teacher engaged in the process of correcting, applying strategies in a graduated way in accordance with Aljaafreh and Lantolf's (1994) typology of implicit/explicit strategies, better learning resulted than when the teacher applied the strategies randomly.

Who Should do the Correcting?

CF may or may not involve the teacher providing the correction. In output-prompting CF, it is left to the student to make the correction. Another possibility, if the student is unable to correct, is for the teacher to invite another student to do so.

The least favored option in the teacher guides is teacher correction, although clearly the teacher has a role to play in prompting the correction. The guides show a clear preference for making students responsible for correction. Hedge (2000) and Scrivener (2005), for example, advised giving students the opportunity to self-correct and, if that fails, inviting another student to perform the correction. However, there is also recognition of the potential dangers of students correcting each other. Ur (1996) noted that asking another student can be very time-consuming and can have a negative impact on the student being corrected. Irrespective of who does the correction, however, there is wide agreement that the teacher needs to ensure that the student who initially made the error finally produces the correct form.

We have seen that some experimental studies have shown that output-prompting feedback, where learners are pushed to self-correct, is more effective than input-providing feedback, where the teacher provides the correction. However, the research also provides plentiful evidence that input-providing feedback consisting of recasts is also effective and, indeed, in some studies (e.g., Mifka Provozic, 2013) it was found to be more effective than output-prompting feedback. I know of no study that has investigated other-student feedback. Seedhouse's (2004) analysis of interactional episodes from a range of different classrooms, however, found that this type of feedback occurred only rarely.

Conclusion

In writing this chapter I have taken the position that to answer the question 'What do we know about CF?' it is necessary to consult both what experienced teachers and teacher educators have to say about CF and what researchers have found out about it. To this end, I took the questions that Hendrickson (1978) addressed and consulted a number of teacher guides to investigate the positions evident in pedagogical accounts of CF and the extensive body of descriptive and experimental studies of CF to examine what research has found out. In so doing I was motivated by my convictions that pedagogy should be research informed and that research will benefit from being pedagogy informed.

The teacher guides present a broadly uniform account of how teachers should conduct CF, which can be summarized as follows:

1. Positive as well as corrective feedback is important.
2. CF needs to be undertaken with care and tact to avoid a negative affective response in students.
3. In accuracy work, CF is necessary; however, in general it should be avoided in fluency work, although brief, unobtrusive feedback is possible.
4. Immediate correction is needed in accuracy work but correction should be delayed in fluency work until the fluency activity has been completed.
5. Teachers need to be selective in what they correct, focusing on 'errors' as opposed to 'mistakes' and on 'global' rather than 'local' errors.
6. A variety of techniques are available for conducting CF and teachers should make use of the range available to them.
7. Ideally the students (either the student who committed the error or another student) rather than the teacher should make the correction, but the teacher should provide clues to help students locate their errors.

By and large, the guides do not attempt to justify these proposals by reference to either theory or research. The proposals seem to reflect what their authors, on the basis of their own experience and knowledge of the pedagogical literature, consider 'best practice.'

To what extent are these proposals supported by the findings of research? The research certainly supports the need to undertake CF. It has shown that it fosters noticing and uptake with repair and leads to acquisition (i.e., greater accuracy in the features corrected). Furthermore the benefits of CF are evident not just in improved accuracy in controlled production, but also in free production.

However, research does not support the avoidance of correction in fluency work. Many studies have shown that correcting learners while they perform communicative tasks assists acquisition and also that such correction need not interfere with the primary focus on meaning. Indeed, a key premise of task-based language teaching is that the 'focus-on-form' (Long, 1991) that CF affords is of crucial importance. However, the potential advantage of delaying feedback in fluency work has not been properly investigated. It remains a possibility that delayed feedback is as or perhaps even more effective than immediate feedback.

The research lends support to the proposal that CF should be selective. However, whereas the guides discuss selection in terms of general types of errors such as global versus local, research has investigated the effects of CF on specific linguistic features. There is no evidence to support the claim that teachers should focus on 'errors' rather than 'mistakes' or on 'global' rather than 'local' errors. In fact, the research points to the efficacy of focusing on local features irrespective of whether they constitute 'mistakes' or 'errors', which in any case teachers are unlikely to be able to distinguish in oral communication.

Research has provided a theory-based taxonomy of strategies rather than the simple list of strategies found in the guides. This affords a more principled way of deciding which strategy to use and has informed experimental studies of CF. The results suggest that output-prompting CF, especially of the explicit kind, is more effective than input providing, especially of the implicit kind, but there is also plenty of evidence to show that the latter is also effective. Like the guides, some researchers have concluded that the best advice that can be given to teachers is to deploy a variety of strategies. One way of combining strategies might be to first employ an output-prompting strategy and then, if the learner fails to correct, to resort to an input-providing strategy, as for example in what Doughty and Varela (1998) called "corrective recasts." Sociocultural theory suggests a different way of applying a variety of strategies. Teachers should opt first for an implicit-type strategy and then move on to increasingly more explicit types until the learner is able to self-correct. It is possible, however, that the most effective strategy is immediate explicit correction.

The guides are clear about the need for students to self-correct. The research that has investigated output-prompting CF supports this, but it also shows that the teacher providing corrections is also effective.

Overall, then, the advice proffered in the guides is supported by the research, but the research also points to a number of ways in which this advice might be revised. The research also demonstrates the complex nature of CF and shows that no single way of conducting CF will be efficient in every instructional context. Perhaps, then, as Ur (1996) suggested, what is most important is to increase teachers' awareness of how CF is conducted through observing lessons. The guides tend to emphasize the affective dimension of CF and neglect consideration of the cognitive dimension. Vásquez and Harvey (2010) showed that engaging teachers in practitioner research can help them to re-evaluate their beliefs about CF and focus on the cognitive aspect of CF.

Finally, the guides also point to a number of issues that the researcher might like to investigate. There is, for example, almost no research that has investigated paralinguistic feedback, but see Loewen and Nakatsukasa (this volume).[3] Perhaps too studies are needed to examine the role of positive feedback in L2 acquisition and, in particular, the relative effectiveness of immediate and delayed CF in task-based instruction. There is also a need to investigate the effect of extensive, unfocused feedback on acquisition over time. This will require longitudinal studies, which currently are lacking.

Notes

1 One study that did investigate positive feedback is Waring (2008). Interestingly, in contrast to the position taken in the teacher guides, Waring concluded that it can have a detrimental effect on learner participation. He argued that from a sociocultural perspective on learning it suppresses "the opportunities for voicing understanding of problems or exploring alternative correct answers, both of which are the stuff that learning is made of" (Waring, 2008, p. 577).
2 In another study (Erlam, Ellis, & Batstone, 2013), however, there was no evidence of any graduated reduction in the level of CF needed to ensure that learners self-corrected their errors. This study also reported that direct, explicit correction was as effective as graduated CF.
3 Nakatsukasa's (2013) thesis investigated feedback involving gestures.

References

Aljaafreh, A., & Lantolf, J. P. (1994). Negative feedback as regulation and second language learning in the Zone of Proximal Development. *The Modern Language Journal, 78*(4), 465–483.

Allwright, R. L. (1975). Problems in the study of the language teacher's treatment of error. In M. K. Burt & H. D. Dulay (Eds.), *On TESOL '75: New directions in second language learning, teaching, and bilingual education* (pp. 96–109). Washington, DC: TESOL.

Ammar, A., & Spada, N. (2006). One size fits all?: Recasts, prompts, and L2 learning. *Studies in Second Language Acquisition, 28*(4), 543–574.

Basturkmen, H., Loewen, S., & Ellis, R. (2004). Teachers' stated beliefs about incidental focus on form and their classroom practices. *Applied Linguistics, 25*(2), 243–272.

Bohlke, D. (2014). Fluency-oriented second language teaching. In M. Celce-Murcia, D. Brinton & M. Snow (Eds.), *Teaching English as a second or foreign language, fourth edition* (pp. 121–135). Boston, MA.: Heinle Cengage.

Bower, J., & Kawaguchi, S. (2011). Negotiation of meaning and corrective feedback in Japanese/English eTandem. *Language Learning & Technology, 15*(1), 41–71.

Brinton, D. (2014). Tools and techniques of effective second/foreign language teaching. In M. Celce-Murcia, D. Brinton & M. Snow (Eds.), *Teaching English as a second or foreign language, fourth edition* (pp. 340–361). Boston, MA: Heinle Cengage.

Burt, M. 1975. Error analysis in the adult EFL classroom. *TESOL Quarterly, 9*(1), 53–63.

Chaudron, C. (1977). A descriptive model of discourse in the corrective treatment of learners' errors. *Language Learning, 27*(1), 29–46.

Corder, S. P. (1967). The significance of learner's errors. *IRAL—International Review of Applied Linguistics in Language Teaching, V*(4), 161–170.

Doughty, C. (2001). Cognitive underpinnings of focus on form. In P. Robinson (Ed.), *Cognition and second language instruction* (pp. 206–257). Cambridge: Cambridge University Press.

Doughty, C., & Varela, E. (1998). Communicative focus on form. In C. Doughty & J. Williams (Eds.), *Focus on form in classroom second language acquisition* (pp. 114–138). Cambridge: Cambridge University Press.

Edge, J. (1989). *Mistakes and correction*. London: Longman.

Egi, T. (2007). Recasts, learners' interpretations, and L2 development. In A. Mackey (Ed.), *Conversational interaction in second language acquisition* (pp. 249–360). New York: Oxford University Press.

Ellis, R., Loewen, S., & Erlam, R. (2006). Implicit and explicit corrective feedback and the acquisition of L2 grammar. *Studies in Second Language Acquisition, 28*(2), 339–368.

Erlam, R., Ellis, R., & Batstone, R. (2013). Oral corrective feedback on L2 writing: Two approaches compared. *System*, *41*(2), 257–268.

Gattegno, C. (1972). *Teaching foreign languages in schools*. New York: Educational Solutions.

Harmer, J. (1983). *The practice of English language teaching*. London and New York: Longman.

Harmer, J. (2007). *The practice of English language teaching, fourth edition*. London: Longman.

Hedge, T. (2000). *Teaching and learning in the language classroom*. Oxford: Oxford University Press.

Hendrickson, J. M. (1978). Error correction in foreign language teaching: Recent theory, research, and practice. *The Modern Language Journal*, *62*(8), 387–398.

Krashen, S., & Terrell, T. (1983). *The natural approach: Language acquisition in the classroom*. Oxford: Pergamon.

Kumaradivelu, B. (1994). The postmethod condition: (E)merging strategies for second/foreign language teaching. *TESOL Quarterly*, *28*(1), 27–48.

Li, S. (2010). The effectiveness of corrective feedback in SLA: A meta-analysis. *Language Learning*, *60*(2), 309–365.

Li, S., Zhu, Y. & Ellis, R. (2016). The effects of the timing of corrective feedback on the acquisition of a new linguistic structure. *The Modern Language Journal*, *100*(1), 276–295.

Lightbown, P. (1998). The importance of timing in focus on form. In C. Doughty & J. Williams (Eds.), *Focus on form in classroom second language acquisition* (pp. 177–196). Cambridge: Cambridge University Press.

Loewen, S., Li, S., Fei, F., Thompson, A., Nakatsukasa, K. Ahn, S., & Chen, X. (2009). Second language learners' beliefs about grammar instruction and error correction. *The Modern Language Journal*, *93*(1), 91–104.

Long, M. (1977). Teacher feedback on learner error: Mapping cognitions. In H. Brown, C. Yorio, and R. Crymes (Eds.), *On TESOL '77* (pp. 278–93). Washington, DC: TESOL.

Long, M. (1991). Focus on form: A design feature in language teaching methodology. In K. de Bot, R. Ginsberg, & C. Kramsch (Eds.), *Foreign language research in cross-cultural perspective* (pp. 39–52). Amsterdam: John Benjamins.

Long, M. H. (2006). *Problems in SLA*. Mahwah, NJ: Lawrence Erlbaum Associates.

Lyster, R. (2004). Differential effects of prompts and recasts in form-focused instruction. *Studies in Second Language Acquisition*, *26*(3), 399–432.

Lyster, R., & Mori, H. (2006). Interactional feedback and instructional counterbalance. *Studies in Second Language Acquisition*, *28*(2), 269–300.

Lyster, R., & Ranta, L. (1997). Corrective feedback and learner uptake. *Studies in Second Language Acquisition*, *19*(1), 37–66.

Lyster, R, & Ranta, L. (2013). The case for variety in corrective feedback research. *Studies in Second Language Acquisition*, *34*(4), 591–626.

Lyster, R., & Saito, K. (2010). Oral feedback in classroom SLA. *Studies in Second Language Acquisition*, *32*(Special Issue 2), 265–302.

Lyster, R., Saito, K., & Sato, M. (2013). Oral corrective feedback in second language classrooms. *Language Teaching*, *46*(1), 1–40.

Lochtman, K. (2002). Oral corrective feedback in the foreign language classroom: How it affects interaction in analytic foreign language teaching. *International Journal of Educational Research*, *37*, 271–283.

Mackey, A. (2006). Feedback, noticing and instructed second language learning. *Applied Linguistics*, *27*(3), 405–430.

Mackey, A., & Goo, J. M. (2007). Interaction research in SLA: A meta-analysis and research synthesis. In A. Mackey (Ed.), *Input, interaction and corrective feedback in L2 learning* (pp. 379–452). Oxford: Oxford University Press.

Mifka Profozic, N. (2013). *The effectiveness of corrective feedback and the role of individual differences in language learning: A classroom study.* Frankfurt am Main: Peter Lang.

Moskowitz, G. (1978). *Caring and sharing in the foreign language class: A sourcebook on humanistic techniques.* Boston, MA: Heinle & Heinle.

Nakatsukasa, K. (2013). *Efficacy of gestures and recasts on the acquisition of L2 grammar.* Unpublished PhD thesis, Michigan State University, US.

Nassaji, H. (2011a). Correcting students' written grammatical errors: The effects of negotiated versus non-negotiated feedback. *Studies in Second Language Learning and Teaching, 1*(3), 315–334.

Nassaji, H. (2011b). Immediate learner repair and its relationship with learning targeted forms in dyadic interaction. *System, 39*(1), 17–29.

Nassaji, H. (2015). *Interactional feedback dimension in instructed second language learning.* London: Bloomsbury Publishing.

Nassaji, H. (2016). Anniversary article: Interactional feedback in second language teaching and learning: A synthesis and analysis of current research. *Language Teaching Research, 20*(4), 535–562.

Nassaji, H., & Swain, M. (2000). A Vygotskian perspective on corrective feedback in L2: The effect of random versus negotiated help on the learning of English articles. *Language Awareness, 9*(1), 34–51.

Nunan, D. (1991). *Language teaching methodology: A textbook for teachers.* London: Prentice Hall.

Rolin-Ianziti, J. (2010). The organization of delayed second language correction. *Language Teaching Research, 14*(2), 183–206.

Russell, J., & Spada, N. (2006). The effectiveness of corrective feedback for the acquisition of L2 grammar. In J. M. Norris & L. Ortega (Eds.), *Synthesizing research on language learning and teaching* (pp. 133–164). Amsterdam: John Benjamins.

Schulz, R. (2001). Cultural differences in student and teacher perceptions concerning the role of grammar instruction. *The Modern Language Journal, 85*(2), 244–58.

Scrivener, J. (2005). *Learning teaching: A guidebook for English language teachers.* Oxford: Macmillan Education.

Seedhouse, P. (2004). *The interactional architecture of the language classroom: A conversation analysis perspective.* Malden, MA: Blackwell.

Sheen, Y. (2004). Corrective feedback and learner uptake in communicative classrooms across instructional settings. *Language Teaching Research, 8*(3), 263–300.

Sheen, Y., & Ellis, R. (2011). Corrective feedback in language teaching. In E. Hinkel (Ed.), *Handbook of research in second language teaching and learning, second edition* (pp. 593–610). New York: Routledge.

Ur, P. (1996). *A course in language teaching: Practice and theory.* Cambridge: Cambridge University Press.

Vásquez, C., & Harvey, J. (2010). Raising teachers' awareness about corrective feedback through research replication. *Language Teaching Research, 14*(4), 421–443.

Waring, H. Z. (2008). Using explicit positive assessment in the language classroom: IRF, feedback, and learning opportunities. *Modern Language Journal, 92*(4), 577–594.

Yang, Y., & Lyster, R. (2010). Effects of form-focused practice and feedback on Chinese EFL learners' acquisition of regular and irregular past tense forms. *Studies in Second Language Acquisition, 32*(2), 235–263.

Appendix A

Research-Based Descriptions of CF Strategies

1. Conversational recasts: reformulations of erroneous utterances that occur in the effort to resolve a communication problem.
2. Didactic recasts: reformulations of erroneous utterances that occur even in the absence of a communicative problem.
3. Explicit corrections: correction that reformulate student utterances together with a clear indication an error has been made.
4. Repetitions: verbatim repetitions of erroneous utterances which may or may not highlight the error by means of intonation.
5. Clarification requests: requests for students to repeat or clarify what they have said (e.g., 'Pardon?' or 'What did you say?').
6. Metalinguistic comments: brief or possibly more extended comments that provide explicit, metalinguistic information about the nature of the error.
7. Elicitations: explicit attempts to elicit the correction from the student by means of questions or partial repetitions of the students' utterances for them to complete by supplying the correct form.
8. Paralinguistic signals: the use of facial expression or gesture to elicit the correct form from the learner.

2

ORAL PEER CORRECTIVE FEEDBACK

Multiple Theoretical Perspectives

Masatoshi Sato

Introduction

Peer corrective feedback (PCF) is a dynamic interaction phenomenon due to its inherently affective and social nature (see Philp & Duchesne, 2016). On the one hand, research has suggested that PCF accelerates L2 development in the same way as corrective feedback (CF) given by other interlocutors, such as teachers and/or L1 speakers, by triggering noticing of gap in the learners' interlanguage (Sippel & Jackson, 2015). On the other hand, PCF is unique because its effectiveness may be mediated by some features that distinguish peer interaction from interaction between learners and the teacher (Sato & Ballinger, 2016). Hence, in the first section of this chapter, research comparing peer interaction with other types of interaction will be reviewed in order to explain the context in which PCF occurs. In particular, I will discuss interactionist research that has examined interactional patterns during peer interaction. In addition, socioculturally oriented research will be discussed, as it has revealed social relationships that are specific to interaction between learners. I will conclude the section by presenting empirical evidence showing PCF's effectiveness.

The second section focuses on the nature of PCF. Unlike teacher CF, learners are providers of CF during peer interaction. In order to provide CF, a learner needs to first detect the error, which may or may not lead to a communication breakdown, in her peer's speech. This act of noticing the error in input may affect the CF provider's L2 development. I will invoke Levelt's (1983) speech production model to explain this mechanism. As far as the quality of PCF—whether it assists L2 learning—is concerned, many studies have reported its positive roles, while some researchers have argued that its impact may be minimal (e.g., Ballinger, 2015) or even detrimental to learning (e.g., Adams, Nuevo, & Egi, 2011). In order to understand the mixed findings, I will focus on two features of peer interaction that may define the extent of PCF effectiveness: (a) learners' interaction mindset toward the task and/or interlocutor prior to and/or during interaction and (b) the social dynamics that learners co-construct during peer interaction. By reviewing pertinent literature, I argue for the importance of the learners' interaction mindset being positive, so that their social dynamics become collaborative; otherwise, some PCF may not be processed to assist L2 development. After discussing the nature of PCF, I will point out methodological challenges of PCF research and propose several research directions.

The vulnerability of PCF to the learners' affective state and social dynamics between learners underscores the importance of instructional intervention so that PCF affects L2 development positively in a consistent manner. In the last section, therefore, I will propose two general approaches to increase the potential of PCF. First, learners can be trained how to interact with each other and how to provide CF to each other. Although learners may become able to detect and correct each other's L2 errors, PCF may still not push L2 development forward when, for instance, learners distrust each other's linguistic abilities. Hence, the second approach that I will discuss concerns the teacher's roles before and during peer interaction activities. In particular, I will make a case that it is pivotal that the teacher constructs a collaborative classroom environment for PCF to be received by a peer in an effective way.

The Context of PCF

Interactional Moves

Interactionist research has shown that L1 interlocutors can be better input providers than L2 partners during interaction (Sato, 2015). For instance, by pairing Japanese English as a foreign language (EFL) learners with English L1 speakers, Pica, Lincoln-Porter, Paninos, and Linnell (1996) reported that L1-speaking interlocutors modified their utterances morphosyntactically and lexically (input modification) more than L2-speaking interlocutors when pairs encountered communication difficulty. However, this rather unsurprising finding does not mean that peer interaction presents less learning opportunity. This is because the way in which interaction drives L2 learning forward is determined not only by the amount and type of input that an L2 learner receives, but also by the amount and type of feedback that a learner receives and the amount and type of output opportunities that interaction and feedback offer (see Gass & Mackey, 2015). In fact, over the last 30 years, comparative research has shown that peer interaction creates learning opportunities more than L1-L2 speaker interaction does in relation to three key interactional moves: CF, modified output, and self-initiated modified output.

First, learners receive CF during peer interaction and even more so than when the interlocutor is an L1 speaker. This finding dates back to Varonis and

Gass (1985), who compared occurrences of "non-understanding routines" and the resulting negotiation of meaning in three types of dyads: L1-L1, L1-L2, and L2-L2 speakers. The analysis revealed that CF, operationalized as a "trigger," was observed more in L2-L2 speaker interaction than in the other dyad types (L1-L1 and L1-L2). In the aforementioned Pica et al.'s (1996) study with adult EFL learners, the researchers also reported that there was significantly more CF in peer interaction (during one of the two tasks) and concluded that peer interaction "did offer data of considerable quality, particularly in the area of feedback" (p. 80). Focusing on child L2 learners (8–13 years old), Oliver (2002) also explored different pairing methods. In her study, 16 L1-L1, 32 L1-L2, and 48 L2-L2 speaker interactions were analyzed in light of negotiation for meaning, including the frequency of three types of CF (comprehension checks, clarification requests, and confirmation checks). The statistical comparisons between the dyad types found that L2-L2 pairs engaged in the most negotiation for meaning, followed by L1-L2 and L1-L1 pairs. Oliver suspected that the lower the proficiency of a pair, the more communication problems they encounter; hence, CF was observed in the pairs with the lowest proficiency, that is, L2-L2 pairs (see also Oliver, Nguyen, & Sato, 2017). Furthermore, Sato and Lyster (2007), who also compared L1-L2 and L2-L2 speaker interactions, found that, in addition to a greater CF frequency during peer interaction than in L1-L2 speaker interaction, the L2-speaking interlocutors provided more output-promoting types of CF (i.e., prompts) than input-providing CF (e.g., recasts), the former of which has been found to give learners more opportunities to self-correct the original utterance.

Second, research has found that learners tend to modify their initial non-target-like utterances (modified output) more when CF was given by a fellow learner than after CF given by L1 speakers (but see counterevidence in Mackey, Oliver, & Leeman, 2003). Shehadeh (1999) examined the interactions between adult English as a second language (ESL) learners and those between the learners and L1 speakers. Having identified more modified output in peer interaction than in L1-L2 speaker interaction during one of the two tasks (i.e., the picture dictation task), the researcher concluded that during peer interaction learners were more likely to "make an initial utterance more accurate and/or more comprehensible to their interlocutor(s)" (p. 644). In an investigation of the effect of feedback type (prompts vs. recasts) and interlocutor type (L1 vs. L2 speakers) on modified output, Sato and Lyster (2007) found modified output to occur less frequently than other types of responses (e.g., ignore feedback) regardless of the type of CF that the L1 interlocutors gave. By examining the longest utterances as well as mean lengths of utterances in L1-L2 and L2-L2 interactions, Sato (2015) reported that learners produced more L2 with a greater complexity when their partner was an L2 speaker. It seems to be the case, therefore, that peer interaction gives learners a context for freely experimenting with the language. In characterizing peer interaction, Philp, Adams, and Iwashita (2014) asserted that during peer interaction, "learners may explore language use with less anxiety of correction and with greater autonomy" (p. 17).

In addition, learners tend to self-correct more while interacting with each other than when they interact with L1 speakers. Shehadeh (2001) showed that 93% of self-initiation led to modified output during L2-L2 speaker interaction, which was proportionally higher than L1-L2 speaker interaction. In a classroom context, Buckwalter (2001) revealed that over 90% of the repair moves were self-initiated, as opposed to other-initiated that included teacher CF (see also Sato, 2007).

In sum, interactionist research has revealed that learners are afforded greater opportunity to shift their attention to formal aspects of language via CF during peer interaction than during L1-L2 speaker interaction. However, as Mackey et al. (2003) pointed out, it is important to examine how CF provided by different interlocutors (L1 vs. L2 speakers) affects L2 development, in addition to an examination of CF frequency during interaction. That is, investigation of the quality of CF is warranted. Interactionist research also suggests that peer interaction provides a richer learning context than L1-L2 interaction especially in the area of output. While Mackey et al. (2003) reported that L1-speaking interlocutors provided more CF, modified output was observed significantly more during L2-L2 speaker interactions than L1-L2 speaker interactions (specifically between young learners). In other words, peer interaction creates an environment in which learners are willing to take up the opportunity created by PCF and to engage in meaningful output practice (see Lyster & Sato, 2013).

Social Dynamics

The nature and effectiveness of PCF have been found to be mediated by social relationships that L2 learners construct together during interaction. Storch (2002) categorized learner relationships by observing 10 pairs of university-level ESL learners working on a range of communicative tasks. Storch identified two dimensions that defined the degree of learner collaboration. The first dimension was equality and pertained to the extent of control that the learners exhibited over the direction of the task. The second dimension was mutuality and was related to learners' level of engagement with their partners' contributions during the task. Based on the degrees of the two dimensions (high vs. low), Storch categorized the pairs into four quadrants. For instance, when a pair showed high equality and high mutuality, this pair was labeled as a collaborative pair. When a pair showed low equality and high mutuality, this pair was labeled as an expert/novice pair (the other two quadrants were dominant/dominant and dominant/passive). Further, Storch analyzed the transcripts in light of possible L2 learning opportunities (e.g., instances suggesting evidence of a transfer of knowledge). The analyses of patterns of relationships and L2 learning opportunities revealed that the collaborative and expert/novice patterns were more conducive to L2 learning than the other patterns.

L2 learning opportunities that emerge when learners establish a collaborative relationship are explained by sociocultural theory. This theory understands that cognition and knowledge are inherently social and are dialogically constructed (Lantolf & Zhang, 2017). Hence, "knowledge is not owned solely by the learner, but is also a property of social settings and the interface between person and social context" (Foster & Ohta, 2005, p. 403). In peer interaction, L2 learning can be conceptualized based on the way in which learners assist each other's learning and achieve a level that they would not necessarily be able to achieve on their own. This support and the subsequent language exchanges is called scaffolding. In this framework, PCF can serve as a mediational tool for scaffolding through which learners "provide expertise to each other" (Brooks & Swain, 2009, p. 69). Donato (1994) observed classroom interaction of American college learners of French who worked on open-ended collaborative tasks. The analysis revealed that of the 32 instances of scaffolding observed during the activity in the first week, 75% of the grammatical structures were used correctly in the following week, showing the effect of scaffolding on L2 learning. Ohta's (2001) corpus of adult learners of Japanese showed that, by engaging in dialogic activities, less proficient learners could support more proficient learners.

To summarize, sociocultural research has evidenced that (a) learners construct a variety of social relationships during peer interaction, (b) some of those relationships are more conducive to L2 learning than others, and (c) the strength of peer interaction lies in its collaborative nature.

Empirical Evidence for PCF

Before delving into the nature of PCF, it is important to highlight research showing the effectiveness of PCF on L2 development. In McDonough (2004), EFL learners in Thailand engaged in communicative tasks in pairs or groups. Based on the amount of PCF and modified output observed during peer interaction, the learners were divided into high-participation (more PCF and modified output) or low-participation groups. The oral production tests administered before and after the communicative tasks showed that the high-participation group demonstrated significant improvement of the target structures (real and unreal conditionals), while the low-participation group did not. In Adams (2007), ESL learners in the United States with various L1 backgrounds engaged in peer interaction. After the tasks, they took tailor-made post-tests in which their knowledge of linguistic structures on which they received PCF during the task were tested. The results showed that 59% of CF episodes resulted in L2 learning.

PCF effectiveness has been experimentally examined as well. In Kim (2013), middle-school Korean EFL learners were assigned to either task-modeling or control groups. Prior to the tasks, the learners in the modeling group were shown video clips in which the researcher and the teacher provided a variety of CF to each other. The analysis of question formation development from the pre-, post- and delayed post-tests indicated that the developmental outcomes of the experimental learners were significantly higher than those in the control group. Kim highlighted that the modeling served "an important role in allocating learners' attentional resources to certain linguistic codes" (p. 28). In Sato and Lyster's (2012) pre-post design, there were four groups, two of which were given PCF training. Another was given communicative tasks only and a fourth acted as a control group. The results showed that the peer-interaction-only group outperformed the control group for oral fluency development (speech rate) but not accuracy (global accuracy), while the two PCF groups outperformed the peer-interaction-only and control groups both for accuracy and fluency. The results underscore that to push accuracy development forward in peer interaction, some attention control device (PCF in this case) may be necessary.

More recently, Sippel and Jackson (2015) designed a quasi-experimental study in which university-level learners of German were divided into teacher-CF, PCF, and control groups. The learners in the PCF group were taught to provide output-promoting CF (prompts) to each other while working in groups. The analysis of L2 development, measured via an oral production task and an untimed grammaticality judgment task, revealed that the experimental groups outperformed the control in both the immediate and delayed post-tests. However, the results of the grammaticality judgment test showed that only the PCF group increased their scores significantly over time, showing a superior effect for PCF over teacher CF. Notably, for the oral production task, the teacher-CF group showed a significant drop from the immediate to delayed post-tests while the PCF group did not show such a tendency. This result suggests a longer lasting effect of PCF. Furthermore, the observational data indicated that the learners in the PCF group received proportionally less CF (38%) than those who were in the teacher-CF group (96% on 40 errors in total), implying a stronger impact for PCF than for teacher CF. Sippel and Jackson accounted for the rather surprising findings by three interaction patterns observed in the data. First, learners tended to self-correct more during peer interaction. Second, learners in the PCF group not only received but also provided CF. Third, those learners engaged in deeper discussion of the target features.

Despite the positive evidence, PCF has been found to affect L2 development negatively at least in one study. Adams et al. (2011) conducted correlational analyses on the frequency of PCF and gain scores on L2 development tests, which yielded a significantly negative correlation for explicit CF. They concluded that "feedback may not play as important a role in learner–learner interaction as it plays in NS–learner interactions" (p. 56). On the contrary, Sato and Lyster (2012) found significantly positive correlations between PCF and L2 development as well as between modified output and L2 development. The polar directions of the correlations in the quantity of PCF indicate a qualitative difference in PCF in the two studies. Some possible factors that caused the quality difference may be learners' social relationships as well as their psychology. Those factors will be discussed in the following sections.

The Nature of PCF

Due to the unique features of peer interaction, understanding PCF requires multiple theoretical perspectives, including those from the mainstream psychology and educational literature, some of which may not apply to teacher CF. (Readers are directed to the introduction to this volume for theories on teacher CF.) For example, learners may trust teacher CF but not PCF, calling for a theoretical account to understand learners' psychology. Also, unveiling the impact of social dynamics that learners construct during group work on learning outcomes may require knowledge from social psychology due to learners' shared roles to accomplish a task, as opposed to the hierarchical relationship between the teacher and learners that arguably ensures teacher CF's corrective force.

Reciprocity and Dual Functions

A peculiar feature of PCF is that it is reciprocal between the interactants: during peer interaction, L2 learners are not only receivers but also providers of CF. In order to understand this feature, Levelt's (1983) perceptual theory of monitoring is useful. Levelt focused on L1 speakers' self-corrections to understand how errors are detected before and after speech production. The theory assumes that self-corrections happen because a speaker is able to "detect any structural deviances which he might as well have detected in somebody else's speech" in his "own inner or overt speech" (p. 46). That is, a speaker can notice an error in his own speech either before actually verbalizing an utterance (but after formulating it in the *formulator*) or after producing it, because the utterance is now heard by the speaker himself (in the *speech-comprehension system*). Relevant to CF, and particularly PCF, is that monitoring errors and the execution of corrected utterances can be triggered by an external factor in the process of "making repairs upon the confirmation or clarification requests of the interlocutor" (Kormos, 2006, p. 135), the only difference being who notices the error. Applying Levelt's L1 speech theories to L2 acquisition, Kormos (1999) argued that monitoring interfaces with SLA theories in several ways. First, because it involves checking of language production not only internally but also externally, it can contribute to noticing the gap between insufficiently automatized knowledge and the input. Second, noticing itself triggered by monitoring is beneficial for L2 development while both processing input and producing output.

Sato and Lyster (2012) drew on Levelt's theory to interpret their findings of PCF. The researchers proposed that PCF serves dual functions to benefit both receivers' and providers' L2 development. For PCF to happen, a learner first needs to detect an error in the input—an error made by her peer—that may result in a communication breakdown (negotiation for meaning) or an exchange that does not involve any communication issue (negotiation for form). In order to do so, he or she must notice the gap between the error and the targetlike production (or at least the targetlike production that he or she believes it is). During the process, the provider may (a) compare the error and her interlanguage, (b) notice that she might as well make the same error and correct it internally, and/or (c) monitor her own CF internally and externally and, possibly, detect the same or another error in her speech. These cognitive processes may contribute to restructuring and consolidation of the provider's L2 knowledge. From the receiver's vantage point, CF given by his peer may trigger noticing and further push the learner to modify the original utterance. Sippel and Jackson (2015) attributed the superior effects of PCF to teacher CF, which was higher in quality (more focused and accurate), to the experimental condition in which the learners were "encouraged to notice not only corrections provided by peers but also mistakes in their peers' speech" (p. 13). Figure 2.1 depicts a proposed dual model of PCF from a monitoring perspective.

Social Aspects

PCF is essentially a social act. Yoshida (2008) investigated factors influencing PCF perceptions and found that the noticeability of PCF depended on learners' social relationships. Specifically, Yoshida asserted that the learners' level of satisfaction with the given PCF was a deciding factor in the effectiveness of the feedback: when learners were dissatisfied with the CF, it was misunderstood or discarded. For example, one of the learners reported that she believed in her partners' meta-linguistic feedback "because he sounded confident" (p. 534). Ballinger (2015) examined interactions of eight pairs of grades 3/4 French immersion learners. The analysis of 22.5 hours of interactions indicated that the learners were able to reciprocally provide linguistic support to each other. However, the correlational analysis between collaborative turns and PCF yielded a non-significance. Ballinger suspected that provision of PCF may indicate either a collaborative relationship or excessive corrective behaviors depending on pair dynamics.

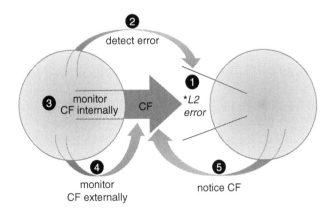

FIGURE 2.1 A Dual Model of Peer Corrective Feedback

Some studies reported social aspects of PCF as its strength. Alcón (2002) compared peer interaction and learner-teacher interaction and measured the development of pragmatic knowledge (requesting strategies). While the observational data showed that the teachers gave more CF than L2 interlocutors, the learners in the peer interaction group exhibited a greater L2 development gain. Alcón accounted for the result by pointing out that learners tested their linguistic hypotheses and "sometimes explained the reason for their new hypothesis" (p. 369) during peer interaction, yet in the teacher-led group, learners were provided with the correct version when they encountered linguistic difficulty. The study implies the effect of collaborative CF on L2 learning. In Brooks and Swain (2009), two pairs of adult ESL learners first jointly wrote a text in which they provided PCF to each other. Afterward, the teacher gave CF on their writing and the teacher CF was discussed by the pairs. The analyses of the audio-recorded interactions during the writing tasks and discussions revealed that the learners switched the role of *expertise* to provide CF to each other, which, in turn, positively affected their learning outcomes (the revised text) more than the teacher CF did.

This research corroborates that PCF effectiveness is mediated by social dynamics during interaction. When a social relationship between learners is collaborative, PCF functions most effectively. However, PCF may be ignored or discarded when learners construct a social relationship characterized by distrust in each other's linguistic abilities, social awkwardness in providing feedback, and embarrassment over being corrected by their peers. In discussing the sociocultural theory, Storch (2017) emphasized that L2 learners are "active agents who assign relevance and significance to certain actions. For example, when receiving CF, learners exercise volitional control over what they notice in the feedback and whether they accept, question, or reject the feedback they receive" (p. 77).

Learner's Interaction Mindset

Different from social dynamics is learner's interaction mindset, which is intrapersonal; a mindset is a thought held by individuals. As Sato (2016) puts it, interaction mindset is "a disposition toward the task and/or the interlocutor prior to and/ or during the interaction."[1] As early as Varonis and Gass (1985), researchers have suspected a connection between learner's affective state and PCF. Based on their finding that there was significantly more CF during peer interaction than during L1-L2 interaction, Varonis and Gass claimed that during peer interaction learners may feel that "they have little to lose by indicating a non-understanding, because they recognize their *shared incompetence*" (emphasis in original, p. 84). Since then, learner's mindset has been explored in relation to interactional behaviors and terms such as *attitudes, perceptions, emotions,* and *orientations* have been used to describe essentially how L2 learners' affective state is related to their engagement levels.

By conducting in-depth interviews with learners who interacted with either another learner or an L1 speaker, Sato and Lyster (2007) found that, on the one hand, learners believed that their English was 'broken English' and L1 speakers' English was 'perfect English.' On the other hand, for peer interaction, they believed that they had more time to decide what to say and felt much more comfortable to test out what they believed to be correct. In another study, Sato (2013) conducted a factor analysis on questionnaire data and interviewed adult EFL learners. Two factor loadings were related to provision (e.g., *I think students should help each other by pointing out each other's grammar errors*) and reception (e.g., *If my classmate points out my grammar errors, I would believe the correction*) of PCF. Overall, the data suggested learners' positive mindset. In the interviews, the learners explained that they did not have to worry about making errors while talking to each other. Storch (2004) sought to answer the question as to why certain pairs constructed a relationship that was more collaborative than others. The interview data with university-level ESL learners revealed that learners' "perceived goals and roles that determine how an activity will be carried out" (pp. 473–474) were reflected in their interactional behaviors; those mindsets were actualized in "the ability to provide and receive valued feedback on one's performance" (p. 474). For example, the learners who provided PCF or perceived PCF positively were those who expressed their perceptions of the benefits of pair work and their intention to complete the task to the best of their ability. As Swain (2013) cautioned, L2 learners' affective states and their cognition are "minimally, interdependent; maximally, they are inseparable/integrated" (p. 196).

The interwoven relationships between learners' mindset, their interactional behaviors with other learners, and their individual learning outcomes have abundantly been reported in the fields of social and educational psychology. For example, the premise of social interdependence theory is that interactants' affective states and the psychological processes that individuals experience while engaging in a group task define the individual learning outcomes. Central to the success of group work is positive interdependence, whereby "individuals perceive that they can attain their goals if and only if the other individuals with whom they are cooperatively linked attain their goals" (Johnson & Johnson, 2009, p. 336). The effect of this psychology has been affirmed in different areas of learning (e.g., moral development) using both quantitative (often with a regression and a hierarchical linear model) and qualitative (e.g., discourse analysis) methods (see, for a meta-analysis, Roseth, Johnson, & Johnson, 2008).

Applying social interdependence theory to L2 research, Sato (2016) collected three data sets from middle-school EFL learners. First, the researcher collected mindset data based on pre-task interviews focusing on peer interaction and PCF. Then, the learners' interactional behaviors such as the quantity and quality of PCF were recorded. In addition, pre- and post-tests were administered consisting of oral and written production tasks on grammatical and lexical aspects. The results showed that the learners who exhibited a positive mindset prior to the task provided more PCF during the task. Those learners showed statistically significant gains in the development tests. Meanwhile, the learners who shared their negative dispositions toward PCF did not provide as much PCF or improve their L2 knowledge significantly over time. Sato concluded that L2 development was mediated by learners' mindset, which in turn affected their interactional behaviors.

Vulnerability

Peer corrective feedback is vulnerable to its social and psychological aspects: for PCF to have a positive impact on L2 learning, an L2 learner may have to (a) approach the task and the interlocutor positively and (b) construct a collaborative relationship with the partner. In Baralt, Gurzynski-Weiss, and Kim (2016), university-level learners of Spanish engaged in peer interaction via face-to-face or computer-mediated modes. In conjunction with a post-task questionnaire, the researchers separately analyzed affective (e.g., "willingness to engage"), social (e.g., "leader or follower"), and cognitive (e.g., "noticing of language and/or interaction features") engagement during interaction. The exploratory analysis led Baralt et al. to conclude that "cognitive attention to form can very much be moderated by learners' affective and social engagement during peer interaction" (p. 234). That is, the more a learner was willing to participate in interaction and the more collaborative a relationship between the learners was, the more attention was drawn to language forms. The evidence suggesting a negative impact of PCF on L2 development (e.g., Adams et al., 2011) may be explained by the social and affective nature of PCF. In other words, PCF's vulnerability to its inherently social and affective nature may be a double-edged sword.

Future Directions

While PCF research has thrived in recent years, it still lags far behind teacher CF research. It needs to be acknowledged first that PCF (and peer interaction) research presents some methodological challenges. In the classroom, unlike student-teacher interaction, multiple pair or group interactions are simultaneously going on, which makes it difficult to capture (audio/video recording) learners' interactional behaviors. Subsequently, the lack of individual scores (e.g., frequency of PCF or modified output) leads to a less rigorous statistical design. In addition, in a communicative classroom, the teacher is often walking around and intervening in peer interaction. While a good teacher should be monitoring and supporting peer interaction, those classroom realities impose a validity threat to findings related to the effects of peer interaction and/or PCF.

Having admitted methodological challenges, I encourage several research designs to further our understanding of the nature of PCF. First, there is a limited amount of research comparing the effect of PCF and teacher CF (cf. Sippel & Jackson, 2015). In addition to the investigation of how much CF occurs in the two contexts, future research should examine their differences in quality (via learner responses or a pre-post design) in the classroom setting. In terms of learner type, more investigation of younger learners is needed (cf. Mackey et al., 2003). Because child L2 learners are developing not only their linguistic knowledge but their cognitive and social skills (Oliver et al., 2017), PCF may serve functionally different roles.

I proposed a dual model of PCF. While cognitive processes that PCF may trigger on both sides of interaction are conceivable, reception and provision of PCF as well as their effects on L2 development need to be experimentally teased apart (see Figure 2.1). Because learners necessarily play the roles of both receivers and providers of PCF during peer interaction, a laboratory study may be necessary to examine the effects of (a) noticing an error in the input, and (b) the subsequent provision of CF. Potentially, this research develops a data-driven theory, because SLA research and, more specifically, input research have not considered what erroneous input would do to the development of accurate L2 knowledge.

Because of the vulnerability of PCF to social dynamics between learners, comparative studies of different learning contexts (e.g., ESL, EFL, content-based language teaching [CBLT], content and language integrated learning [CLIL], and computer-mediated communication [CMC]) are warranted. Another important direction is related to learners' affective states. Such research may involve a rigorous quantitative design (e.g., a correlational model including questionnaire results and learning gains) or a nuanced qualitative design (e.g., a combination of in-depth interviews prior to interaction and observation of actual interaction). Caution is needed when designing such a study; a learner's mindset may be fluid and it could be altered during interaction or when reflecting on the interaction after the task. Because of the intricate relationships between affective, social, and cognitive aspects of L2 learning, I would encourage future research to incorporate theories and methodologies from cognitive, educational, and social psychology research.

Finally, experimental studies of pedagogical interventions are much needed. Due to observational and comparative research, we know by now how peer interaction and PCF affects L2 learning to a great extent. We know to a much lesser extent, however, how we can enhance peer interaction's and PCF's effectiveness. Future research can replicate the interventions outlined in this chapter or try out different interventions that are pedagogically viable and feasible. The following section discusses some of those pedagogical efforts.

Pedagogical Implications

For many L2 learners, even when they are able to notice their classmates' errors, it may be difficult to correct them due to the social and psychological nature of PCF. In Philp, Walter, and Basturkmen (2010), learners reported that they hesitated to provide PCF because of (a) their proficiency (e.g., readiness to correct as a learner), (b) task-related discourses (e.g., interruption during a role-play), and (c) social relationship (e.g., face saving). Not only may a learner's mindset stop him/her from giving PCF to his/her peer but, even when he/she decided to correct his/her peer's error (consciously or not), the feedback may lack linguistic focus. Toth's (2008, p. 269) observation data of teacher-led and learner-led discourses led him to conclude that the benefit of PCF comes "at the expense of consistency in attention to the target form." Furthermore, PCF often lacks a pedagogical (corrective) force, again due to its social nature. This is exactly where pedagogical interventions are necessary, first to ensure that PCF occurs and second to ensure that it affects L2 development positively.

One way to assist L2 learners to autonomously pay attention to language forms is to model interactions. In Kim and McDonough (2011), learners in the experimental group were shown videotaped interaction between the teacher and the researcher whereby they modeled "collaborative pair dynamics with both interlocutors providing feedback, responding to questions, and sharing ideas" (p. 187). The results indicated that learners in the experimental group not only produced more language-related episodes (a sign of attention to form), but they also resolved the linguistic issues more successfully. Another way of promoting PCF is to provide learners with activities designed specifically to train them to become more effective interactants. Sato and Ballinger (2012) examined CF training in two learning contexts: adult EFL learners in Japan and child French immersion students in Canada. In both contexts, the training resulted in an increase in both quantity and quality of PCF. More recently, Fujii, Ziegler, and Mackey (2016) conducted an experiment in which metacognitive instruction, entitled "How to be an active learner: Feedback, negotiation, and noticing," was implemented. The learners in the experimental group, who were shown models of CF and practiced how to give CF with the teacher, detected significantly more errors and provided proportionally more PCF than those in the control group.

After making sure that PCF does occur during communicative activities, it is equally important to ensure that the provided PCF has a positive impact on L2 learning. Here, the teacher plays (and should play) an important role before and during peer interaction activities by constructing a collaborative learning environment in the classroom. By operationalizing classroom interaction as "an engagement with other learners and teachers in joint activities that focus on matters of shared interest and that contain opportunities for learning" (pp. 159–160), Walqui (2006) proposed three scales of classroom scaffolding to promote learners' autonomous learning. First, the teacher needs to set up a support structure by, for instance, creating a non-threatening learning environment. Second, the teacher should make sure that the learners know what they are supposed to do. Third, the teacher should monitor the learners to make sure that scaffolding among them is being practiced. An example of such pedagogical intervention is Davin and Donato (2013), who examined the impact of dynamic assessment, a teacher's scaffolding technique pertaining to CF. The analysis of small-group activities in content-based Spanish classes showed that the learners used the mediational tool (i.e., CF) to support each other's linguistic growth and the support was facilitated by the dynamic assessment implemented prior to the peer interaction activities.

Some caution is needed when implementing peer interaction interventions, however. First, the teacher should not over-monitor peer interaction. Philp et al. (2014) asserted that peer interaction is "generally felt to be less stressful than teacher-led interaction, precisely because it will not be carefully monitored" (p. 198). Sato and Ballinger (2016) also concluded that "[t]eachers cannot and probably should not manage all peer interaction, lest they override one of its key advantages—the absence of an authority figure" (p. 21). Second, the teacher needs to be patient in witnessing the effect of a pedagogical effort. Unlike other pedagogical techniques delivered by the teacher (e.g., teacher CF), altering how L2 learners interact with each other requires a longitudinal, step-by-step lesson plan to guide them. Such a pedagogical effort also requires continued, patient effort to assist them with the use of interaction strategies.

Note

1 This operationalization of "mindset" differs from that based on implicit theories (see Dweck, 2006). The construct of mindset in mainstream psychological research (fixed vs. growth) concerns assumptions that "individuals make about various human attributes, such as intelligence or personality" (Mercer & Ryan, 2010, p. 437).

References

Adams, R. (2007). Do second language learners benefit from interacting with each other? In A. Mackey (Ed.), *Conversational interaction in second language acquisition: A collection of empirical studies* (pp. 29–51). Oxford: Oxford University Press.

Adams, R., Nuevo, A., & Egi, T. (2011). Explicit and implicit feedback, modified output, and SLA: Does explicit and implicit feedback promote learning and learner–learner interactions? *Modern Language Journal, 95*(s1), 42–63.

Alcón, E. (2002). Relationship between teacher-led versus learners' interaction and the development of pragmatics in the EFL classroom. *International Journal of Educational Research, 37*(4), 359–377.

Ballinger, S. (2015). Linking content, linking students: A cross-linguistic pedagogical intervention. In J. Cenoz & D. Gorter (Eds.), *Multilingual education: Between language learning and translanguaging* (pp. 35–60). Cambridge: Cambridge University Press.

Baralt, M., Gurzynski-Weiss, L., & Kim, Y. (2016). The effects of task complexity and classroom environment on learners' engagement with the language. In M. Sato & S. Ballinger (Eds.), *Peer interaction and second language learning: Pedagogical potential and research agenda* (pp. 209–239). Amsterdam: John Benjamins.

Brooks, L., & Swain, M. (2009). Languaging in collaborative writing: Creation of and response to expertise. In A. Mackey & C. Polio (Eds.), *Multiple perspectives on interaction: Second language research in honor of Susan M. Gass* (pp. 58–89). New York: Routledge.

Buckwalter, P. (2001). Repair sequences in Spanish L2 dyadic discourse: A descriptive study. *The Modern Language Journal, 85*(3), 380–397.

Davin, K., & Donato, R. (2013). Student collaboration and teacher directed classroom dynamic assessment: A complementary pairing. *Foreign Language Annals, 46*(1), 5–22.

Donato, R. (1994). Collective scaffolding in second language learning. In J. Lantolf & G. Appel (Eds.), *Vygotskian approaches to second language research* (pp. 33–56). Norwood, NJ: Ablex.

Dweck, C. (2006). *Mindset: The new psychology of success*. New York: Random House.

Foster, P., & Ohta, A. (2005). Negotiation for meaning and peer assistance in second language classrooms. *Applied Linguistics, 26*(3), 402–430.

Fujii, A., Ziegler, N., & Mackey, A. (2016). Peer interaction and metacognitive instruction in the EFL classroom. In M. Sato & S. Ballinger (Eds.), *Peer interaction and second language learning: Pedagogical potential and research agenda* (pp. 63–89). Amsterdam: John Benjamins.

Gass, S., & Mackey, A. (2015). Input, interaction, and output in second language acquisition. In B. VanPatten & J. Williams (Eds.), *Theories in second language acquisition* (2nd ed., pp. 180–206). New York: Routledge.

Johnson, D., & Johnson, R. (2009). An educational psychology success story: Social interdependence theory and cooperative learning. *Educational Researcher, 38*(5), 365–379.

Kim, Y. (2013). Effects of pretask modeling on attention to form and question development. *TESOL Quarterly, 47*(1), 8–35.

Kim, Y., & McDonough, K. (2011). Using pretask modelling to encourage collaborative learning opportunities. *Language Teaching Research, 15*(2), 183–199.

Kormos, J. (1999). Monitoring and self-repair in L2. *Language Learning, 49*(2), 303–342.

Kormos, J. (2006). *Speech production and second language acquisition*. Mahwah, NJ: Lawrence Erlbaum.

Lantolf, J., & Zhang, X. (2017). Concept-based instruction: Promoting L2 development through principles of sociocultural theory. In S. Loewen & M. Sato (Eds.), *The handbook of instructed second language acquisition* (pp. 146–165). New York: Routledge.

Levelt, W. (1983). Monitoring and self-repair in speech. *Cognition, 14*(1), 41–104.

Lyster, R., & Sato, M. (2013). Skill acquisition theory and the role of practice in L2 development. In M. García Mayo, M. Gutierrez-Mangado, & M. Martínez Adrián (Eds.), *Contemporary approaches to second language acquisition* (pp. 71–92). Amsterdam: John Benjamins.

McDonough, K. (2004). Learner-learner interaction during pair and small group activities in a Thai EFL context. *System, 32*(2), 207–224.

Mackey, A., Oliver, R., & Leeman, J. (2003). Interactional input and the incorporation of feedback: An exploration of NS-NNS and NNS-NNS adult and child dyads. *Language Learning, 53*(1), 35–66.

Mercer, S., & Ryan, S. (2010). A mindset for EFL: Learners' beliefs about the role of natural talent. *ELT Journal, 64*(4), 436–444.

Ohta, A. (2001). *Second language acquisition processes in the classroom: Learning Japanese*. Mahwah, NJ: Lawrence Erlbaum.

Oliver, R. (2002). The patterns of negotiation for meaning in child interactions. *The Modern Language Journal, 86*(1), 97–111.

Oliver, R., Nguyen, B., & Sato, M. (2017). Child instructed SLA. In S. Loewen & M. Sato (Eds.), *The handbook of instructed second language acquisition.* (pp. 468–487) New York: Routledge.

Philp, J., Adams, R., & Iwashita, N. (2014). *Peer interaction and second language learning*. New York: Routledge.

Philp, J., & Duchesne, S. (2016). Exploring engagement in tasks in the language classroom. *Annual Review of Applied Linguistics, 36*, 50–72.

Philp, J., Walter, S., & Basturkmen, H. (2010). Peer interaction in the foreign language classroom: What factors foster a focus on form? *Language Awareness, 19*(4), 261–279.

Pica, T., Lincoln-Porter, F., Paninos, D., & Linnell, J. (1996). Language learners' interaction: How does it address the input, output, and feedback needs of L2 learners? *TESOL Quarterly, 30*(1), 59–84.

Roseth, C., Johnson, D., & Johnson, R. (2008). Promoting early adolescents' achievement and peer relationships: The effects of cooperative, competitive, and individualistic goal structures. *Psychological Bulletin*, *134*(2), 223–246.

Sato, M. (2007). Social relationships in conversational interaction: A comparison between learner-learner and learner-NS dyads. *JALT Journal*, *29*(2), 183–208.

Sato, M. (2013). Beliefs about peer interaction and peer corrective feedback: Efficacy of classroom intervention. *The Modern Language Journal*, *97*(3), 611–633.

Sato, M. (2015). Density and complexity of oral production in interaction: The interactionist approach and an alternative. *International Review of Applied Linguistics in Language Teaching*, *53*(3), 307–329.

Sato, M. (2016). Collaborative mindset, collaborative interaction, and L2 development: An affective-social-cognitive model. *Language Learning*, *67*(2). Advanced online publication.

Sato, M., & Ballinger, S. (2012). Raising language awareness in peer interaction: A cross-context, cross-method examination. *Language Awareness*, *21*(1–2), 157–179.

Sato, M., & Ballinger, S. (2016). Understanding peer interaction: Research synthesis and directions. In M. Sato & S. Ballinger (Eds.), *Peer interaction and second language learning: Pedagogical potential and research agenda* (pp. 1–30). Amsterdam: John Benjamins.

Sato, M., & Lyster, R. (2007). Modified output of Japanese EFL learners: Variable effects of interlocutor vs. feedback types. In A. Mackey (Ed.), *Conversational interaction in second language acquisition: A collection of empirical studies* (pp. 123–142). Oxford: Oxford University Press.

Sato, M., & Lyster, R. (2012). Peer interaction and corrective feedback for accuracy and fluency development: Monitoring, practice, and proceduralization. *Studies in Second Language Acquisition*, *34*(4), 591–626.

Shehadeh, A. (1999). Non-native speakers' production of modified comprehensible output and second language learning. *Language Learning*, *49*(4), 627–675.

Shehadeh, A. (2001). Self- and other-initiated modified output during task-based interaction. *TESOL Quarterly*, *35*(3), 433–457.

Sippel, L., & Jackson, C. N. (2015). Teacher vs. peer oral corrective feedback in the German language classroom. *Foreign Language Annals*, *48*(4), 688–705.

Storch, N. (2002). Patterns of interaction in ESL pair work. *Language Learning*, *52*(1), 119–158.

Storch, N. (2004). Using activity theory to explain differences in patterns of dyadic interactions in an ESL class. *The Canadian Modern Language Review*, *60*(4), 457–480.

Storch, N. (2017). Sociocultural theory in the L2 classroom. In S. Loewen & M. Sato (Eds.), *The handbook of instructed second language acquisition* (pp. 69–84). New York: Routledge.

Swain, M. (2013). The inseparability of cognition and emotion in second language learning. *Language Teaching*, *46*(2), 195–207.

Toth, P. (2008). Teacher- and learner-led discourse in task-based grammar instruction: Providing procedural assistance for L2 morphosyntactic development. *Language Learning*, *58*(2), 237–283.

Varonis, E., & Gass, S. (1985). Non-native/non-native conversations: A model for negotiation of meaning. *Applied Linguistics*, *6*(1), 71–90.

Walqui, A. (2006). Scaffolding instruction for English language learners: A conceptual framework. *International Journal of Bilingual Education and Bilingualism*, *9*(2), 159–180.

Yoshida, R. (2008). Learners' perception of corrective feedback in pair work. *Foreign Language Annals*, *41*(3), 525–541.

3

THE TIMING OF ORAL CORRECTIVE FEEDBACK

Paul Gregory Quinn and Tatsuya Nakata

Introduction

The timing of corrective feedback (CF) refers to the juncture in the instructional sequence when learners' errors are addressed. CF can be provided immediately after an error, or it can be delayed until a later point in time. Most research into orally provided CF has been conducted on types of CF provided immediately following errors. However, there is an emerging interest in investigating delayed CF and in comparing the effects of immediate to delayed CF. This chapter begins by considering how theoretical explanations for second language (L2) development have influenced the views about when CF should be provided and the interest in investigating that question. Then, three frameworks that explain why immediate and delayed CF might facilitate L2 development are outlined. Next, an overview is provided of the empirical findings on the timing of oral CF. This overview is followed by guidance for future research. The chapter concludes with a discussion of potential pedagogical implications of CF timing research.

Theoretical Influences on When to Correct

Views about when to provide CF have been influenced by theoretical explanations about how L2s are learned. Behaviourist-oriented theorists, like Brooks (1960), recommended avoiding errors like sin to prevent learners from focusing on incorrect examples of speech. They feared conditioning learners into accidentally learning those examples as if they were accurate models. If errors were to be treated, they were to be dealt with immediately, and then focus was to be quickly shifted. However, after Corder (1967) argued that errors were important indicators of learner progress, theorists such as Chastain (1971) and Fanselow (1977) suggested that teachers might delay CF to give themselves time to analyze and respond to errors effectively. With the advent of the communicative approach to language teaching, theorists like Krashen persuaded many to replace the question of when to provide CF with the question of whether to provide CF at all. Krashen (1985) theorized that CF was unnecessary, positing instead that comprehensible input was the only necessary component for L2 acquisition. A resurgence in the interest of investigating CF developed as empirical research indicated that comprehensible input was not a sufficient explanation for all L2 development (e.g., Swain, 1985), and the interest in investigating CF increased steadily with the accumulation of empirical findings that instruction which included attention to language form was helpful in L2 development (e.g., Norris & Ortega, 2000).

Lyster and Ranta's (1997) descriptive study of the types of CF that teachers provided in classrooms greatly influenced the direction of this renewed interest in CF. The study fueled an interest in how to provide CF. In particular, the CF types known as explicit correction, recasts, and prompts have been investigated extensively in contemporary CF research. In explicit correction, learners are informed that their utterance is incorrect and a corrected model is provided to them. Recasts are a type of CF in which learners' inaccurate utterances are paraphrased and repeated back to them in the correct form. Prompts employ cues to encourage learners to notice that they have said something inaccurately and to self-correct. These three CF types have almost invariably been investigated in studies in which CF has been provided immediately after errors. Indeed, until recently, there has been little need to discuss the question of the timing of CF because orally provided CF has almost uniformly only referred to immediate CF. As Hunter (2007) reflected, "it is as if error treatment falling outside the immediate discourse is irrelevant" (p. 42).

Arguably, another reason there has been little investigation of CF timing is that unlike immediate CF, there are no generally accepted theoretical explanations about how delayed CF could facilitate L2 development. Given that immediate CF has been the default kind of orally provided CF in studies, there has been little motivation to explain how delayed CF could facilitate development. Conversely, the effectiveness of immediate CF is regularly explained in two ways: (1) immediate cognitive comparison, or (2) skill acquisition induced through prompting. Immediate cognitive comparison explains the effectiveness of the types of CF, such as recasts, that Ranta and Lyster (2007) refer to as reformulations. As Ellis (2006) argues, the function of these types of CF is to provide input in the form of accurate models that learners can mentally compare with their errors. Doughty (2001) argues that recasts facilitate development by allowing for an immediate cognitive comparison which causes restructuring of the learner's knowledge. Doughty contends that to be effective the comparison should occur within the "cognitive window of opportunity" (p. 257). This window refers to the less than 60 seconds that humans can maintain active mental representations in working memory, which, according to Cowan (1995), is the activated component of long-term memory that facilitates the processing and storage of new sensory input.

The second explanation about how immediate CF facilitates L2 development is skill acquisition theory. This theory posits that humans learn by first learning factual information about a skill and then practicing until the skill is proceduralized into a behaviour that eventually becomes automatic. DeKeyser (2007) argues that the theory can be applied to L2 acquisition. Drawing upon DeKeyser's argument, Ranta and Lyster (2007) propose that CF in the form of prompts may facilitate proceduralization in communicative practice because prompts encourage learners to retrieve a learned grammar rule and reattempt to produce the language more accurately with that rule in mind. Continually doing so proceduralizes accurate usage. Despite the differences in the theoretical positions supporting immediate CF, these diverse perspectives share the assumption that CF is best provided within communicative interaction, and thus only support immediate CF.

However, there are theoretical frameworks from cognitive psychology that L2 researchers could adopt to explain the effectiveness of delayed and immediate CF. One such framework is the distributed practice effect, which predicts that delayed CF increases learning more than immediate CF. According to the distributed practice effect, introducing longer intervals between study opportunities of a given item leads to better long-term retention than shorter intervals or no intervals at all (e.g., Cepeda, Pashler, Vul, Wixted, & Rohrer, 2006). For instance, the distributed practice effect suggests that studying a list of words four times over one hour would lead to better retention than studying it for the same number of times in ten minutes. Although previous L2 research on the distributed practice effect has been conducted mostly in the field of vocabulary acquisition (e.g., Karpicke & Bauernschmidt, 2011; Nakata, 2015; Nakata & Webb, in press), research suggests that the distributed practice effect can also be observed in grammar acquisition. In Bird (2010), for instance, 38 Malay learners of English studied English tenses (simple past, present perfect, and past perfect) under short and long spacing conditions. The short spacing condition used spacing of 3 days, and the long spacing condition used spacing of 14 days. Bird found that long spacing contributed to significantly higher scores than short spacing on the post-test conducted 60 days after the treatment. Even though these results are not from a CF study, they suggest that introducing long intervals between study opportunities also increases L2 grammar acquisition. Note that by definition, delayed CF introduces longer intervals between study opportunities of a given item than immediate CF. The distributed practice effect, as a result, suggests that delaying CF may increase learning.

Transfer appropriate processing is another framework that could explain L2 knowledge development from either immediate or delayed CF. Transfer appropriate processing posits that memories are best recalled in conditions similar to those in which they were encoded (Morris, Bransford, & Franks, 1977). Researchers such as Spada and Lightbown (2008) have hypothesized that transfer appropriate processing might have an impact on instructed L2 acquisition. They suggest that learners who are instructed on grammar structures during communicative practice might score significantly better on a test of those structures that takes the form of a communicative task than on a discrete point grammar test. Concomitantly, different learners who learned the same grammar feature by learning the rules of the feature outside of a communicative task might score higher on a discrete grammar point test than on a test in the form of a communicative task. Another way of looking at this interpretation of transfer appropriate processing is that providing grammar instruction that is integrated into communicative activity may lead to an increase in procedural (potentially even implicit) grammar knowledge while providing isolated grammar instruction may lead to an increase in explicit (i.e., declarative) knowledge. Because immediate CF is provided during a communicative activity, it is arguably integrated grammar instruction. If CF were to be delayed until after a communicative activity, arguably, it could be considered isolated grammar instruction. If Spada and Lightbown's (2008) interpretation of transfer appropriate processing were extended to immediate and delayed CF, delayed CF should lead to better results on tests of explicit (i.e., declarative) knowledge than immediate CF does, but immediate CF should result in better outcomes in tests of procedural (i.e., implicit) knowledge. Thus, in this interpretation, transfer appropriate processing would predict that L2 development could result from both immediate and delayed CF.

Another framework which might explain L2 development that results from immediate and delayed CF is reconsolidation theory (e.g., Nader & Einarsson, 2010). This theory holds that the act of reminding a participant of a previously learned pattern causes a reactivation of a long-term mental representation of it. This reactivation of the mental representation makes it labile, or susceptible to influence. If that labile representation is present when a new stimulus (such as the forming of a new mental representation caused by the learning of a new similar pattern) occurs, the mind mixes the two mental representations together as it attempts to store or reconsolidate the original memory. Thus, the reactivated long-term mental representation is interfered with by the new mental stimulus and it is altered to include some component of that new stimulus. Research has shown that this alteration effect occurs in declarative (Walker, Brakefield, Hobson, & Stickgold, 2003) and procedural memory (Hupbach, Gomez, Nadel, & Hardt, 2007).

Arguably, reactivation and reconsolidation could underlie the changes in L2 knowledge that result from CF. In the case of immediate CF, for example, upon hearing a grammar error, a teacher can provide a prompt that compels the learner to try again. At that juncture, the learner may accurately self-correct and proceed with her communication. Alternatively, she may make an error. Put differently, she may reactivate her inaccurate long-term mental representation of how to form that grammar structure. In that case, that inaccurate mental representation will now be labile and susceptible to alteration. If the teacher provides an accurate reformulation of the grammar structure, and that stimulus enters the learner's mind as a similar mental representation to the original inaccurate mental representation, then the process of reconsolidation could cause a novel, more accurate mental representation of how to form the grammar structure to be stored in the learner's long-term memory. This novel long-term mental representation may still not be entirely accurate, but it would represent a positive development in interlanguage. Over time, that representation may be exposed to more CF that leads to further restructuring. Reactivation and reconsolidation could also occur with delayed CF. In this case, teachers would record errors and provide the prompts that initiate the process after some delay. For example, teachers could use what Rolin-Ianziti (2010) refers to as teacher-initiated student correction. That is, delayed CF could be provided at the end of a communicative activity by teachers asking questions to the student who made the error that compel him to meaningfully communicate his point again. For example, if the student made a past progressive error while explaining what he was doing at ten o'clock the previous evening, the teacher might ask the student to remind her of his actions at ten o'clock. As in the case of immediate CF, the teacher's prompt will either result in accurate production or the reactivation of the learner's inaccurate long-term mental representation of how to form the grammar structure. At that juncture, the same process as was outlined above for immediate CF would be followed.

In summary, theoretical influences play an important role in CF timing research. There are theoretical explanations for why immediate and delayed CF may be effective. However, determining whether delayed CF is as effective in leading to L2 development as immediate CF is an empirical question which has received little investigation. As argued below, the dearth of CF timing studies and the inconsistency among their findings demonstrate a need for more empirical CF timing research.

Empirical Findings about the Timing of Orally Provided CF

Research on the timing of orally provided CF can be divided into investigations of immediate and delayed CF and investigations comparing immediate to delayed CF. As discussed above, until recently, studies of orally provided CF have almost invariably investigated CF that was provided immediately. The findings of several meta-analyses of this research (none of which included delayed CF studies) indicate that immediate CF facilitates L2 development and that awareness of the corrective intent of CF plays an important role in its effectiveness (e.g., Li, 2010; Lyster & Saito, 2010).

Very few studies have investigated delayed CF. Two studies that did so focused only on describing how delayed CF was provided without seeking evidence of L2 development. Rolin-Ianziti (2010) analyzed how French teachers delayed CF to avoid interrupting role plays. The teachers recorded learners' errors, and after the role plays, they provided CF using teacher-initiated correction and teacher-initiated student correction. In the former, teachers reminded the learners of their errors and provided the accurate models for them. In the latter, as illustrated above, teachers used prompts to provoke learners to attempt to say something that they had previously said inaccurately. Whether learners subsequently produced the correct version or not, the teachers provided the accurate version and had the learners repeat it.

Hunter (2012) observed a different means of providing delayed CF in an American university ESL program. Teachers noted errors that they overheard while students chatted about trivial topics. Then, teachers created audio-recorded corrections that contained accurate models of the errors. These were made available within 24 hours, along with practice exercises for students to use to learn from their errors.

An exhaustive search of the L2 research literature revealed only a handful of studies that have compared the effects of immediate and delayed orally provided CF on L2 development. So few studies have investigated this question that it is necessary to report unpublished studies like Siyyari's (2005) master's thesis research. The timing of CF was compared on errors made on four grammar forms: "I wish," three forms of causative clause, second conditional sentences, and "should have + past participle." In a period of 12 classes, 4 teachers provided CF to 60 Iranian adult English learners in a series of dictogloss (Wajnryb, 1990) text reconstruction tasks that elicited the 4 grammar forms. Thirty learners received immediate CF in the form of recasts. The other 30 learners received delayed CF in the form of explicit CF on errors after the task. Pre- and post-tests featuring sentence completion questions compelled the use of the four grammar forms. For each form, Siyyari found that immediate and delayed CF resulted in significant improvement from the pre- to post-tests, but he found no significant differences between the immediate and delayed CF. However, when he aggregated the scores from all the grammar forms, Siyyari found that the immediate CF group significantly outperformed the delayed CF group.

Varnosfadrani (2006) also compared immediate and delayed CF in his unpublished doctoral dissertation. Twenty-eight Iranian adult English learners participated in two dictogloss tasks. In the first task, learners were provided with immediate explicit CF on grammar errors. In the second task, the same learners received delayed CF after the task in the form of a reminder of the error they made, followed by explicit CF. Varnosfadrani measured the effectiveness of the treatments by creating tailor-made tests for each learner composed of items with grammar forms that they had received CF on. He found no significant differences between the immediate and delayed CF treatments.

Both preceding studies share limitations due to internal validity issues. Neither had control groups that did not receive CF. Without a control group, improvement that occurs over time cannot be dependably attributed to the CF treatments. That is, if a control group that received no CF were present and outperformed by the treatment groups that only differed because they included CF, then the outperformance could be more dependably attributed to CF. Another serious validity problem was that both confounded CF type and timing. Their use of one type of CF for immediate CF and a different type of CF for delayed CF means that they compared CF type as much as they compared CF timing. No results could be confidently attributed to a difference in CF timing alone.

To avoid validity issues, Quinn (2014) conducted a tightly controlled laboratory-based experimental comparison of the developmental effects of immediate and delayed CF. Ninety ESL learners with a variety of L1s were randomly assigned to three conditions: immediate CF, delayed CF, and a control group that received no CF. Quinn conducted the same three-week procedure with each participant individually. In the first week, learners completed an oral production test, a timed aural grammaticality judgment test, and a written error correction test on the English passive construction in the simple present, present perfect, and simple past forms. In the second week, learners received a mini-lesson on the English passive voice to ensure that they had some explicit instruction in the passive prior to engaging in tasks where their use of the passive would be the focus of CF. Then, according to learners' conditions, Quinn provided or did not provide CF while each learner individually engaged in three 10-minute communicative tasks with him. The three tasks that were designed to elicit use of the passive voice were an information gap task, a picture-cued story-retelling task, and a role play. To avoid any confounding variables, the type and amount of CF provision was strictly controlled to be uniform. Twelve provisions of teacher-initiated student correction (Rolin-Ianziti, 2010) were provided for each learner. Thus, the only differences between the three treatment conditions were that the no CF condition received no CF, immediate CF learners received CF immediately after an error, and the delayed CF learners received CF after each task. Immediately following the treatment and one week after that, learners again completed the three tests that they had taken prior to the treatment. On all test types, Quinn found a significant improvement from pre- to post-tests. However, he found no significant differences between any of the treatment conditions.

Li, Ellis, and Zhu (2016) also compared the developmental effects from immediate and delayed CF provided on the English passive voice. Li et al.'s study was classroom based and they elected to study the passive as a completely new structure for their 120 adolescent English learners in four intact classrooms in China. These classes made up the four conditions in the study: immediate CF, delayed CF, task only, and test only. Learners took pre-tests one week before engaging in treatment tasks, which were followed by immediate post-tests and two-week delayed post-tests. Knowledge of the passive was assessed at each testing juncture, with an untimed grammaticality judgment test to assess explicit knowledge and an elicited imitation test to assess implicit knowledge. The treatment tasks engaged learners in practicing and then performing two dictogloss tasks that elicited the passive. Immediate CF learners were corrected as soon as errors were made with corrective recasts (Doughty & Varela, 1998). Thus, once an error was made, the teacher repeated the utterance using prosodic emphasis to highlight the part that was inaccurate. If the student self-corrected accurately, the task continued. If not, the teacher provided the accurate model. For delayed CF learners, their errors were noted, and CF was delayed until after both dictogloss tasks. Then, CF was provided by reminding the learner about a wrong utterance that the learner had produced and asking him to correct it. From that juncture, CF followed the same process as the immediate CF. For the task-only learners, errors were not corrected. Finally, test-only learners took the pre- and post-tests, but did not do dictogloss tasks or receive CF. Li et al. found that all their conditions improved significantly from pre- to post-tests for the elicited imitation measure of implicit knowledge. Because there were no significant differences between conditions, they concluded that the improvement came only as a result of a test practice effect.

For the grammaticality judgment measure of explicit knowledge, Li et al. (2016) again found significant improvement over time. Moreover, on the delayed post-test, they found that immediate CF learners significantly outperformed the test-only but not the task-only learners. That is, they found that doing dictogloss tasks with or without CF helped learners, but they could not attribute the development solely to CF. However, they found that only immediate CF learners scored significantly better than task-only learners when they analyzed test items that contained regular verbs. Moreover, when they analyzed the scores on the delayed post-test for test items that used verbs that had been in the dictogloss tasks, they found that only the immediate CF learners significantly outperformed the task-only learners. Thus, Li et al. concluded that immediate CF learners demonstrated some advantages over delayed CF learners in explicit L2 knowledge development.

In summary, the majority of comparative analyses found no differences between immediate and delayed CF, and delayed CF never significantly outperformed immediate CF. However, Siyyari (2005) found that immediate CF significantly outperformed delayed CF in an aggregate analysis of his results, and Li et al. (2016) found significant advantages for immediate CF in the cases of regular passive verbs and verbs that participants had encountered in the instructional treatment. The dearth and inconsistency of the findings in the research of CF timing clearly indicate the need for future research.

Considerations for Future Research of the Timing of CF

Future CF timing research has many issues to consider. Perhaps the most important is how to distinguish between the constructs of immediate and delayed CF. CF that is directly adjacent to an error is immediate, so the definition of immediate CF is relatively uncontentious. The vexing question is when does immediate CF cease being immediate and become delayed?

One proposed delineation between the constructs of immediate and delayed CF can be derived from Doughty's (2001) window of cognitive opportunity. As explained, Doughty posited it best for immediate cognitive comparison to occur within the approximately one-minute duration of working memory. Presumably, any CF beyond that boundary would no longer be contiguous to the original commission of the error, and as such would be delayed CF. Quinn (2014) used this psycholinguistic demarcation to define delayed CF. Delayed CF was provided after each of three communicative tasks, which meant that the delayed CF ranged from one to ten minutes after an error. However, some might argue that it is counterintuitive to accept that immediate CF provided 59 seconds after an error is a different construct than delayed CF that is provided 61 seconds after an error.

A second option might be referred to as the pedagogical construct definition of delayed CF, meaning CF that is defined as delayed because it is provided after tasks. Put differently, it is CF that is provided as a subsequent pedagogical activity, separate from the execution of the communicative task. In all the studies reviewed above, delayed CF was provided some time after the communicative task that the error occurred in. However, the amount of that delay varied greatly from study to study, from the end of a task, to the end of all tasks, to the next day. In fact, Li et al. (2016) argue that because the CF in Quinn's (2014) study was delayed only until the end of each task, some of that CF should not be considered delayed CF, but rather as pre-task instruction for the subsequent tasks. Thus, Li et al. argue that delayed CF is CF that occurs after all tasks are complete, or put differently, end-of-lesson CF. Hunter's (2012) delayed CF was provided 24 hours after the errors were committed. Some might argue that CF delayed so long is more akin to remedial instruction than to delayed CF. Do all three of these versions of delayed CF really represent the same construct? The different results in Quinn (2014) and Li et al. (2016) might suggest that end-of-task CF and end-of-lesson CF are potentially two different constructs. The question is an empirical one that is well worth investigating.

Another consideration regarding construct definition is how CF is provided. Quinn (2014) and Li et al. (2016) both attempted to avoid confounding CF type with CF timing. Quinn's laboratory context allowed him to strictly control CF to ensure that immediate and delayed CF were provided in precisely the same way. Consider how the error "The eggs wash" in Quinn's picture-cued story retelling task was addressed. For immediate CF, when the learner made the error, Quinn pointed at the picture of the eggs that were being washed, and said "Could you try this one again?" Regardless of the learner's response, Quinn said "O.K., we say 'the eggs are washed.' Could you repeat that please?" The learner was allowed to repeat it, and the task continued. For delayed CF, after the task was completed, Quinn pointed at the picture of the eggs being washed and followed the same correction verbatim.

Li et al. (2016) concede that their immediate and delayed CF were slightly different. Their immediate CF was initiated by a repetition, so when a learner made an error such as "The driver was arrest," the teacher corrected by saying, "The driver WAS ARREST?" (p. 282). Their delayed CF was initiated by an elicitation such as the teacher saying "Tom, you said 'the driver wanted to run away, but he stopped by a policeman.' Can you say it, correctly?" (p. 283). To address this issue of difference, they explain that different types of prompts are often treated as equivalent in CF research literature. However, arguably they could have avoided this potential confounding of CF timing and type by using the same phrasing for immediate and delayed CF. That is, for both the immediate and the delayed CF, the teacher could have said, "Tom, you said 'the driver was arrest.' Can you say it correctly?" Clearly, the way that the timing of CF was provided differed in the two studies. CF type research has demonstrated that different types of CF lead to different results (e.g., Lyster, 2004). Thus, it is important to keep this consideration in mind when drawing general conclusions about the comparisons between immediate and delayed CF from studies that operationalize CF differently.

Beyond the issues of construct definition, future CF timing investigation should follow the trend toward more careful research design. For example, Quinn (2014) included a control group that received the exact same instruction as the two CF conditions without CF in order to more confidently attribute differential results to the presence of CF in the two CF conditions. However, the only development that was found was the development over time, and that development was equivalent for the control and CF groups. This result made it impossible to disentangle the effects of instruction from the effects of instruction with CF, or even from a practice effect from taking the same tests three times. Li et al. (2016) cleverly included not only a task-only condition, but also a test-only true control condition that allowed them to ameliorate that issue. Future CF timing researchers would be wise to include task-only and test-only control groups.

Future research would also benefit from longer treatment periods. Both Quinn (2014) and Li et al. (2016) took great care to employ a variety of measures and to use immediate and delayed post-tests to bolster confidence in their findings. However, had their treatments taken place over multiple sessions rather than as one-shot treatments, they may have seen more differences emerge as a result of the increased amount of instruction. More CF timing research is needed, and carefully designing that research in line with a consideration of the preceding issues will increase confidence in future results.

Pedagogical Implications of CF Timing Research

L2 researchers regularly urge caution in drawing pedagogical implications from their research. In this case, caution is quite appropriate given the validity problems in some CF timing studies and the small number of investigations. Notwithstanding that, one pedagogical implication that can probably be drawn without too much controversy is that teachers should feel confident in providing immediate and delayed CF. As discussed above, the results of meta-analyses attest to the effectiveness of immediate CF (e.g., Li, 2010; Lyster & Saito, 2010). In addition, Quinn (2014) and Siyyari (2005) found that significant development resulted over time from instruction that included delayed CF. The question most teachers want answered is "When is it best to provide CF?" Unfortunately, the research has not provided a decisive response because research results have differed. While Quinn (2014) and Varnosfadrani (2006) found no differences in the effectiveness of immediate and delayed CF, Li et al. (2016) and Siyyari (2005) found instances in which immediate CF demonstrated significant advantages over delayed CF. These differences were likely due to the differing methodologies the researchers employed in their studies, especially in the ways that delayed CF was operationalized. As Li et al. argued, because the delayed CF in Quinn's study was provided between tasks, learners may have been able to make use of what they gained from the delayed CF in subsequent tasks. Thus, there may be a pedagogical advantage in providing delayed CF between tasks rather than providing it at the end of a lesson. In fact, Li et al.'s method of providing delayed CF may have caused their delayed CF to be less effective than their immediate CF. Unlike their immediate CF, which only repeated the learner's error, their delayed CF informed the learner when the error was made, repeated the error, and then asked for the correct form. Thus, their immediate CF was akin to the learner salvaging a meaningful communication by trying to communicate more accurately, while their delayed CF was more akin to the learner displaying to a teacher that she could solve a grammar problem. Perhaps immediate and delayed CF are most effective when they encourage learners to re-attempt communication rather than when they ask learners to display their ability to solve grammar problems. Another implication that might be drawn from Li et al.'s work is that the question of when it is best to provide CF may not be nuanced enough. Li et al. did not find that immediate CF was always better than delayed CF, but rather that immediate CF was more effective in the development of specific variables (i.e., regular verbs and items that learners had previously encountered). This finding suggests that immediate and delayed CF may be differentially effective for different variables. More CF timing research is required before more pedagogical implications can be agreed upon with an adequate degree of confidence.

References

Bird, S. (2010). Effects of distributed practice on the acquisition of second language English syntax. *Applied Psycholinguistics, 31*(5), 635–650.

Brooks, N. (1960). *Language and language learning, second edition.* New York: Harcourt, Brace and World, Inc.

Cepeda, N. J., Pashler, H., Vul, E., Wixted, J. T., & Rohrer, D. (2006). Distributed practice in verbal recall tasks: A review and quantitative synthesis. *Psychological Bulletin, 132*(3), 354–380.

Chastain, K. (1971). *The development of modern language skills: Theory to practice.* Chicago, IL: Rand McNally.

Corder, S. P. (1967). The significance of learners' errors. *International Review of Applied Linguistics, 5*(1–4), 161–169.

Cowan, N. (1995). *Attention and memory: An integrated framework.* New York: Oxford University Press.

DeKeyser, R. M. (2007). *Practice in a second language: Perspectives from applied linguistics and cognitive psychology*. New York: Cambridge University Press.

Doughty, C. (2001). Cognitive underpinnings of focus on form. In P. Robinson (Ed.), *Cognition and second language instruction* (pp. 206–257). New York: Cambridge University Press.

Doughty, C., & Varela, E. (1998). Communicative focus on form. In C. Doughty & J. Williams (Eds.), *Focus on form in classroom second language acquisition* (pp. 114–138). Cambridge: Cambridge University Press.

Ellis, R. (2006). Researching the effects of form-focused instruction on L2 acquisition. *AILA Review, 19*(1), 18–41.

Fanselow, J. (1977). The treatment of error in oral work. *Foreign Language Annals, 10*(5), 583–593.

Hunter, J. (2007). *The question of error*. Unpublished doctoral dissertation (module 1). University of Birmingham, UK.

Hunter, J. (2012). 'Small talk': Developing fluency, accuracy, and complexity in speaking. *ELT Journal, 66*(1), 30–41.

Hupbach, A., Gomez, R., Hardt, O., & Nadel, L. (2007). Reconsolidation of episodic memories: A subtle reminder triggers integration of new information. *Learning & Memory, 14*(1–2), 47–53.

Karpicke, J. D., & Bauernschmidt, A. (2011). Spaced retrieval: Absolute spacing enhances learning regardless of relative spacing. *Journal of Experimental Psychology: Learning, Memory, and Cognition, 37*(5), 1250–1257.

Krashen, S. D. (1985). *The input hypothesis*. London: Longman.

Li, S. (2010). The effectiveness of corrective feedback in SLA: A meta-analysis. *Language Learning, 60*(2), 309–365.

Li, S., Ellis, R., & Zhu, Y. (2016). The effects of the timing of corrective feedback on the acquisition of a new linguistic structure. *Modern Language Journal, 100*(1), 276–295.

Lyster, R. (2004). Differential effects of prompts and recasts in form-focused instruction. *Studies in Second Language Acquisition, 26*(3), 399–432.

Lyster, R., & Ranta, L. (1997). Corrective feedback and learner uptake. *Studies in Second Language Acquisition, 19*(1), 37–66.

Lyster, R., & Saito, K. (2010). Oral feedback in classroom SLA: A meta-analysis. *Studies in Second Language Acquisition, 32*(2), 265–302.

Morris, D. D., Bransford, J. D., & Franks, J. J. (1977). Levels of processing versus transfer appropriate processing. *Journal of Verbal Learning and Verbal Behavior, 16*(5), 519–533.

Nader, K., & Einarsson, E. O. (2010). Memory reconsolidation: An update. *Annals of the New York Academy of Sciences, 1191*(1), 27–41.

Nakata, T. (2015). Effects of expanding and equal spacing on second language vocabulary learning: Does gradually increasing spacing increase vocabulary learning? *Studies in Second Language Acquisition, 37*(4), 677–711.

Nakata, T., & Webb, S. (in press). Does studying vocabulary in smaller sets increase learning? The effects of part and whole learning on second language vocabulary acquisition. *Studies in Second Language Acquisition*.

Norris, J,. & Ortega, L. (2000). Effectiveness of L2 instruction: A research synthesis and quantitative meta-analysis. *Language Learning, 50*(3), 417–528.

Quinn, P. (2014). *Delayed versus immediate corrective feedback on orally produced passive errors in English*. Unpublished doctoral dissertation, University of Toronto, Canada.

Ranta, L., & Lyster, R. (2007). A cognitive approach to improving immersion students' oral language abilities: The awareness-practice-feedback sequence. In R. M. DeKeyser (Ed.), *Practice in a second language: Perspectives from applied linguistics and cognitive psychology* (pp. 141–160). Cambridge: Cambridge University Press.

Rolin-Ianziti, J. (2010). The organization of delayed second language correction. *Language Teaching Research*, *14*(2), 183–206.

Siyyari, M. (2005). *A comparative study of the effect of implicit and delayed, explicit focus on form on Iranian EFL learners' accuracy of oral production.* Unpublished MA thesis, Iran University of Science and Technology, Iran.

Spada, N., & Lightbown, P.M. (2008). Form-focused instruction: Isolated or integrated? *TESOL Quarterly*, *42*(2), 181–207.

Swain, M. (1985). Communicative competence: Some roles of comprehensible input and comprehensible output in its development. In S. Gass & C. Madden (Eds.), *Input in second language acquisition* (pp. 235–253). Rowley, MA: Newbury House.

Varnosfadrani, A. D. (2006). *A comparison of the effects of implicit / explicit and immediate / delayed corrective feedback on learners' performance in tailor-made tests.* Unpublished PhD thesis, University of Auckland, New Zealand.

Wajnryb, R. (1990). *Grammar dictation.* Oxford: Oxford University Press.

Walker, M. P., Brakefield, T., Hobson, J. A., & Stickgold, R. (2003). Dissociable stages of human memory consolidation and reconsolidation. *Nature*, *425*(6958), 616–620.

PART II

Computer-Mediated Corrective Feedback

4

COMPUTER-ASSISTED CORRECTIVE FEEDBACK AND LANGUAGE LEARNING

Trude Heift and Volker Hegelheimer

Introduction

The provision of immediate and individualized learner feedback has been a central topic in Computer-Assisted Language Learning (CALL) ever since the first CALL programs were developed in the early 1960s. Corrective feedback in CALL has largely focused on learner-computer interactions by exploiting the strengths of different technology-mediated pedagogical approaches to second language (L2) learning and teaching in providing explicit and implicit feedback. Yet, due to the technological advances that occurred over the past decades, CALL applications have varied greatly in the ways in which errors in learner language have been processed and communicated to the learner. With the advent of the World Wide Web, increased storage and faster processing speeds, for instance, corrective feedback is no longer limited to generic computer responses to mechanical, written practice of selected grammatical phenomena and lexical items. Instead, these technological innovations have resulted in more individualized and error-specific learner-computer feedback by also extending it to essay writing. This chapter reviews research on learner-computer feedback in CALL by focusing on two CALL environments which are designed to assist language learners with their written language: Tutorial CALL and systems for Automatic Writing Evaluation (AWE).

Tutorial CALL follows a deductive teaching approach by presenting explicit explanations of grammatical concepts and by focusing language practice on graded and discrete grammatical points. The grammar learning activities mainly consist of short, sentence-based practice and cover isolated grammatical forms which are presented as multiple choice, fill-in-the-blank, match or rank, and reassemble or translate small chunks of text items (Hubbard & Bradin Siskin, 2004; Schulze & Heift, 2013). One of the main differences among Tutorial CALL programs lies in the ways in which learner responses are processed and evaluated. To a large extent, these computational algorithms determine the different types and levels of specificity of the corrective feedback the CALL program provides. In its simplest form of error processing, the computer application is based on monolithic string-matching algorithms and binary knowledge of answer processing that compare the learner input with a pre-stored, correct answer (e.g., Williams, Davis & Williams, 1981). As a result of this computationally limited error-processing technique, the feedback is very general in that it does not identify or explain the source of error. In contrast, Intelligent Language Tutoring Systems (ILTSs) rely on Natural Language Processing (NLP) and techniques of Artificial Intelligence (AI). Based on this complex linguistic processing of students' textual input, ILTSs can detect a wide variety of learner errors and thus provide contextual learner feedback and instructional guidance.

Unlike Tutorial CALL, which emphasizes form-focused instruction at the sentence level for mainly grammar teaching, AWE systems evaluate word-processed essays. As with Tutorial CALL, the feedback in AWE programs focuses primarily on error correction, but these systems also include summative scoring, as well as a range of formative assessment features. Pre-writing tools in the form of graphic organizers, for instance, also make available an emphasis on idea development. The impact of automated feedback in AWE on improving student writing is limited, but growing. While AWE systems provide a type of feedback that might complement a larger, comprehensive approach, much still has to be learned, however, about the context in which these programs are best employed and the types of learners who best benefit from feedback strategies that mostly rely on learner autonomy.

In the following sections, we situate these two distinct CALL environments in their respective SLA theories and then illustrate their goals and functionalities with concrete examples of the different feedback types. For each of the technologies, the chapter further reviews existing research and identifies pedagogical implications for the L2 classroom.

Tutorial CALL

In Tutorial CALL, the computer takes on the role of a *tutor* (Levy, 1997) by evaluating learner responses and presenting new material in one-to-one interactions. In early Tutorial CALL applications, learners were provided with mechanical practice of selected and graded grammatical phenomena, such as the use of verb conjugations, in the form of drills, similar to those commonly found in the face-to-face classroom during the prevalence of the Audio-Lingual Method up to the 1970s. The focus of Tutorial CALL applications was on repetition and immediate feedback, which were provided while allowing students to work at their own pace and time. Later applications placed an increased focus on record keeping and the individualization of the learning experience by paying particular attention to branching, that is, the individualization of practice sequences based on prior student performance (Burston, 1989).

One of the main differences among Tutorial CALL programs lies in the ways in which learner responses are processed and evaluated. These computational algorithms determine the distinct ways in which the CALL application responds to learner errors and thus the varying levels of specificity of corrective feedback.

Tutorial CALL applications, which are based on string-matching algorithms and binary knowledge of answer processing, compare the learner input with a pre-stored, correct answer (e.g., Williams et al., 1981). For instance, the ESL grammar activity given in Example (1) illustrates a typical Tutorial CALL exercise which asks the learner to complete the sentence with the correct verb form.

Example (1):

Prompt: The population of India _____ (have increased,
                  increased, has increased) since 1992.
Learner response: *increased*
System response: *Wrong, try again!*

If the student answers with the simple past 'increased', the system will identify that an error has occurred and respond with a generic error message (e.g., *Wrong, try again!*). However, even if the student chooses the correct answer 'has increased' but misspells it, the CALL program will provide the same error message and thus not make a distinction between different error types. Accordingly, and due to the underlying less sophisticated algorithm of processing learner input, the feedback the CALL program generates is limited to a yes/no response.

More detailed feedback on error type and location is achieved by implementing pattern matching or error anticipation techniques (see Heift & Vyatkina, in press). These algorithms search for variations on the correct response (e.g., inversions of characters, extra characters, missing words, or extra words) or are based on a collection of likely errors which commonly is established by means of a contrastive analysis between the L1 and L2 that the system targets in the learner response (see e.g., Liou, Wang & Hung-Yeh, 1992), respectively. However, the main challenge for these types of Tutorial CALL applications remains the same. As long as the error processing techniques rely on more or less sophisticated string-matching algorithms to provide students with contextual corrective feedback and/or additional instructional guidance, they have to be based on the anticipation of each and every possible correct and erroneous answer in order for them to be robust and comprehensive. If one does not compare the students' input string to the strings of anticipated answers, the computer needs to be capable of a much more sophisticated linguistic analysis of student input to detect errors and provide corrective feedback and contextual instructional guidance. Broadly speaking, this approach is taken in ICALL, which enriches the L2 grammar learning experience by providing contextual learner feedback and instructional guidance based on the complex linguistic processing of students' textual input.

ICALL integrates NLP and AI modeling into CALL. NLP techniques model 'understanding' of human language by a computer by producing a formal linguistic representation of learner input with the goal to provide error-specific corrective feedback, and instructional guidance and scaffolding. AI techniques can be used to model the individualized learning experience, thus aiming at learning programs that come closer to natural language interaction between humans than has been the case with traditional Tutorial CALL.

ILTSs are generally grounded in interactionist Second Language Acquisition (SLA) theory (Gass, 1997; Long, 1996) by, however, illustrating a different type of interaction and noticing process than originally developed for the face-to-face classroom. Their focus is on learner-computer interactions by emphasizing computer reactions and responses to learner output, error detection, and error-specific feedback and by drawing the learners' attention to a gap between their interlanguage and the target language through salient modified language input. ILTSs are primarily designed to support form-focused instruction by identifying ill-formed grammatical constructions in learner output and providing informative, error-specific feedback.

Accordingly, and based on sophisticated NLP technologies, an ILTS identifies and interprets errors as well as correct constructions in learner input and then generates pedagogically appropriate, informative learner feedback by instructing the learner as to the exact location and source of an error. Example (2) illustrates such error-specific, metalinguistic feedback with a sentence-building activity which requires the learner to form a German sentence by providing missing articles and inflections.

Example (2):

Prompt:	Kind / im / Garten / spielen
	child / in the / garden / to play
Learner response:	★Die Kind spielt im Garten.
Correct answer:	Das Kind spielt im Garten.
	The child is playing in the garden.

If the student incorrectly provides the article *Die* for the noun *Kind*, the ICALL system informs the learner that an error has occurred with the article of the neuter noun. In addition, an ILTS is capable of distinguishing among different types of errors. For instance, if the student misspells a word (e.g., ★*speilt* instead of *spielt*), the system also instructs the learner accordingly. Unlike Tutorial CALL, ICALL is able to provide appropriate feedback to a large range of unanticipated errors that the student may make.

A number of ILTSs are used in regular L2 curricula: *E-Tutor* (Heift, 2010) for L2 German, *Robo-Sensei* (Nagata, 2009) for L2 Japanese, and *Tagarela* (Amaral &

Meurers, 2011) for L2 Portuguese. These ICALL systems provide feedback on spelling, morphological, syntactic, and semantic errors for L2 grammar practice. Due to the more sophisticated NLP analysis of ILTSs, their learning environments and activity types are also less restricted than those found in online L2 workbooks and especially than those found in more traditional Tutorial CALL activities (see Example 1).

Research in Tutorial CALL

In view of the powerful capacity of ICALL systems for generating error-specific feedback to learners, researchers have examined the effectiveness of different types of corrective feedback on learners' L2 performance to determine its impact on learning outcomes and/or learner-computer interactions. One of the early ICALL studies, for instance, investigated different feedback types for learning Japanese particles and found that error-specific metalinguistic feedback (see Example 2) that explained the functions and semantic relations of nominal relations in a sentence was more effective than generic, traditional feedback (e.g., *Wrong, try again!*) (Nagata, 1993). A number of studies followed (e.g., Bowles, 2005; Heift, 2004; Heift & Rimrott, 2008; Lado, Wood Bowden, Stafford, & Sanz, 2014; Murphy, 2007; Nagata, 1996; Petersen, 2010; Pujolà, 2002; Rosa & Leow, 2004) that generally supported the benefits of error-specific feedback in a CALL environment. However, a few studies also showed little or no advantage of metalinguistic feedback. For instance, Moreno (2007) investigated the effects of metalinguistic feedback compared to feedback that only signalled whether the student input was right or wrong. While both types led to an increase in scores on the immediate post-test, feedback without metalinguistic information was superior on the delayed post-test (see also Sanz & Morgan-Short, 2004). Similarly, Kregar (2011) examined the effects of text enhancement and metalinguistic feedback on the acquisition of L2 Spanish verbal aspect and found that metalinguistic feedback was less effective than text enhancement.

In addition to these studies which investigated a *reactive* focus on form, that is, feedback that the ICALL system provides in response to learner input, a few studies have also examined *pre-emptive* focus on form which provides learners with relevant metalinguistic information before difficulties arise. The goal here is to reduce potential frustration by marking critical features in the language task to assist learners in task completion (Ellis, Basturkmen & Loewen, 2001). According to Ellis (1993), pre-emptive focus on form also assists in providing learners with explicit knowledge which helps improve performance through monitoring and facilitate acquisition through noticing. Heift (2013), for instance, investigated the impact of pre-emptive focus on form which consisted of exercise-specific grammar and vocabulary hints that the CALL system provided when students started an exercise. She showed that for different proficiency levels (beginner and early intermediate) of adult learners of German, pre-emptive focus on form was significantly more effective than not providing any assistance before students attempted to complete a task. Furthermore, according to retrospective interviews with some of the study participants, pre-emptive focus on form helped them to avoid some errors, thus also leading to a more positive learning experience.

While the research above focused on learning outcomes by studying the effectiveness of different feedback types, some studies have also considered learner strategies with respect to corrective feedback in CALL. For instance, Brandl (1995), studying L2 learners of German, found that lower achieving learners, as determined by an initial placement test of reading comprehension, had a more limited set of strategies for processing feedback than learners of higher achievement levels. Similarly, a study by Vinther (2005) investigated the difference in learner strategies employed by low- and high-achieving Danish university students of English as a foreign language. Her study confirmed Brandl's (1995) results by showing that high-performing students were more likely to make use of cognitive strategies throughout program use, while lower performing students employed only a few cognitive strategies, favoring affective strategies more, at least at the beginning of program use.

Similarly, some studies also examined learner error correction behavior in response to distinct feedback types, thus focusing on the learning process as opposed to learning outcomes. The range of possible reactions and/or responses to corrective feedback is generally referred to as learner uptake. Research from face-to-face instruction (e.g., Lyster, 2007) proposes that successful learner uptake is a good predictor of learning. Even in instances where no learning takes place at a particular moment, the research suggests that learners notice the feedback and process it, thereby increasing the likelihood of learning. As a result, researchers tend to view learner uptake as facilitative of L2 acquisition and examine its role when teaching L2 grammar with technology. For instance, Heift's (2002) study revealed that, when students were provided with error-specific feedback, the majority of them (85%) sought to correct errors on their own most of the time instead of looking up a correct answer made available to them in her ICALL system (see also Hegelheimer & Chapelle, 2000).

Overall, this line of research has shown that students generally benefit from explicit, metalinguistic feedback because they subsequently perform better on particular target language structures and/or because students' grammatical awareness is subsequently raised. Nevertheless, there are a number of conflating factors, such as feedback amount and timing, or, more generally, the long-term impact of CALL feedback on L2 learning which make the research less conclusive and requires further investigation.

In contrast to Tutorial CALL applications which, commonly, are limited to grammatical errors at the sentence level, systems for automatic writing evaluation provide feedback for word-processed essays. The following sections describe different types of AWE-generated feedback from an SLA perspective and review research that has been conducted in writing classrooms. We conclude with suggestions for future research and pedagogical applications in L2 writing classes.

Automatic Writing Evaluation

Since the initial development of a scoring engine in 1996 (Page, 2003), the last 20 years have witnessed a rapid development of Automated Essay Scoring (AES) systems. Outfitted with error detection and scoring engines, AWE tools such as *Criterion* (Educational Testing Service, https://criterion.ets.org), *MYAccess!* (Vantage learning, http://www.myaccess.com), *WriteToLearn* (Pearson Education, http://www.writetolearn.net), *CyWrite* (Iowa State University, https://cywrite. engl.iastate.edu/), and *Research Writing Tutor* (*RWT*) (Iowa State University, http://circlcenter.org/events/cyberlearning-2015/gallery-walk/research-writing-tutor/) are able to analyze a wide range of lexical, syntactic, semantic, and discourse structures and to provide feedback on the linguistic features of student writing.

AWE tools use a variety of computational methods and algorithms. AWE systems such as *Criterion* (Burstein, Chodorow, & Leacock, 2004; Burstein, Tetreault, & Madnani, 2013), *IntelliMetric* (Rudner, Garcia, & Welch, 2006; www.vantagelearning. com/products/intellimetric/), *CyWrite*[1] (Feng, Saricaoglu, & Chukharev-Hudilainen, 2016) and *RWT* (Cotos & Pendar, 2016) use Natural Language Processing and statistical techniques. Other AWE programs, like the *Intelligent Essay Assessor* (Landauer, Laham, & Foltz, 2003), are trained in Latent Semantic Analysis (LSA).

With regard to identifying and reporting learner errors, AWE programs provide two different types of corrective feedback: *explicit* and *implicit*.

Explicit or *direct* feedback pertains to a situation in which the computer specifies an error in student writing and provides language learners with the correct form. Students can click on a detected mistake in order to view its pop-up comments and editing suggestions. As illustrated in Examples (3)–(6), feedback in *Criterion* not only identifies different error types (e.g., a missing or extra articles) but also highlights those in student essays. *CyWrite,* a web-based AWE tool developed at Iowa State University, for instance, provides instant feedback on spelling errors, run-on sentences, subject-verb agreement, quantifiers, and articles (Feng et al., 2016). *WriteToLearn* (Pearson Education) is another example of machine-generated direct corrective feedback. These AWE systems can all locate erroneous instances and suggest possible corrections, even though not all suggestions yield correct sentences (see Example 6).

Example (3):

Learner written discourse: These products and services are actually giving us **problem** besides making our life easier.

Criterion feedback: You may need to use an article before this word. Consider using the article **a**.

Example (4):

Learner written discourse: Football is my **favorit*** sport.

CyWrite feedback: You have a spelling error. Please fix. Suggestions: favorite.

Example (5):

Learner written discourse:	Tai Chi is **one★ of★** the popular and well-known exercise in China.
CyWrite feedback:	You cannot use "one of" with a singular or uncountable noun. You have used "one of" incorrectly here.

Example (6):

Learner written discourse:	My family **had★ got★** a really hard time.
WriteToLearn feedback:	It looks like you have used the wrong tense of the verb "got" when combined with the helper verb "had".
WriteToLearn suggestions:	got/had gotten/had been getting/gotten.

In order to explain the nature of an error explicitly, metalinguistic feedback in AWE programs is presented to learners in various forms. *Criterion*'s feedback briefly describes definitions and functions of discourse features, such as introductory material, thesis statements and main ideas, etc. In addition, "Writer's Handbook" in *Criterion* instructs students to rectify their mistakes with explanations of error types, example sentences, model essays, and further instructional materials. *MYAccess* features "Word Bank" to enrich students' vocabulary knowledge and "Activity Bank" to provide additional lessons. The *RWT*'s Demonstration Module allows students to access examples of rhetorical structures in published papers of their disciplines.

In contrast to *explicit* feedback, *implicit* or *indirect* corrective feedback also identifies and signals the error to the student; however, the AWE program does not offer any corrections. As with teacher-provided implicit feedback in L2 writing, students are left identifying and rectifying the error themselves. In *Criterion*, *MYAccess!*, and *WriteToLearn*, implicit feedback on student writing performance can be provided in the form of holistic and trait scores. Unlike a holistic score that is given as a single score and reflects the overall quality of an essay, trait scores provide feedback on each of the evaluative criteria for the writing task. Students can also view visual reports on their progress and a score guide that helps interpret machine-generated scores. For example, a trait descriptor of grammar, usage, and mechanics under the "Conventions" category in *Criterion* describes a proficient-level essay as including some errors that do not generally prevent understanding.

Unlike written corrective feedback in traditional L2 writing research, which commonly focuses on accuracy-related features (e.g., Bitchener, Young, & Cameron, 2005; Chandler, 2003; Ferris, 1999; Truscott, 1996), automated corrective feedback has also been extended to rhetorical and discourse features. The *Research Writing Tutor* (the *RWT*, Cotos, 2012) is an innovative AWE tool that aims at the rhetorical quality in academic writing for advanced graduate students.

Automated feedback in the *RWT* is generated by comparing the learners' writing to a collection of published articles. The *RWT* provides color-coded feedback and evaluative comments on rhetorical functions in students' submitted texts. Based on an analytical summary of rhetorical functions and evaluative remarks, students are encouraged to revise their drafts to address writing conventions of their disciplines.

Research in AWE-Generated Corrective Feedback

Previous learner-focused research of AWE tools can be classified into three distinct areas: research that (a) evaluates the reliability of automated feedback, (b) investigates the impact of AWE-based corrective feedback on L2 learning, and (c) explores learners' perceptions of machine-generated corrective feedback.

The reliability of AWE corrective feedback is primarily determined by the error detection and scoring engines as the core components of AWE systems (Chapelle, Cotos & Lee, 2015). Prior research has focused on assessing the accuracy of computer-provided feedback by comparing automated feedback with feedback given by writing teachers. Results show that the accuracy of machine-generated feedback, for example, *Criterion* and *CyWrite*, varied across error types (Feng et al., 2016; Ranalli, Link, & Chukharev-Hudilainen, 2016). Reliability of scoring engines in AWE tools has also been fairly inconclusive. Several studies found high correlations between computer-generated scores and human scores (Attali, Bridgeman, & Trapani, 2010; Burstein et al., 2004; El-Ebyary & Windeatt, 2010; Warschauer & Ware, 2006). Other studies (James, 2006; Li, Link, Ma, Yang, & Hegelheimer, 2014; Wang & Brown, 2007) found low to moderate positive correlations between machine-generated scores and instructors' ratings.

Numerous studies also investigated the impact of automated corrective feedback on students' writing performance and revealed mixed results. Some studies (Chodorow, Gamon, & Tetreault, 2010; Warschauer & Grimes, 2008) demonstrated learners' improvement largely for surface linguistic features such as grammar and mechanics at the word or sentence levels. A study by Wang and Wang (2012), for instance, showed that the employment of *Writing RoadmapTM 2.0* (WRM) could help improve word choice, fluency, spelling, and grammatical control in student writing. Kellogg, Whiteford and Quinlan (2010) found that error reduction in terms of mechanics, usage, grammar, and style could be transferred in student writing, but holistic scores showed little improvement. Chapelle et al. (2015) studied meaning-focused corrective feedback and confirmed evidence of learners' increased focus on discourse meaning after using the *Intelligent Academic Discourse Evaluator* (a former version of the *Research Writing Tutor*). Regarding the effect of computer-provided corrective feedback on draft revisions, Attali (2004) showed that 71% of students did not revise their drafts and 48% of those who made revisions did so only once. In the same vein, findings in the study by Chapelle et al. (2015) showed that 51% of the students did not attempt to make changes of *Criterion*-detected errors, although direct, indirect, or metalinguistic feedback was provided with suggested corrections. Nevertheless, Huffman (2015) observed that students extensively employed the Demonstration Module's concordancing tool in the *RWT* for rhetorical examples in authentic published works in response to automated feedback. In surveying previous studies for written production measures, Stevenson and Phakiti (2013) suggested that there has been scant evidence that AWE feedback has a positive effect on the quality of student writing. Consequently, as of yet, there is little empirical evidence of the transferability of AWE feedback to a more general improvement in L2 writing proficiency (Warschauer & Grimes, 2008).

In order to shed light on how learners perceive AWE-generated feedback, a large body of research has examined learners' preferences for AWE compared to teacher-provided feedback by collecting evidence through observations, questionnaires and interviews. Several studies indicate that learners generally appreciate the usefulness of computer-generated feedback (Cassandra, Dexter, & Riedel, 2008; Chen & Cheng, 2008; Huffman, 2015) while, at the same time, valuing instructors' feedback (Hyland & Hyland, 2006; Yang, 2004) or peer feedback (Lai, 2010) over automated feedback. As Yang (2004) explained, this may be largely due to the fact that instructor-provided feedback is meaning focused, while feedback given by AWE tools is generally form focused. Another possible explanation might relate to the trustworthiness of AWE feedback on draft revisions of student essays (Chapelle et al., 2015; Scharber, Dexter, & Riedel, 2008). Scharber et al. (2008), for instance, found that students' awareness of affordances and limitations of AWE tools could affect their trust in automated feedback. Similarly, Huffman (2015) reported students' wavering trust due to their observations of *RWT* feedback inaccuracies. However, Li, Link, and Hegelheimer (2015) highlight that learners' views may likely depend on the learners' language proficiency and instructors' use and perspectives of AWE. Interestingly, the authors also found that *Criterion*-provided feedback could motivate draft revisions and, hence, help to improve writing accuracy across multiple drafts.

In summary, while previous research on AWE has undoubtedly provided some insight into the effectiveness of its tools, there is a scarcity of research evidence, especially with regard to whether automated AWE feedback results in accuracy development and retention over time. For this, longitudinal examinations of writing samples of L2 learners are needed. In addition, the effect of different types of AWE corrective feedback on L2 writing accuracy and writing fluency (i.e., an ability to write an essay quickly with minimal errors) needs to be determined. In order to facilitate this type of research, AWE systems such as *CyWrite* must include mechanisms to allow for varying corrective feedback and detecting different error types depending on the focus of the teacher, the student, and/or the researcher. Finally, the distinct writing environments in which AWE tools and corrective feedback are employed need to be closely examined. Warschauer and Grimes (2008), for instance, noted that AWE tools tend to be misused, with insufficient time scheduled for them. Thus, maximizing the full potentials of computer-provided feedback in writing classes also largely depends on how instructors deploy the tools.

Conclusion and Pedagogical Implications

This chapter outlined two CALL environments designed to assist language learners with their grammar and writing by providing corrective feedback of varying degrees of specificity and focus. Both Tutorial CALL and AWE provide language learners with feedback on their written language. Yet, Tutorial CALL emphasizes form-focused instruction at the sentence level for mainly grammar teaching, while AWE systems evaluate word-processed essays. Taking these two technologies in combination, however, they provide an opportunity for learners to work on vital L2 skills independently of the face-to-face L2 classroom.

The gold standard for corrective feedback provided by CALL technology is to achieve a level of accuracy close to that of a learner-teacher interaction independent of whether the tools are used during teacher-directed classroom instruction or for self-study outside the classroom. As discussed throughout the chapter, significant progress toward that goal has been made and although there remains room for improvement, particularly with regard to the accuracy of error identification, computer-generated corrective feedback has increasingly taken on a significant role in grammar and vocabulary practice and, more generally, in writing instruction. The usefulness of computer-generated corrective feedback largely lies in enabling learner self-study and practice of the target language by identifying and explaining error sources and, with regard to L2 essay writing, allowing for draft revision. At the same time, language instructors are central to the successful realization of these new opportunities and affordances of L2 learning and independent of the particular technologies used.

Like with any CALL tool employed in the L2 classroom, the involvement of instructors is crucial, as they can trigger, stimulate, monitor, and guide in-class as well as outside-class activities. As for the use of AWE tools, more specifically, these systems must be thoroughly introduced so that L2 learners can become cognizant of their advantages and disadvantages. According to Feng et al. (2016), for instance, variable error-type detection reliability makes it difficult to provide anything but nuanced suggestions to learners as to when to trust AWE engines. As a result, pedagogically sound advice on the use of AWE tools might consist of instructing L2 learners on how to self-educate, so that they learn when and how much faith to put into automatically generated error detections.

In classroom settings, pedagogical practices on using corrective feedback in AWE programs (*Criterion*, in this instance) can be implemented during in-class activities of peer review exercises, or editing and revising tasks (Link, Dursun, Karakaya, & Hegelheimer, 2014). As for peer review exercises, for example, students may examine the automated corrective feedback they receive and then collaborate with classmates on how to interpret and negotiate such feedback.

In editing and revising tasks, writing instructors can deploy automated corrective feedback on a focused error to help guide the design of revision exercises. As for independent study activities, computer-generated feedback systems may promote learner autonomy in writing practice (Link et al., 2014), thus also making effective use of the benefits offered by computer-generated corrective feedback. For instance, students may employ a grammar checker for draft revisions and take advantage of supplementary instructional material for error explanations, rhetorical function clarifications, or model essays. However, teachers and language learners alike need to be able to use these technologies in ways that are most conducive to successful language learning. Key in the future development of computer-generated feedback is to equip the tools with mechanisms that allow for research of vast and reliable user data.

Note

1 The CyWrite project (https://cywrite.engl.iastate.edu/wp/) was initiated by Volker Hegelheimer and Carol Chapelle in 2013 and, since then, the CyWrite team has been led by Evgeny Chukharev-Hudilainen.

References

Amaral, L., & Meurers, D. (2011). On using intelligent computer-assisted language learning in real-life foreign language teaching and learning. *ReCALL, 23*(1), 4–24.
Attali, Y. (2004). Exploring feedback and revision features of *Criterion*. Paper presented at the National Council on Measurement in Education San Diego, April 12–16, 2004.
Attali, Y., Bridgeman, B., & Trapani, C. (2010). Performance of a generic approach in automated essay scoring. *The Journal of Technology, Learning and Assessment, 10*(3), 1–17.
Bitchener, J., Young, S., & Cameron, D. (2005). The effect of different types of corrective feedback on ESL student writing. *Journal of Second Language Writing, 14*(3), 191–205.
Bowles, M. (2005). *Effects of verbalization condition and type of feedback on L2 development in a CALL task*. PhD dissertation, Georgetown University, US.
Brandl, K. (1995). Strong and weak students' preferences for error feedback options and responses. *Modern Language Journal, 79*(2), 194–211.
Burstein, J., Chodorow, M., & Leacock, C. (2004). Automated essay evaluation: The Criterion online writing system. *AI Magazine, 25*(3), 27–36.
Burstein, J., Tetreault, J., & Madnani, N. (2013). The E-rater® automated essay scoring system. In M. D. Shermis, & J. Burstein (Eds.), *Handbook for automated essay scoring: Current applications and new directions* (pp. 55–67). New York: Routledge.
Burston, J. (1989). Towards better Tutorial CALL: A matter of intelligent control. *CALICO Journal, 6*(4), 75–89.
Cassandra, S., Dexter, S., & Riedel, E. (2008). Students' experiences with an automated essay scorer. *The Journal of Technology, Learning and Assessment, 7*(1), 4–44.
Chandler, J. (2003). The efficacy of various kinds of error feedback for improvement in the accuracy and fluency of L2 student writing. *Journal of Second Language Writing, 12*(3), 267–296.
Chapelle, C. A., Cotos, E., & Lee, J. (2015). Validity arguments for diagnostic assessment using automated writing evaluation. *Language Testing, 32*(3), 385–405.

Chen, C., & Cheng, W. (2008). Beyond the design of automated writing evaluation: Pedagogical practices and perceived learning effectiveness in EFL writing classes. *Language Learning & Technology*, *12*(2), 94–112.

Chodorow, M., Gamon, M., & Tetreault, J. (2010). The utility of article and preposition error correction systems for English language learners: Feedback and assessment. *Language Testing*, *27*(3), 419–436.

Cotos, E. (2012). Towards effective integration and positive impact of automated writing evaluation in L2 writing. In G. Kessler, A. Oskoz & I. Elola (Eds.), *Technology across writing contexts and tasks, CALICO Monograph Series* (Vol. 10, pp. 81–112). San Marcos, TX: CALICO.

Cotos, E., & Pendar, N. (2016). Discourse classification into rhetorical functions for AWE feedback. *CALICO Journal*, *33*(1), 92–116.

Educational Testing Service (n.d.). *Criterion*. Available at https://criterion.ets.org.

El-Ebyary, K., & Windeatt, S. (2010). The impact of computer-based feedback on students' written work. *International Journal of English Studies*, *10*(2), 121–142.

Ellis, R. (1993). The structural syllabus and second language acquisition. *TESOL Quarterly*, *27*, 91–113.

Ellis, R., Basturkmen, H., & Loewen, S. (2001). Preemptive focus on form in the ESL classroom. *TESOL Quarterly*, *35*, 407–432.

Feng, H-H., Saricaoglu, A., & Chukharev-Hudilainen, E. (2016). Automated error detection for developing grammar proficiency of ESL learners. *CALICO Journal*, *33*(1), 49–70.

Ferris, D. (1999). The case for grammar correction in L2 writing classes: A response to Truscott (1996). *Journal of Second Language Writing*, *8*(1), 1–10.

Gass, S. (1997). *Input, Interaction and the Second Language Learner*. Mahwah, NJ: Lawrence Erlbaum.

Hegelheimer, V., & Chapelle, C. (2000). Methodological issues in research on learner–computer interactions in CALL. *Language Learning & Technology*, *4*(1), 41–59.

Heift, T. (2002). Learner control and error correction in ICALL: Browsers, peekers and adamants. *CALICO Journal*, *19*(2), 295–313.

Heift, T. (2004). Corrective feedback and learner uptake in CALL. *ReCALL*, *16*(2), 416–431.

Heift, T. (2010). Developing an intelligent tutor. *CALICO Journal*, *27*(3), 443–459.

Heift, T. (2013). Preemptive feedback in CALL. In A. Mackey & K. McDonough (Eds.), *Interaction in Diverse Educational Settings* (pp. 189–207). Philadelphia: John Benjamins.

Heift, T., & Rimrott, A. (2008). Learner responses to corrective feedback for spelling errors in CALL. *System*, *36*(2), 196–213.

Heift, T., & Vyatkina, N. (in press). Technologies for teaching and learning L2 Grammar. In C.A. Chapelle & S. Sauro. (Eds.), *The Handbook of Technology in Second Language Teaching and Learning*. Hoboken, NJ: Wiley-Blackwell.

Hubbard, P. & Bradin Siskin, C. (2004). Another look at Tutorial CALL. *ReCALL*, *16*, 448–461.

Huffman, S. (2015). *Exploring learner perceptions of and interaction behaviors using the Research Writing Tutor for research article Introduction section draft analysis*. Unpublished doctoral dissertation, Iowa State University, US.

Hyland, K., & Hyland, F. (2006). Feedback on second language students' writing. *Language Teaching*, *39*(2), 83–101.

Iowa State University (n.d.). *CyWrite*. Available at https://cywrite.engl.iastate.edu/.

Iowa State University (n.d.). *Research Writing Tutor*. Available at http://circlcenter.org/events/cyberlearning-2015/gallery-walk/research-writing-tutor/.

James, C. (2006). Validating a computerized scoring system for assessing writing and placing students in composition courses. *Assessing Writing, 11*(3), 167–178.

Kellogg, R., Whiteford, A., & Quinlan, T. (2010). Does automated feedback help students learn to write? *Journal of Educational Computing Research, 42*(2), 173–196.

Kregar, S. (2011). *Relative effectiveness of corrective feedback types in computer-assisted language learning.* PhD dissertation, Florida State University, US.

Lado, B., Bowden, H., Stafford, C. and Sanz. C. (2014). A fine-grained analysis of the effects of negative evidence with and without metalinguistic information in language development. *Language Teaching Research, 18,* 320–344.

Lai, Y. (2010). Which do students prefer to evaluate their essays: Peers or computer program. *British Journal of Educational Technology, 41,* 432–454.

Landauer, T. K., Laham, R. D., & Foltz, P. W. (2003). Automated scoring and annotation of essays with the Intelligent Essay Assessor. In M. Shermis & J. Bernstein (Eds.), *Automated essay scoring: A cross-disciplinary perspective* (pp. 87–112). Mahwah, NJ: Lawrence Erlbaum Associates.

Levy, M. (1997). *Computer-assisted language learning. Context and conceptualisation.* Oxford: Clarendon.

Li, J., Link, S., & Hegelheimer, V. (2015). Rethinking the role of automated writing evaluation (AWE) feedback in ESL writing instruction. *Journal of Second Language Writing, 27,* 1–18.

Li, Z., Link, S., Ma, H., Yang, H., & Hegelheimer, V. (2014). The role of automated writing evaluation holistic scores in the ESL classroom. *System, 44*(1), 66–78.

Link, S., Dursun, A., Karakaya, K., & Hegelheimer, V. (2014). Towards best ESL practices for implementing automated writing evaluation. *CALICO Journal, 31*(3), 323–344.

Long, M. (1996). The role of the linguistic environment in second language acquisition. In W. Ritchie, & T.K. Bhatia (Eds.), *Handbook of Second Language Acquisition* (pp. 413–468). San Diego, CA: Academic Press.

Lyster, R. (2007). *Learning and Teaching Languages through Content: A Counterbalanced Approach.* Amsterdam: Benjamins.

Moreno, N. (2007). *The effects of type of task and type of feedback on L2 development in CALL.* PhD dissertation, Georgetown University, US.

Murphy, P. (2007). Reading comprehension exercises online: The effects of, feedback, proficiency and interaction. *Language Learning & Technology, 11*(3), 107–129.

Nagata, N. (1993). Intelligent computer feedback for second language instruction. *Modern Language Journal, 77*(3), 330–338.

Nagata, N. (1996). Computer vs. workbook instruction in second language acquisition. *CALICO Journal, 14*(1), 53–75.

Nagata, N. (2009). Robo-Sensei's NLP-based error detection and feedback generation. *CALICO Journal, 26*(3), 562–579.

Page, E. (2003). Project essay grade: PEG. In M. D. Shermis & J. C. Burstein (Eds.), *Automated essay scoring: A cross-disciplinary perspective* (pp. 43–54). Mahwah, NJ: Lawrence Erlbaum.

Pearson Education (n.d.). *WriteToLearn.* Available at http://www.writetolearn.net.

Petersen, K. (2010). *Implicit corrective feedback in computer-guided interaction. Does mode matter?* PhD dissertation, Georgetown University.

Pujolà, J. T. (2002). CALLing for help: Researching language learning strategies using help facilities in a web-based multimedia program. *ReCALL, 14*(2), 253–262.

Ranalli, J., Link, S., & Chukharev-Hudilainen, E. (2016). Automated writing evaluation for formative assessment of second language writing: Investigating the accuracy and usefulness of feedback as part of argument-based validation. *Educational Psychology*, *37*(1), 8–25.

Rosa, E., & Leow, R. (2004). Computerized task-based exposure, explicitness and type of feedback on Spanish L2 development. *Modern Language Journal, 88*, 192–217.

Rudner, L., Garcia, V., & Welch, C. (2006). An evaluation of the IntelliMetric essay scoring system. *Journal of Technology, Learning, and Assessment, 4*(4). Retrieved from www.jtla.org.

Sanz, C., & Morgan-Short, K. (2004). Positive evidence versus explicit rule presentation and explicit negative feedback: A computer-assisted study. *Language Learning, 54*(1), 35–78.

Scharber, C., Dexter, S., Riedel, E. (2008). Students' experiences with an automated essay scorer. *Journal of Technology, Learning, and Assessment, 7*(1). Retrieved from http://www.jtla.org.

Schulze, M., & Heift, T. (2013). Intelligent CALL. In M. Thomas, H. Reinders and M. Warschauer (Eds.), *Contemporary Computer-Assisted Language Learning* (pp. 249–265). London and New York: Continuum.

Stevenson, M., & Phakiti, A. (2013). The effects of computer-generated feedback on the quality of writing. *Assessing Writing, 19*(1), 51–65.

Truscott, J. 1996. The case against grammar correction in L2 writing classes. *Language Learning, 46*(2), 327–369.

Vantage Learning (n.d.). *IntelliMetric.* Available at www.vantagelearning.com/products/intellimetric/.

Vantage Learning (n.d.). *MYAccess!* Available at http://www.myaccess.com.

Vinther, J. (2005). Cognitive processes at work in CALL. *Computer Assisted Language Learning, 18*(4), 251–271.

Wang, J., & Brown, M. S. (2007). Automated essay scoring versus human scoring: a comparative study. *Journal of Technology, Learning, and Assessment, 6*(2). Retrieved from http://www.jtla.org.

Wang, F., & Wang, S. (2012). A comparative study on the influence of automated evaluation system and teacher grading on students' English writing. *Procedia Engineering, 29*, 993–997.

Warschauer, M., & Ware, P. (2006). Automated writing evaluation: Defining the classroom research agenda. *Language Teaching Research, 10*(2), 1–24.

Warschauer, M., & Grimes, G. (2008). Automated writing assessment in the classroom. *Pedagogies: An International Journal, 3*(1), 22–36.

Williams, A., Davies, G. & Williams, I. (1981). *Apfeldeutsch.* London: Wida Software.

Yang, N. (2004). Using MYAccess in EFL writing. In *The proceedings of 2004 International Conference and Workshop on TEFL & Applied Linguistics* (pp. 550–564). Taipei, Taiwan: Ming Chuan University.

5

PEER CORRECTIVE FEEDBACK IN COMPUTER-MEDIATED COLLABORATIVE WRITING

Neomy Storch

Introduction

A peer feedback activity is generally implemented in a writing class as a reciprocal activity, whereby two students exchange their drafts and provide each other with feedback, including corrective feedback (CF), on these drafts. The feedback can be delivered in the form of comments written on the drafts or on a checklist, comments provided via face-to-face or computer-mediated (CM) interaction, or a combination of these forms. Liu and Hansen (2002) summarize the many pedagogical and social benefits of peer feedback. Pedagogically, reading a peer's text exposes the learner to different ways of expressing ideas. Furthermore, evaluating a peer's text can help develop critical reading skills and audience awareness. Liu and Hansen also note that in peer feedback activities, the feedback is provided in a non-threatening context and may thus encourage exploratory talk. Socially, engaging with peers about writing and deliberating about similar concerns may help build collegial ties.

However, the literature on peer feedback has also identified some of the difficulties that L2 learners experience in peer feedback activities, particularly in the provision of CF. Learners often admit to lacking confidence in their ability to provide CF and distrusting the accuracy of the feedback provided by fellow L2 learners (e.g., Guardado & Shi, 2007; Sengupta, 1998; Tsui & Ng, 2000). This distrust may explain why a large proportion of peer feedback is not incorporated in revised drafts (e.g., Connor & Asenavage, 1994). Learners may also resent being asked to provide CF because they believe this to be the role of the teacher, the only real source of language expertise in the classroom (Sengupta, 1998). These views together with the expressed lack of confidence can lead to learner disengagement in peer feedback activities (Liu & Hansen, 2002). Yet for any feedback to be useful, it requires learners to notice it and engage with it. Deep levels of conceptual processing of linguistic information, including information provided via feedback, are associated with greater retention (e.g., Moranski & Toth, 2016; Qi & Lapkin 2001; Storch, 2008).

One way of addressing these concerns with CF is to implement collaborative writing activities. I begin by defining collaborative writing and then briefly review the literature on CF provided by peers working on such tasks in the face-to-face environment. This discussion provides the necessary background to the main focus of this chapter: research findings on peer CF when the collaborative writing activities are CM and the pedagogical implications of these findings.

Collaborative Writing in the Face-to-Face Environment

Collaborative writing is an activity that involves two or more writers co-authoring a text and sharing responsibility for the jointly composed text (Storch, 2013). It should be noted that collaborative writing is distinct from cooperative writing. Although both approaches result in the creation of one joint text, the processes leading to the creation of the text and when the peer feedback is provided differ. Cooperation implies some division of labour, with contributors taking individual responsibility for specific subtasks or for composing certain sections of the text. Thus, in cooperative writing peer CF is likely to take place when a section has been drafted by one contributor and/or when the whole text has been assembled. In collaborative writing, the co-authors are involved in all stages of the text construction. Peer feedback can occur not only once the draft is complete, but throughout the writing process when a learner notices an error in the evolving text and during deliberations on how to best express ideas. Admittedly, the distinction between collaborative and cooperative writing may not always be very clear cut. What may begin as a collaborative activity may become cooperative and vice versa.

The following extract exemplifies the nature of peer CF in collaborative writing. The extract comes from a study conducted in Australia with advanced ESL learners, where learners were asked to compose a text discussing the merits of exams as an assessment procedure (Wigglesworth & Storch, 2009). The extract shows two instances of CF that occur in the process of co-constructing the text. The first instance occurs when Emily (Line 277) suggests to Matt, the scribe, an alternative word choice (encouraging vs. forcing), feedback readily accepted by Matt (Line 278) and incorporated into the joint text. The second instance occurs when Emily deliberates about the appropriate word form (a revision vs. revising). Her deliberations elicit feedback from Matt (Line 280). In solitary writing, the writer relies on their own linguistic knowledge to resolve any uncertainties about language choice. In collaborative writing, uncertainties can be resolved with assistance from the co-author or by a pooling of linguistic resources.

Extract 1: Corrective feedback during collaborative writing

276	Mat:	By forcing the students to revising
277	Emily:	encouraging would be a nicer word
278	Mat:	ha ha ha. In the encouraging the students ...
279	Emily:	to take the initiative yeah, great ... to take initiatives to start revising ... to start a revision. Oh no, to start revising, no?
280	Mat:	mmm ... . To start revising

A number of studies (see review in Storch, 2013) have documented the nature of peer CF during collaborative writing, showing evidence of learners engaging in negotiations about language use, in explorations of alternative forms of expression, and providing explanations of grammatical conventions. These studies show that the CF provided during collaborative writing deals with problems that have been identified by the learners themselves and that any explanations provided are accessible (e.g., use of L1, simple metalanguage). Thus the feedback provided is more likely to be understood and retained. For example, Brooks and Swain (2009) found that peer feedback provided by learners during a joint writing activity was more enduring than the CF provided by a native speaker expert on the completed draft.

Research on collaborative writing undertaken in a range of L2 settings has also shown that during deliberations about language learners pool their linguistic resources and reach resolutions that are mostly correct (e.g., Fernández Dobao, 2012; Storch, 2002; Storch & Aldosari, 2010; Swain, 1998). There is also evidence that texts produced collaboratively are grammatically more accurate than texts produced by learners writing individually (e.g., Fernández Dobao, 2012; Storch, 2005; Storch & Wigglesworth, 2007). Most importantly, perhaps, research has shown that the negotiations during collaborative writing lead to language learning (e.g., Brooks & Swain, 2009; Storch, 2002; Watanabe & Swain, 2007).

To summarize, corrective feedback provided during collaborative writing has a number of pedagogical benefits. It is timely and expedient because it is contingently responsive to the learners' needs as they arise in the process of text composition, it is accessible, and is more readily accepted and incorporated. Learners are more likely to be motivated to provide peer CF on a text over which they share responsibility and ownership than is the case in peer feedback activities, where the text reviewed is the property of the author.

However, it is important to note that simply assigning students to work in pairs or small groups does not mean that they will necessarily collaborate and engage productively in the provision of CF. Research by Storch (2001, 2002) has shown that if learners form a cooperative relationship or a dominant/passive relationship, where one learner takes control of the task and the other contributes very little, there is very little provision or engagement with CF in the joint writing activity. Such relationships are less conducive to language learning (see Kim & McDonough, 2008; Storch, 2002; Watanabe & Swain, 2007).

The studies on collaborative writing cited above have been conducted in classrooms with learners interacting face to face. Nowadays, as CM language instruction is becoming more pervasive, interest in collaborative writing has shifted to this new environment.

Computer-Mediated Collaborative Writing and Peer CF

Much has been written about the learning potentials of CM instruction, including first generation web tools for communication such as chat rooms and second generation tools such as wikis and Google Docs. Wikis and Google Docs are of greatest relevance to collaborative writing research because they are considered dedicated collaborative writing platforms. The main distinction between these two platforms is that wikis are asynchronous, whereas Google Docs are synchronous.

These platforms offer a number of pedagogical advantages. They are relatively easy to use and lend themselves to small and large group collaborative writing projects. They extend and facilitate the opportunities for learners to engage in collaborative writing outside the confines of the physical classroom, with each learner having access to the latest version of the joint draft. Furthermore, they have a number of important built-in features such as dedicated discussion spaces assigned to particular pages and a log of contributions, which saves every revision made. The log enables writers to reject revisions and revert to a previous version. The log also enables teachers (and researchers) to monitor each learner's contribution to the activity.

Studies on L2 learners' revision behavior when working on collaborative writing tasks using these two platforms can be divided into three strands: (a) studies investigating the CF provided on peers' contributions, (b) studies investigating the level of learners' engagement with the CF provided, or deliberations about language choice in the discussion space or via the use of other CM means, and (c) studies comparing the nature and level of engagement with peer CF in the face-to-face and CM environments.

CF Provided on Peers' Contributions

Research on peer feedback in wiki or Google Docs projects has investigated revisions that peers make to the posted contributions of other learners in the group. This research (e.g., Arnold, Ducate, & Kost, 2009; Kessler, 2009; Mak & Coniam, 2008) has distinguished between revisions made to the posted contributions for content (meaning changes) and revisions made to the language used (formal changes); that is, CF. The findings of these studies are mixed.

A number of studies (e.g., Aydin & Yilduz, 2014; Bui, 2015; Elola & Oskoz, 2010; Kessler, 2009; Kessler, Bikowski & Boggs, 2012; Lund & Smørdal, 2006; Mak & Coniam, 2008) that compared meaning changes and formal changes reported that meaning-related changes predominated. For example, Mak and Coniam's (2008) study, conducted with Year 7 ESL learners in Hong Kong, reported that the students paid very little attention to the grammatical accuracy of the collaboratively produced wiki. They seemed more willing to add ideas to peers' contributions than to edit their peers' contributions for language errors. These findings may be attributable to the students' relatively young age (11) and their low L2 proficiency. However, studies conducted with adult learners of advanced L2 proficiency reported similar results. For example, Kessler's (2009) study with advanced EFL learners found that only 17% of revisions made to peers' posted contributions dealt with language errors, compared to 54% that dealt with content. Kessler noted that in some cases, students added ideas or altered superficial aspects of texts (e.g., fonts) while ignoring the many grammatical errors in the texts. Similar findings were reported by Kessler et al. (2012) in a study with advanced ESL learners working on a collaborative writing task using Google Docs. The study found that the students mainly revised peers' contributions for meaning rather than form, and that feedback on form focused on errors in spelling and punctuation, with very little attention paid to errors in grammatical accuracy.

Kessler (2009), using retrospective interviews, found that the absence of CF was not related to the students' lack of knowledge of grammatical rules but because they felt that the errors did not interfere with meaning. In the interviews that Lund (2008) conducted with his EFL learners working on wiki projects, all the learners expressed concerns with the inexpert editing of their peers. Although the learners were aware that wikis enable previous versions to be restored, they nevertheless were unhappy when members of their group changed or altered something that they felt was well written and accurate. Lund claims that these attitudes to peer CF testify to notions of ownership; that is, that contributions to the collaborative wiki text are perceived as the property of the author rather than of the collective. In the study conducted by Elola and Oskoz (2010), which compared L2 learners' approaches and perceptions of composing essays individually and in pairs using wikis, survey responses showed that students expressed a preference to work on grammatical accuracy on their own and thought it inappropriate to comment on the accuracy of their partner's contribution because such comments may be perceived as offensive and affect their working relationship.

However other studies found evidence of learners editing each other's postings for language use (e.g., Arnold et al., 2009, 2012; Kost, 2011; Lee, 2010). For example, Kost (2011) found more revisions relating to language use than to style among her L2 (German) learners working on wiki projects. Similarly, the beginner learners of Spanish in Lee's (2010) study attended to language errors during the revision stage of their wiki page.

What may explain these contradictory findings is the nature of the tasks used and implementation conditions. For example, in Lee's (2010) study, the tasks required the use of particular grammatical structures or lexical items. Aydun and Yilduz's (2014) study, where EFL learners completed three different wiki-based writing tasks (argumentative, informative, and decision making), found that students provided some CF on all three tasks but that the argumentative task elicited the most CF. The researchers explained their findings by reference to task complexity, arguing that the more cognitively demanding argumentative task may encourage learners to focus on language form in their feedback. However, it should be noted that CF in all three tasks dealt mainly with word choice and errors in spelling. There was much less attention paid to errors in grammar.

Among the implementation conditions, teacher intervention also seems to affect revision behavior in CM collaborative writing. Lund and Smørdal (2006) reported that students began to provide more CF on contributions following the teacher's intervention. In Lee's (2010) study, the teacher played a very active role. The teacher assigned students to groups to ensure that each group had one high-proficiency learner. The teacher also provided explicit instructions throughout, encouraging learners to focus on the targeted features and to provide each other with corrective feedback. Nevertheless, Lee noted that although CF was provided as the semester progressed, a large proportion (40%) of the students remained reluctant to edit their peers' postings because they lacked confidence in their own writing. Arnold et al.'s (2009) study compared the editing behavior of German L2 learners in teacher guided and unguided wiki book review assignments. Although all students made revisions to language and content, there were significantly more revisions for language use than content in the guided class. However, a re-analysis of the data (Arnold, Ducate, & Kost, 2012), revealed that in the teacher-guided class, students edited their own contributions more so than their peers' contributions. The authors suggest that the guided approach, where the teacher provided feedback on preliminary wiki drafts, emphasized accuracy and seemed to encourage learners to focus primarily on editing their own contributions.

Group size in wiki and Google Docs projects may be another important factor impacting on revision behavior. The lack of peer CF reported in Kessler's (2009) study could be attributed to group size. Kessler had the entire class of 40 students working on the one wiki page. In contrast, studies reporting evidence of peer CF employed pairs (e.g., Kost, 2011) or small groups of three to four (e.g., Arnold et al., 2009). Arnold et al. (2012) also found less evidence of 'free riders' (participants who made no contribution to the revisions) in pairs than in small groups.

Engagement with the CF Provided or Deliberations about Language Choice

A number of studies have looked not only at the log of contributions, but also at the discussion spaces of wikis and Google Docs or discussions via other CM means of communication, investigating the quality of learners' engagement with any corrections offered or deliberations about language choice. These studies report little evidence of learners' deliberations about language (e.g., Elola & Oskoz, 2010; Lund & Smørdal, 2006; Oskoz & Elola, 2012). For example, Lund and Smørdal (2006) reported that metalinguistic discussions in discussion spaces were sparse, with contributions generally confined to only one member of the group. In Elola and Oskoz's (2010) study, wikis were supplemented with chats (voice or text based). The researchers found that most of the negotiations that occurred in the chats dealt with issues related to content, with only 10% devoted to language use (grammar, vocabulary, and editing). Questionnaires completed by the learners revealed that they perceived chats as suitable mostly for negotiating about the content and organization of their essays rather than language.

These findings may be related to the relationships learners form when working on CM collaborative writing tasks. The students in Lee's (2010) study mentioned in their final interviews that group dynamics affected their revision behavior. Analysis of group dynamics for patterns of interactions (e.g., Bradley, Lindström & Rystedt 2010; Kost 2011; Li, 2013; Li & Zhu, 2013) confirmed that, as in the case of face-to-face collaborative writing tasks, relationships learners form when working on wikis or Google Doc projects impact on the provision and response to the peer CF. For example, Li (2013) found that the CF provided in pairs which formed a dominant/defensive pattern was often ignored. Li and Zhu's (2013) study of triads producing wiki pages reported that in the triad that worked collaboratively as a collective, the learners edited each other's posting and deliberated about language use in the discussion space. However, in the triad that formed a dominant/withdrawn pattern, suggestions made by the two dominant participants were often ignored or reversed.

Comparing Peer CF Provided Face-to-Face and CM Collaborative Writing

One way of verifying the impact of the mode of communication on the nature of peer feedback in collaborative writing activities is to use a within-group research design. In such studies, researchers compare the behavior of the same group of learners completing similar tasks in the two environments (i.e., face-to-face vs. online). To date, very few studies have used this research design.

An early study by Tan, Wigglesworth, and Storch (2006, 2010) compared the interaction of six pairs of L2 learners of Chinese in a university setting. This longitudinal classroom-based study (conducted over a 10-week term) compared learners' interaction on a range of collaborative writing tasks (e.g., translation, narrative). Using a counterbalanced design, each task had two similar versions. One version was completed in class in the face-to-face mode and all talk was audio recorded; the other version was completed outside class time using MSN messenger (a chatting program that has since been discontinued). The study found more episodes of learners providing and engaging with CF when interacting face-to-face than in the CM environment (Tan et al., 2010). An examination of the relationships that learners formed showed that although in both environments there was evidence of learners working collaboratively on some or most of the tasks, evidence of learners forming a cooperative relationship was found only in the CM environment (Tan et al., 2006). When cooperating, members of the dyad tended to take turns in composing sentences, with little peer feedback provided on these individually composed sentences.

A more recent experimental study by Rouhshad (2014) compared L2 learners completing a collaborative writing task face-to-face and when using Google Docs. Using a counterbalanced design, 12 pairs of ESL learners (pre-university) completed two similar versions of a problem-solving task that required them to produce a short, jointly written report. The learners were explicitly encouraged at the outset to provide each other with CF. Yet despite this encouragement, and the fact that learners spent more time composing in the online environment, Rouhshad found very few instances of CF in this environment. Furthermore, whereas engagement with the CF and deliberations about language in the face-to-face environment was extensive, this was not the case in the CM environment.

Analysis of the data for the relationships learners formed when composing their reports jointly in the two environments (Rouhshad & Storch, 2016) showed that in the face-to-face environment collaboration predominated. However, when the same pairs composed reports in Google Docs they tended to cooperate or form a dominant/passive relationship. In the cooperative pattern, there was a clear division of labour, with one learner taking on the role of the scribe, the other the role of the editor. Although the 'editor' provided some corrective feedback, there was very little engagement with the CF and the scribe often ignored the feedback provided. In the dominant/passive pairs, the dominant learner composed the text and engaged in some self-corrections with little input from the passive learner.

Extracts 2 and 3 taken from Rouhshad's (2014) study contrast the same two learners' interactions when engaging in collaborative writing in the two environments. Extract 2 is taken from the pair's interaction in Google Docs. The pair formed a cooperative relationship, with a clear division of labour. Feri was the scribe and wrote most of the text independently in the large window. Tina took on the role of the language editor and, in the discussion space, provided CF on what Feri wrote (e.g., Turn 42). In most instances Feri did not respond to Tina's suggested amendments. Thus, although Tina provided CF, there was limited response to or engagement with these suggestions.

Extract 2: Peer CF in a cooperative relationship (Google Docs)

37 Feri:	I start the 2nd reason
38 Tina:	Ok
	Stop
	2ndly … Ahhh wat is the 2nd reason
39 Feri:	The personality?
40 Tina:	Her good behaviour
41 Feri:	Oh
42 Tina:	Whatever … But briefly
	Ok 2nd the future
	add 'the' … .
	spelling 'moreOver'
	Full stop after mother

Extract 3 shows the same two learners engaged in the face-to-face version of the collaborative writing activity. The pattern of interaction is clearly collaborative, with both learners engaging in the deliberations about the word form to use. It begins with Feri providing CF, suggesting that the noun form does not sound correct and that the adjective should be used (Lines, 82, 84). Tina engages with the suggested CF, and provides a metalinguistic explanation for why the noun should be used (e.g., Lines 85, 89), ultimately persuading Feri about the correct word form.

Extract 3: Peer CF in a collaborative relationship (face-to-face)

82 Feri:	his value a little bit weird
83 Tina:	ha?
84 Feri:	value because we just think he is more … valuable. We discuss
85 Tina:	I think his value will the noun
86 Feri:	"he is more valuable than sally."
87 Tina:	because I use
88 Feri:	yeah
89 Tina:	because here so we have the noun, the noun phrase
90 Feri:	his value
91 Tina:	that's all right value

Exit interviews conducted with the participants by Rouhshad (2014) suggested that the main reasons why learners provided little CF in the CM environment was the focus on meaning rather than accuracy (see also Aydun & Yilduz, 2014; Kessler, 2009); they admitted that they only offered CF if they felt that the error was grave and they were confident about their correction. Another reason was the concern of causing offense. Such concerns were also reported by other researchers (e.g., Elola & Oskoz, 2010; Mak & Coniam, 2008) and suggest that the text was not perceived as a jointly owned text.

What the findings of these two studies suggest is that the mode of communication does impact on the nature of learners' behavior when engaging in collaborative writing tasks. It impacts on the relationship learners are likely to form and subsequently on the amount of peer CF provided and on the depth of engagement with this feedback. I discuss these findings and the pedagogical implications of these findings in the section that follows.

Conclusion and Pedagogical Implications

Research on collaborative writing tasks has now provided sufficient evidence to suggest that the implementation of these tasks in the face-to-face environment does encourage learners to provide peer CF and engage with the feedback, particularly when the learners form a collaborative relationship. Working collaboratively means that the text is co-constructed with all members of the dyad/small group contributing to the decision making about what ideas to include in the text and how to express these ideas. This research also suggests that careful pairing of students (Kim & McDonough, 2008; Storch & Aldosari, 2013) and pre-modeling of collaborative dialogues (Kim & McDonough, 2011) encourages learners to form collaborative relationships. These instructional strategies may be even more pertinent to the implementation of CM collaborative writing tasks.

Studies on CM collaborative writing highlight the importance of careful attention to the nature of the tasks used and the implementation conditions if the instructional goal is to elicit learners' attention to language. In the CM environment, meaning-focused tasks (e.g., reports, argumentative essay) may not draw attention to form (see Mak & Coniam, 2008) unless these tasks are carefully structured (see Lee, 2010). Furthermore, unless there is active teacher intervention (e.g., Arnold et al., 2009), students may not provide CF on peers' contributions nor engage in deliberations about language. This behavior may be attributed to the cooperative relationships learners form when engaging in CM collaborative writing. These relationships seem to alter how the task is carried out and more importantly the sense of text ownership; contributions are perceived as owned by the author rather than by the collective.

One factor which may explain why learners are more likely to cooperate when engaging in CM collaborative writing is the lack of social presence in this environment. The term social presence was coined by Short, Williams, and Christie (1976), and refers to the salience of the other person in the interaction. It encompasses a sense of physical proximity and psychological intimacy caused by, for example, eye contact or a smile. In the online environment, the absence of social presence may explain lack of attention and engagement with language form (Baralt, Gurzynski-Weiss, & Kim, 2016).

In the online environment, social presence may take time to develop and this has implications for the frequency and duration of CM collaborative writing projects in L2 classes. Findings from longitudinal studies (e.g., Ducate, Anderson & Moreno, 2011; Lee, 2010; Mak & Coniam, 2008) show that students often hesitate at the beginning of a wiki project to edit their peers' contribution, but that this initial discomfort dissipates over time, as they become more comfortable about working with each other. It is this element of time which may explain why some of the pairs in Tan et al.'s (2006) study, a longitudinal, classroom-based study, collaborated in the CM environment as well as when working face-to-face, whereas the learners in Rouhshad's (2014) experimental study, who participated in the CM collaborative writing activity on only one occasion, formed cooperative relationships. Other studies conducted in a range of online learning environment (e.g., Arnold & Ducate, 2006; Zhao, Sullivan, & Mellenius, 2014) have also shown that once social presence is established, students are more likely to engage with each other, to share perspectives, and reflect on others' perspectives (Murphy, 2004). These findings suggest that CM collaborative writing activities need to be implemented on more than one occasion. Over time, the sense of social presence may develop, encouraging learners to form collaborative relationships and become more comfortable about providing and engaging with CF in dialogues about language use evident in face-to-face collaborative writing (see Extracts 1 and 3).

One other strategy to consider is a blended approach, combining different channels of communication. Oskoz and Elola (2012) suggested supplementing wikis with synchronous, web-based voice applications. The combination of voice or text chats and image has been found to increase learners' sense of social presence (Yamada, 2009). Zorko (2009) found that a combination of wikis and face-to-face interaction encouraged her L2 learners to provide each other with CF, although other researchers who combined these two modes of communication (e.g., Bui, 2015) did not find that it encouraged learners to provide each other with CF on their posting. Clearly more investigations are needed to investigate an optimal way of implementing a blended approach to collaborative writing that also incorporates some of the other suggestions (e.g., careful selection of tasks, teacher intervention).

As a number of scholars have pointed out (e.g., Kessler, 2013a, b; Yamada, 2009), in today's technologically driven world, language educators need to recognize the potential that new technologies offer language learning. At the same time, it is important that we investigate and continue to critically evaluate the impact these new technologies have on learners' interaction, including peer feedback. While some Web 2.0 applications may have the potential to facilitate collaboration, it does not necessarily mean that using the technology will result in collaborative learning in the same way that simply assigning students to work in a group means that they will work as a group. As language educators, we need to plan and implement collaborative writing tasks, in both the face-to-face and CM environment, to create conditions conducive to collaboration and language learning.

References

Arnold, N., & Ducate, L. (2006). Future foreign language teachers' social and cognitive collaboration in an online environment. *Language Teaching & Technology, 10*(1), 42–66.

Arnold, N., Ducate, L., & Kost, C. (2009). Collaborative writing in wikis: Insights from a culture project in a German class. In L. Lomicka & G. Lord (Eds.), *The next generation: Social networking and online collaboration in foreign language learning* (pp. 115–144). San Marcos, TX: CALICO.

Arnold, N., Ducate, L., & Kost, C. (2012). Collaboration or cooperation? Analyzing group dynamics and revision processes in wikis. *CALICO Journal, 29*(3), 431–448.

Aydin, Z., & Yilduz, S. (2014). Using wikis to promote collaborative EFL writing. *Language Learning & Technology, 18*(1), 160–180.

Baralt, M., Gurzynski-Weiss, L., & Kim, Y. (2016). Engagement with the language: How examining learners' affective and social engagement explains successful learner-generated attention to form. In M. Sato & S. Ballinger (Eds.), *Peer interaction and second language learning. Pedagogical potentials and research agenda* (pp. 209–240). Amsterdam/Philadelphia: John Benjamins.

Bradley, L., Lindström, B., & Rystedt, H. (2010). Rationalities of collaboration for language learning in a wiki. *ReCALL, 22*(2), 247–265.

Brooks, L., & Swain, M. (2009). Languaging in collaborative writing: Creation of and response to expertise. In A. Mackey & C. Polio (Eds.), *Multiple perspectives on interaction in SLA* (pp. 58–89). Mahwah, NJ: Lawrence Erlbaum.

Bui, T. H. G. (2015). *Using collaboration and technology to enhance Vietnamese students' English writing skills.* Unpublished PhD thesis, Queensland University of Technology, Australia.

Connor, U., & Asenavage, K. (1994). Peer response groups in ESL writing classes: How much impact on revision? *Journal of Second Language Writing, 3*(3), 257–276.

Ducate, L., Anderson, L., & Moreno, N. (2011). Wading through the world of wikis: An analysis of three wiki projects. *Foreign Language Annals, 44*(3), 495–524.

Elola, I., & Oskoz, A. (2010). Collaborative writing: Fostering foreign language and writing conventions development. *Language Learning & Technology, 14*(3), 51–71.

Fernández Dobao, A. (2012) Collaborative writing tasks in the L2 classroom: Comparing group, pair, and individual work. *Journal of Second Language Writing, 21*(1), 40–58.

Guardado, M., & Shi, L. (2007). ESL students' experiences of online peer feedback. *Computers and Composition, 24*(4), 443–461.

Kessler, G. (2009). Student-initiated attention to form in wiki-based collaborative writing. *Language Learning & Technology, 13*(1), 79–95.

Kessler, G. (2013a). Collaborative language learning in co-constructed participatory culture. *CALICO Journal, 30*(3), 307–322.

Kessler, G. (2013b). Teaching ESL/EFL in a world of social media, mash-ups, and hyper-collaboration. *TESOL Journal, 4*(4), 615–632.

Kessler, G., Bikowski, D., & Boggs, J. (2012). Collaborative writing among second language learners in academic web-based projects. *Language Learning & Technology, 16*(1), 91–109.

Kim, Y. (2008). The contribution of collaborative and individual tasks to the acquisition of L2 vocabulary. *The Modern Language Journal, 92*, 114–130.

Kim, Y., & McDonough, K. (2008). The effect of interlocutor proficiency on the collaborative dialogue between Korean as a second language learners. *Language Teaching Research, 12*(2), 211–234.

Kim, Y., & McDonough, K. (2011). Using pretask modelling to encourage collaborative language learning opportunities. *Language Teaching Research, 15*, 183–199.

Kost, C. (2011). Investigating writing strategies and revision behaviour in collaborative writing projects. *CALICO Journal, 28*(3), 606–620.

Lee, L. (2010). Exploring wiki-mediated collaborative writing: A case study in an elementary Spanish course. *CALICO Journal, 27*(2), 260–276.

Li, M. (2013). Individual novices and collective experts: Collective scaffolding in wiki-based group writing. *System, 41*(3), 752–769.

Liu, J., & Hansen, J. (2002). *Peer response in second language writing classrooms.* Ann Arbor, MI: University of Michigan Press.

Li, M., & Zhu, W. (2013). Patterns of computer-mediated interaction in small writing groups using wikis. *Computer Assisted Language Learning, 26*(1), 61–82.

Lund, A. (2008). Wikis: a collective approach to language production. *ReCALL, 20*(1), 35–54.

Lund, A., & Smørdal, O. (2006). Is there space for the teacher in a wiki? Proceedings of the 2006 International Symposium on Wikis (WikiSym '06) (pp. 37–46). Odense, Denmark: ACM Press.

Mak, B., & Coniam, D. (2008). Using wikis to enhance and develop writing skills among secondary school students in Hong Kong. *System, 36*(3), 437–455.

Moranski, K., & Toth, P. (2016). Small-group meta-analytic talk and Spanish L2 development. In M. Sato & S. Ballinger (Eds.), *Peer interaction and second language learning: Pedagogical potentials and research agenda* (pp. 291–319). Amsterdam/Philadelphia: John Benjamins.

Murphy, E. (2004). Recognising and promoting collaboration in an online asynchronous discussion. *British Journal of Educational Technology, 35*(4), 421–431.

Oskoz, A., & Elola, I. (2012). Understanding the impact of social tools in the FL writing classroom: Activity theory at work. In G. Kessler, A. Oskoz, & I. Elola (Eds.), *Technology across writing contexts and tasks* (pp. 131–153). San Marcos, TX: CALICO.

Qi, D. S., & Lapkin, S. (2001) Exploring the role of noticing in a three-stage second language writing task. *Journal of Second Language Writing, 10*(4), 277–303.

Rouhshad, A. (2014). *The nature of negotiations in computer-mediated and face-to-face modes with/without writing modality.* Unpublished PhD thesis, the University of Melbourne, Australia.

Rouhshad, A., & Storch, N. (2016). A focus on mode: Patterns of interaction in face-to-face and computer-mediated contexts. In M. Sato & S. Ballinger (Eds.), *Peer interaction and second language learning. Pedagogical potentials and research agenda* (pp. 267–290). Amsterdam/Philadelphia: John Benjamins.

Sengupta, S. (1998). Peer evaluation: 'I'm not the teacher.' *ELT Journal, 52*(1), 19–28.

Short, J., Williams, E., & Christie, B. (1976). *The social psychology of telecommunications.* London: John Wiley.

Storch, N. (2001). How collaborative is pair work? ESL tertiary students composing in pairs. *Language Teaching Research, 5*(1), 29–53.

Storch, N. (2002). Patterns of interaction in ESL pair work. *Language Learning, 52*(1), 119–158.

Storch, N. (2005). Collaborative writing: Product, process and students' reflections. *Journal of Second Language Writing, 14*(3), 153–173.

Storch, N. (2008). Metatalk in a pair work activity: Level of engagement and implications for language development. *Language Awareness, 17*(2), 95–114.

Storch, N. (2013). *Collaborative writing in L2 classrooms.* Bristol, UK: Multilingual Matters.

Storch, N., & Aldosari, A. (2010). Learners' use of first language (Arabic) in pair work in an EFL class. *Language Teaching Research, 14*(4), 355–375.

Storch, N., & Aldosari, A. (2013). Pairing learners in pair work activity. *Language Teaching Research, 17*(1), 31–48.

Storch, N., & Wigglesworth, G. (2007). Writing tasks: Comparing individual and collaborative writing. In M. del Pilar Garcia-Mayo (Ed.), *Investigating tasks in formal language learning* (pp. 157–177). Clevedon: Multilingual Matters.

Swain, M. (1998). Focus on form through conscious reflection. In C. Doughty and J. Williams (Eds.), *Focus on form in classroom second language acquisition* (pp. 64–81). Cambridge: Cambridge University Press.

Tan, L., Wigglesworth, G., & Storch, N. (2006). Patterns of pair interaction and mode of communication: Comparing face-to-face and computer-mediated communication. Paper presented at the Annual Congress of ALAA, University of Queensland, Australia.

Tan, L., Wigglesworth, G., & Storch, N. (2010). Pair interactions and mode of communication: Comparing face-to-face and computer-mediated communication. *Australian Review of Applied Linguistics, 33*(3), 1–24.

Tsui, A., & Ng, M. (2000). Do secondary L2 writers benefit from peer comments? *Journal of Second Language Writing, 9*(2), 147–170.

Watanabe, Y., & Swain, M. (2007). Effects of proficiency differences and patterns of pair interaction on second language learning: Collaborative dialogue between adult ESL learners. *Language Teaching Research, 11*(2), 121–142.

Wigglesworth, G., & Storch, N. (2009). Pairs versus individual writing: Effects on fluency, complexity and accuracy. *Language Testing, 26*(3), 445–466.

Yamada, M. (2009). The role of social presence in learner-centred communicative language learning using synchronous computer-mediated communication: Experimental study. *Computers & Education, 52*, 830–833.

Zhao, H., Sullivan, K., & Mellenius, I. (2014). Participation, interaction and social presence: An exploration of collaboration in online peer review groups. *British Journal of Educational Technology, 45*(5), 807–819.

Zorko, V. (2009). Factors affecting the way students collaborate in a wiki for English language learning. *Australasian Journal of Educational Technology, 25*(5), 645–665.

6

INTERACTIONAL FEEDBACK IN SYNCHRONOUS COMPUTER-MEDIATED COMMUNICATION

A Review of the State of the Art

Nicole Ziegler and Alison Mackey

Introduction

Numerous studies and meta-analyses have demonstrated benefits of interactional feedback for second language development (see Keck, Iberri-Shea, Tracy-Ventura, & Wa-Mbaleka, 2006; Mackey & Goo, 2007; Nassaji, 2015, 2016; Russell & Spada, 2006; Ziegler, 2016a for recent reviews). By providing negotiation and feedback opportunities, acquisition is supported through "the connection of input, internal learner capacities, particularly selective attention, and output in productive ways" (Long, 1996, pp. 451–452). These negotiations for meaning, as well as the provision of negative evidence via corrective feedback, offer opportunities for learners to identify gaps between their interlanguage (IL) and the target language (TL), as well as to produce modified output (Long, 1996; Swain, 2005), thereby providing learners with the potential to reap both receptive and productive linguistic benefits from interaction. These benefits have been found to hold for adults as well as children in a wide range of first–second language pairings and in classroom, laboratory, and naturalistic contexts (Mackey, 2012).

There is now a growing body of research examining interaction within the context of synchronous computer-mediated communication (SCMC), which also suggests positive benefits for interaction within technology-supported environments (e.g., Blake, 2000; de la Fuente, 2003; Lai & Li, 2011; Sauro, 2011; Sauro & Smith, 2010; Smith, 2004, 2005, 2010; Ziegler, 2016b). This research provides compelling evidence that interactional features found to be beneficial to L2 development in face-to-face (FTF) contexts, such as negotiation for meaning, corrective feedback, and modified output, can and do occur in computer-assisted language learning (CALL) environments as well (e.g., Beauvois, 1992; Lee, 2001). Building on previous meta-analytic and synthetic research (Mackey & Goo, 2007;

Sauro, 2011; Ziegler, 2016a), our aim in this chapter is to provide a comprehensive review of interactional feedback and technology research from the past few decades to aid the reader in understanding its development and status quo.

Interactional Features

Long's (1996) update to the original interaction hypothesis addressed the ways in which interaction provides negative evidence, which can be defined as input that provides direct or indirect evidence of ungrammatical forms. Negative evidence, which facilitates L2 development by indicating to learners that there was an issue with their language production, potentially drawing their attention to gaps between their IL and the TL, is provided through interlocutors' feedback on learners' L2 utterances (Leeman, 2003, 2007), often during the process of negotiation for meaning. Through negotiation, output can be modified to be made more comprehensible, as well as more salient (e.g. Mackey, 2012; Pica, 1994, 1996; Swain, 1985, 1995).

Overall, research has shown that receiving feedback and participating in negotiation, the concept of which has expanded in recent research to include interactional modifications occurring in response to other forms of implicit and explicit feedback, including recasts and metalinguistic feedback as well as modified output (Mackey, 2012), may support learners' L2 development by providing both positive and negative evidence. By facilitating learners' noticing of erroneous utterances and directing their attention to the TL, this provision of positive and negative evidence may prepare learners to be more observant regarding future instances of linguistic input, as well as provide them with multiple opportunities to confirm, modify, or reject hypotheses they have formed regarding the L2 (Gass & Mackey, 2007).

Interactional Feedback and Computer-Mediated Communication

Building on the idea that CALL might be developed to reflect ideal conditions for L2 development, an early position paper by Chapelle (1998) identified features of interaction that could be directly applied to instruction in a computer-mediated environment, such as making key linguistic features salient, supporting modified interaction between the learner and the interlocutor, and providing opportunities for learners to notice their errors, to modify their output, and to receive comprehensible input. Based on hypotheses regarding ideal second language acquisition (SLA) conditions, such as the importance of interaction, exposure to comprehensible input, and opportunities for output and feedback (Long, 1996; Pica, 1994). These principles were later expanded upon by Doughty and Long (2003) to include features of task-based language learning and teaching. Using Chapelle's suggestions for instructional designs as a framework to investigate the basic tenets and features of the interaction approach in CALL contexts, researchers sought to demonstrate the potential for computer-mediated communication (CMC) to direct learners' attention to specific target language features and to provide learners with opportunities to negotiate for meaning, to receive comprehensible input and corrective feedback, and to produce modified output (Smith, 2004).

Negotiation for Meaning in SCMC

Within the body of CALL research conducted during the early 1990s, only a few studies examined the nature of learners' interactions. For example, in her often-cited early investigation of computer-assisted class discussions, Chun (1994) examined the quantity and quality of language produced by learners of German as a foreign language. Results indicated that learners provided corrective feedback and negotiated for meaning in the form of clarification requests. Building on Chun's (1994) early work, Pellettieri (2000) examined intermediate-level Spanish learners' negotiation of form and meaning during communicative tasks carried out using text-chat. Findings indicated that the patterns of interaction were similar to those found in non-native speakers' (NNS) oral conversation, with instances of negotiation triggered by inappropriate responses or lack of comprehension. Pellettieri (2000) also found that learners used clarification requests and confirmation checks to negotiate for meaning and provided one another with corrective feedback during meaning-focused exchanges. These results led Pellettieri (2000, p. 59) to conclude that text-based SCMC provided an environment facilitative of negotiation of meaning and interaction and, importantly, that because learners in a written SCMC context may have more time to process and monitor their language, written SCMC may play a "significant role in the development of grammatical competence among classroom language learners."

Blake (2000) also used SCMC text–chat tasks to encourage negotiation between intermediate learners of Spanish, finding that these negotiations were most often triggered by lexical misunderstandings, echoing findings in the FTF interaction literature (cf. Mackey, Gass & McDonough, 2000). Similarly, in an influential early line of work, Smith (2003) examined the amount and types of negotiation occurring when learners encountered novel lexical items during jigsaw and decision-making tasks in text-chat, finding that learners do negotiate for meaning when miscomprehension occurs in a computer-mediated environment.

Research in CMC has also examined the effects of specific types of technology on the quantity and type of negotiation that learners produce. For example, Jepson's (2005) comparison found that a greater number of repair moves took place in voice chat than in text chat. Smith (2009) examined the relationship between negotiated interaction and the use of scrolling or cursor movement, with results indicating that negotiation was negatively affected by increased scrolling activity and mouse movement. Smith (2010) also investigated the relationship between learners' eye movements and uptake, while Wang (2006) took the study of interaction and technology one step further by examining the role of visual cues, such as facial expressions or gestures, in negotiation routines during video conferences. In addition, other, more recent studies have demonstrated the potential impact of the communication mode on the provision of feedback, with learners receiving recasts in SCMC outperforming those that received feedback in FTF contexts (e.g., Yilmaz, 2012; Yilmaz & Yuksel, 2011).

However, recent meta-analyses suggest that the interaction agenda has not been pursued as thoroughly and systematically in CMC contexts as it has been in FTF contexts (e.g., Ziegler, 2016a). For example, the overall body of research specifically focusing on feedback type remains somewhat limited, and only a handful of studies have investigated the impact of implicit and explicit corrective feedback in SCMC on L2 development (e.g., Loewen & Erlam, 2006; Sauro, 2009; Yilmaz, 2012). Possibly because of this lack of variety in recent studies, the results remain mixed, with a few studies finding no differences in efficacy across recasts and metalinguistic feedback (Loewen & Erlam, 2006; Sauro, 2009) and others finding advantages for explicit correction compared to recasts on immediate and delayed posttests, as well as across production and comprehension measures (e.g., Yilmaz, 2012). Most of this research has been conducted in text-chat environments, although recently Monteiro (2014) examined the effectiveness of oral metalinguistic feedback and recasts during video-conference interactions, finding no significant differences in the development of learners' implicit and explicit knowledge across groups.

Noticing and Focus on Form in SCMC

Schmidt's well-known Noticing Hypothesis (Schmidt, 2001) posits that noticing is a necessary condition for SLA. Some scholars have suggested that SCMC might provide learners with additional opportunities for noticing, and thus more developmental opportunities than might be encountered in FTF interaction, due to the possibility of increased saliency, more opportunities to review input and output, and longer times for processing and planning production (Beauvois, 1992; Pellettieri, 2000; Smith, 2004, 2005; Smith & Gorsuch, 2004; Warschauer, 1995, 1997). This is particularly true of text-chat exchanges, as learners are presented with a written record of the interaction, which may provide added opportunities for learners to attend more closely to the form and content of the input, while still maintaining the real-time feel of conversation (Pellettieri, 2000; Smith, 2003). Because SCMC may increase learners' opportunities to notice target items in the input, as well as to notice gaps between their IL and the TL, we can speculate that it may be *more* facilitative of noticing certain target forms than FTF interaction. For example, Payne and Whitney (2002) reported that learners described noticing their mistakes more frequently in SCMC chat environments than in FTF interaction, while Sotillo (2009), Shekary and Tahririan (2006), and Blake (2005) found evidence of learners noticing the gap between their IL and the TL during text-chat interactions. Similarly, Bower and Kawaguchi (2011) found that although negotiation occurred most often due to communication problems, providing learners with the opportunity to visually review their interaction through chat logs leads to increased rates of correction, possibly because learners' attention is directed toward their interlanguage, thereby potentially leading to improvement. Lai and Zhao (2006) also showed that text-chat resulted in improved noticing of errors and interactional feedback, providing further evidence of the possible opportunities for SCMC to enhance noticing. Finally, the results of Lai, Fei, and Roots (2008) indicated that the amount of noticing was impacted by learners' working memories or the contingency of feedback, with findings demonstrating that learners noticed 53% of contingent recasts compared to noticing only 35% of non-contingent recasts. Of course, noticing and learning are not isomorphic, as McDonough and Mackey (2006) point out in their study of FTF interaction, where responses in the form of immediate repetitions of contingent recasts, which suggest noticing of them, were not associated with linguistic development. Nevertheless, the Lai et al. (2008) study still suggests that future research is warranted.

Besides noticing, empirical research has also demonstrated that SCMC may encourage learners to focus on form (Blake, 2000; Salaberry, 2000; Shekary & Tahririan, 2006; Yilmaz & Yuksel, 2011), as well as potentially enhancing negotiation for form and meaning (Lee, 2002). In recent years, methodological advancements and the use of eye-tracking technology have also been helpful as researchers have tried to tease apart the relationship between recasts, noticing, and uptake, providing important information regarding what learners attended to in terms of feedback during the interaction (Smith, 2010, 2012). For example, drawing on learners' eye-gaze records, Smith (2010) found that learners noticed lexical recasts more frequently than grammatical recasts, with those recasts resulting in successful uptake, leading to short- and middle-term gains. Building on these findings, Smith (2012) added stimulated recall protocols to measure learners' noticing of corrective feedback, specifically recasts, in SCMC. Results indicated that although learners had similar viewing activity for various linguistic categories, morphological target items were noticed less frequently than syntactic and semantic categories, confirming results found in FTF work. Similarly, Smith and Renaud (2013) found that learners attended to recasts targeting both lexical and grammatical items, with learners demonstrating L2 learning gains between 20% and 33% on posttests, while the results of Gurzynski-Weiss and Baralt (2014) provide further evidence for the noticing of feedback targeting lexical items over other target forms. Overall, then, these results support previous findings in FTF contexts that feedback targeting lexical items was noticed more than feedback on other types of target items (e.g., Mackey, Gass, & McDonough, 2000; Nabei & Swain, 2002).

Researchers have also argued that learners seem to notice instances of negotiation significantly more in SCMC than in FTF contexts (Yuksel & Inan, 2014). However, on this topic, studies have produced conflicting results, with some finding no differences in terms of the amount of noticing across modes of interaction (e.g., Ziegler, in press). For example, Gurzynski-Weiss and Baralt (2014, 2015) found that there were no differences across SCMC and FTF modes in terms of noticing, a finding potentially attributed to the additional time for writing, reading, and processing messages in text-based SCMC contexts. In 2011, Baralt and Gurzynski-Weiss reported that learners in SCMC environments spent more time on tasks than those in FTF interactions, arguing in a later study that the additional time required to complete SCMC tasks is allocated to task completion rather than focus on form (Gurzynski-Weiss & Baralt, 2014). However, the results of Gurzynski-Weiss and Baralt (2015) also indicated that partial modified output was a greater predictor of noticing in text-based SCMC than in FTF interaction, suggesting that the available opportunities for learners to visually compare erroneous utterances with modified output might be important in noticing. Again, more research is needed to better understand these interesting trends.

Interlocutor Characteristics and Interactional Feedback in SCMC

Research has also examined the role an interlocutor may have in negotiation, with studies investigating how interactions between native or non-native speaking interlocutors might impact noticing (Sotillo, 2000) and negotiation in web-based chat programs (Toyoda & Harrison, 2002; Tudini, 2003). For example, Toyoda and Harrison (2002) found that the provision of feedback during synchronous text-chat interactions in an online virtual university campus environment led learners to produce output modified by both native speaker (NS) and NNS interlocutors.

Tudini (2003) also investigated learner and NS dyads, examining whether text-chats between NNSs and NSs of Italian provided negotiation opportunities during open-ended tasks. Results indicated that negotiation for meaning and modified output opportunities occur in synchronous CMC, with NS interlocutors also providing instances of corrective feedback during the interactions. More recently, Bueno-Alastuey (2010) examined the impact of dyad composition on pronunciation in video chat, finding that learner dyads with different L1s seem to be the most beneficial for improving L2 pronunciation in terms of modified output and achievement, although improvement was also found for learner dyads with shared L1s. Overall, results suggest that dyads consisting of learners with different L1s may participate in more negotiation and produce more modified output than learners interacting with NSs or learners with the same L1, a finding that classroom instructors have long understood to be true.

Interactional Feedback, L2 Development, and the Use of New Technologies in SCMC

Although the initial investigations in CALL sought to describe interactional features and feedback, focusing on observational studies of discourse in CMC, the last few decades have yielded a rich body of empirical evidence demonstrating the efficacy of interactional features in computer-mediated environments, with studies demonstrating positive benefits for a wide range of L2 skills, including comprehension (e.g., Yanguas, 2012), vocabulary (e.g., Smith, 2004), proficiency (e.g., Payne & Whitney, 2002), and the quality and quantity of pragmatic strategies (e.g., Sykes, 2005, 2014). For example, findings have demonstrated the positive benefits of interaction in text-based SCMC in terms of improved grammatical competence (e.g., Sauro, 2009), more complex language (e.g., Böhlke, 2003; Kern, 1995; Kitade, 2000; Warschauer, 1995), and increased accuracy (Salaberry, 2000). Research has also found opposing trends, with some studies finding no differences across modalities (e.g., Gurzynski-Weiss & Baralt, 2015; Parlak & Ziegler, 2016). These findings suggest that although modality may sometimes play a role, other factors, such as individual differences, may also be mediating factors (Sauro, 2012).

More recently, research has sought to investigate the effects of a wider range of technologies, web applications, and tools, including audio and video chat programs such as Skype, FaceTime, and Google Hangouts. Although the body of research examining oral chat is still somewhat small, this is clearly an area of growth and requires further investigation. For example, Bueno-Alastuey (2010, 2013) found that interaction in synchronous video chat had positive effects on learners' pronunciation by encouraging negotiation, noticing, and the production of modified output. However, some studies report differences in negotiation patterns between audio and FTF or video interactions (Parlak & Ziegler, 2016; Yanguas, 2010), while others report advantages for audio SCMC over video SCMC or FTF for comprehension, as well as no differences across modality in terms of oral production (Yanguas, 2012). More recently, in their longitudinal investigation of the efficacy of recasts during video-based interactions, Saito and Akiyama (in press) found significant gains in English learners' comprehension, fluency, and lexical and grammatical skills. However, they report no significant improvements in terms of accentedness and pronunciation. In another study, Akiyama and Saito (2016) examined the benefits of video-based interaction and corrective feedback on L2 learning outcomes. Results indicated benefits for vocabulary and grammar, although fluency and comprehensibility of speech did not significantly improve. These mixed results highlight the need for further research in these areas, as the impact of modality on L2 learning outcomes remains unclear. Replications also need to be carried out so that results are directly comparable (cf. Mackey, 2012).

Research has also examined the efficacy of Web 2.0 tools, such as social media and forums. These tools are interaction driven, highlighting the important role that interactional features, including feedback, negotiation, and output, are likely to play in L2 instructional contexts utilizing these technologies. These technologies offer opportunities for increased learner interaction, including negotiation and feedback provision, as well as opportunities to produce output in the target language (Baten, Bouckaert, & Yingli, 2009; Lee, 2006; Peterson, 2006). For instance, multiuser object-oriented (MOO) collaborations have been shown to provide opportunities for interaction and negotiation (Schwienhorst, 2004).

With the potential to extend the benefits found in MOOs, multiuser virtual environments (MUVEs) allow learners to use both voice and text-chat in a 3D virtual world, thereby increasing the options available to learners for opportunities to receive feedback and participate in negotiation. In addition, MUVEs offer learners the option to use avatars to communicate with other learners through real-time chat and gestures, potentially enhancing motivation, participation, willingness to communicate (Peterson, 2012), and production (Cooke-Plagwitz, 2008). Research has demonstrated that learners in the 3D virtual world of Second Life actively participated in interaction and negotiation for meaning (e.g., Zheng, Li, & Zhao, 2008), although some authors note that the context-specific tasks might influence the quantity and quality of the interaction (e.g., Jauregi, Canto, de Graaff, Koenraad, & Moonen, 2011). These results are similar to those of Peterson (2006), who found that task type affected negotiation, with decision-making tasks resulting in the most frequent negotiation.

Overall, Web 2.0 technologies offer researchers fertile grounds for examining interaction and L2 development, particularly regarding collaborative and community-based learning, in which learners can form structured networks and create theme-based groups to support learning and interaction. Since many of these tools are already an indispensable aspect of many learners' daily lives (McBride, 2009), educators may find their students more receptive or enthusiastic to L2 instruction situated within these contexts. Interestingly, a potential obstacle to the contribution of Web 2.0 technologies to L2 development is Google Translate, as well as similar apps and products. Although translation tools may be used to support L2 learning outcomes, such as the development of vocabulary and grammar, as automatic speech recognition and translation improve, the authentic, real-world communicative need for learners to interact in an L2 might decrease in virtual and online environments, thereby reducing the opportunities for negotiation and feedback.

Comparing Interactional Feedback in FTF and SCMC

Research has also made direct comparisons between interaction in FTF and SCMC to examine whether there are interactional similarities between the two modes. For example, research has successfully demonstrated that both contexts provide learners with opportunities to negotiate for meaning (Fernández-Garcia & Martínez-Arbelaiz, 2002) and provide an environment facilitative for corrective feedback, including recasts (Lai & Zhao, 2006). In one of the first direct comparisons of FTF and computer-mediated interaction, de la Fuente (2003) investigated whether interaction occurring in SCMC was as effective as FTF interaction in promoting receptive and productive lexical knowledge. Results indicated that learners in both the FTF and SCMC groups demonstrated receptive and productive gains in L2 vocabulary development, although findings suggested that FTF may be more beneficial for immediate oral productive acquisition. However, in order to maintain comparability between modes, de la Fuente (2003) imposed strict limits on the time permitted for negotiation. This takes away from the essential nature of SCMC and may have played a role in inhibiting learners from taking part in the negotiations necessary to successfully notice and acquire the target forms. As previous research has suggested that SCMC negotiations are likely to experience potentially extended delays between triggers and indicators (e.g., Lai et al., 2008; Smith, 2003, 2012), these temporal restrictions may have impacted the results. For instance, there is a short time delay in text-chat between the initiation of the utterance and its receipt by the interlocutor. More importantly, SCMC does not adhere to the same pattern of turn adjacency found in FTF interaction. Rather, negotiation triggers may be followed by an indicator, but are initially unaddressed, only to be answered later after a repeat indicator in subsequent turns. These delays between triggers, indicators, and responses are referred to as a split negotiation routine (Smith, 2003), and highlight the possibility that negotiation and the efficacy of feedback may be hampered by time restrictions due to the complex nature of split negotiation routines in SCMC.

Comparative studies between SCMC and FTF environments have also provided encouraging evidence for the use of technology in the classroom. For example Murphy (2011) examined the role of corrective feedback provided during social interaction in asynchronous and synchronous chats. Results suggested that feedback contributed to learners' improved confidence and self-evaluation, while the social aspects served as a source of motivation for students, demonstrating the positive impact of SCMC on affective factors.

Similar to FTF interaction research (Keck et al., 2006; Mackey & Goo, 2007), lexical items have also been found to be more facilitative of negotiation than grammatical items in SCMC (Blake, 2000; Fernández-Garcia & Martínez-Arbelaiz, 2002; Pellettieri, 2000; Tudini, 2003). For example, Pellettieri (2000) found instances of negotiation were triggered more frequently by lexically related rather than grammatically related communication problems, with the same results reported by Tudini (2003). In addition, de la Fuente's (2003) results indicated that learners in both FTF and SCMC negotiated interaction groups demonstrated greater comprehension of lexical items than learners in a non-negotiated interaction group. Long (2007) has also argued that the type of target form may be an influencing factor on the effectiveness of interactional feedback in facilitating L2 development. The results of Mackey and Goo's (2007) meta-analysis, which suggest that interaction was more effective in supporting lexical development than grammatical development, provide further evidence that learners may participate in negotiation more frequently regarding lexical items than grammatical items. Overall, these findings indicate that oral FTF interaction and SCMC display many of the same features and learning outcomes, with learners receiving similar opportunities for negotiation and feedback in both contexts.

Although some researchers have pointed out the differences between FTF and SCMC interaction, such as in structure or turn-taking patterns (Smith, 2004;

Toyoda & Harrison, 2002), other researchers have argued that because learners are still able to receive and produce visual and situational cues in video SCMC, it provides similar social signals as in FTF interaction (Lee, 2007). Although research has found similarities in performance across learners in video SCMC and FTF contexts, these similarities do not seem to extend to audio SCMC interaction. For instance, research has demonstrated differences in learners' negotiation patterns between in audio interaction and in FTF or video interaction, a difference attributed to the lack of visual input in the audio SCMC group Yanguas, 2010. Yanguas' findings also suggest that overall interactional patterns in oral SCMC were more similar to those found in FTF contexts than those of written CMC, indicating that there are important implications of restricting learners' input to aural or literal forms. However, learners' performance on listening comprehension measures indicated advantages for audio SCMC contexts over video SCMC or FTF contexts (Yanguas, 2012), suggesting that there may be positive benefits to audio conferencing for some measures over other forms of SCMC. Overall, more research is needed to determine the relative effectiveness of aural and visual forms of SCMC on learners' written and oral production and recognition.

Pedagogical Implications

As the use of technology in the classroom continues to grow, methodologically sound, well-grounded, relevant research can be used to responsibly inform educational practices. Perhaps most relevant for the classroom, empirical findings suggest that overall, teachers should not be concerned about negative effects in terms of how interactional feedback is experienced during the processes of SCMC. In other words, learners participating in interaction in computer-mediated contexts will have similar or possibly improved opportunities to benefit from negotiation, feedback, noticing, and focus on form. These findings are particularly important for distance-learning programs, suggesting that participating in computer-mediated contexts means that learners are likely to experience positive developmental benefits associated with FTF interaction. In addition, research has demonstrated benefits for both oral and written skills development, as well as receptive and productive learning. Overall, these results are highly encouraging, as they provide evidence for the wide-ranging efficacy of interaction in SCMC. The positive benefits associated with interaction in SCMC in lexical, grammatical, and phonological skills, ranging from measures of overall proficiency to assessments of individual target items, illustrates the potential applications of SCMC in promoting L2 learning outcomes and they give instructors encouraging evidence that CMC can be successfully used independently or as a supplement to FTF within the classroom. Furthermore, when interpreted alongside other important descriptive or observational findings in the field, such as those indicating the SCMC may promote more equal participation (e.g., Chun, 1994; Kern, 1995; Warschauer, 1995) or reduce anxiety (Abrams, 2003; Kelm, 1992), instructors may find that the integration of SCMC components into their classrooms is likely to provide learners with numerous linguistic, pragmatic, affective, and communicative benefits.

The availability of technology provides educators and researchers with unique opportunities to not only integrate cutting-edge technology into the L2 classroom, but to pursue research agendas that are continuously pushing the boundaries of CALL and how it might facilitate L2 development. Instructors seeking to integrate SCMC technology into their classrooms today have many free options, including video, audio, and text-chat products as well as Web 2.0 tools, that are likely to appeal to a range of students. Instructors interested in incorporating technology into the L2 classroom can be encouraged by the empirical results suggesting that SCMC need not be restricted to distance learning contexts, but can be integrated successfully into more traditional classroom settings to support and enhance learners' L2 development.

References

Abrams, Z. I. (2003). The effect of synchronous and asynchronous CMC on oral performance in German. *Modern Language Journal, 87*(2), 157–167.

Akiyama, Y., & Saito, K. (2016). Development of comprehensibility and its linguistic correlates: A longitudinal study of video-mediated telecollaboration. *Modern Language Journal, 100*(3), 585–609.

Baralt, M., & Gurzynski-Weiss, L. (2011). Comparing learners' state anxiety during task-based interaction in computer-mediated and face-to-face communication. *Language Teaching Research, 15*(2), 201–229.

Baten, L., Bouckaert, N., & Yingli, K. (2009). The use of communities in a virtual learning environment. In M. Thomas (Ed.), *Handbook of research on Web 2.0 and second language learning* (pp. 137–155). London: IGI Global.

Beauvois, M. H. (1992). Computer-assisted classroom discussion in the foreign language classroom: Conversation in slow motion. *Foreign Language Annals, 25*(5), 455–464.

Blake, R. (2000). Computer-mediated communication: A window on L2 Spanish interlanguage. *Language Learning & Technology, 4*(1), 120–136.

Blake, R. J. (2005). Bimodal CMC: The glue of language learning at a distance. *CALICO Journal, 22*(3), 497–511.

Böhlke, O. (2003). A comparison of student participation levels by group size and language stages during chatroom and face-to-face discussions in German. *CALICO Journal, 21*(1), 67–87.

Bower, J., & Kawaguchi, S. (2011). Negotiation of meaning and corrective feedback in Japanese/English eTandem. *Language Learning & Technology, 15*(1), 41–71.

Bueno-Alastuey, M. C. (2010). Synchronous-voice computer-mediated communication: Effects on pronunciation. *CALICO Journal, 28*(1), 1–20.

Bueno-Alastuey, M. C. (2013). Interactional feedback in synchronous voice-based computer mediated communication: Effect of dyad. *System, 41*(3), 543–559.

Chapelle, C. (1998). Analysis of interaction sequences in computer-assisted language learning. *TESOL Quarterly, 32*(4), 753–57.

Chun, D. M. (1994). Using computer networking to facilitate the acquisition of interactive competence. *System, 22*(1), 17–31.

Cooke-Plagwitz, J. (2008). New directions in CALL: An objective introduction to Second Life. *CALICO Journal, 25*(3), 547–557.

De la Fuente, M. J. (2003). Is SLA interactionist theory relevant to CALL? A study on the effects of computer-mediated interaction on L2 vocabulary acquisition. *Computer Assisted Language Learning, 16*(1), 47–81.

Doughty, C., & Long, M. (2003). Optimal psycholinguistic environments for distance foreign language learning. *Language Learning & Technology, 7*(3), 50–80.

Fernández-Garcia, M., & Martínez-Arbelaiz, A. (2002). Negotiation of meaning in non-native speaker–non-native speaker synchronous discussions. *CALICO Journal, 19*(2), 279–294.

Gass, S. M., & Mackey, A. (2007). Input, interaction, and output in second language acquisition. In B. Van Patten and J. Williams (Eds.), *Theories in second language acquisition: An introduction* (pp. 175–199). Mahwah, NJ: Lawrence Erlbaum Associates.

Goo, J., & Mackey, A. (2013). The case against the case against recasts. *Studies in Second Language Acquisition, 35*(1), 127–165.

Gurzynski-Weiss, L., & Baralt, M. (2014). Exploring learner perception and use of task-based interactional feedback in FTF and CMC modes. *Studies in Second Language Acquisition, 36*(1), 1–37.

Gurzynski-Weiss, L., & Baralt, M. (2015). Does type of modified output correspond to learner noticing of feedback? A closer look in face-to-face and computer-mediated task-based interaction. *Applied Psycholinguistics, 36*(6), 1393–1420.

Iwasaki, N., & Oliver, R. (2003). Chat-line interaction and negative feedback. *Australian Review of Applied Linguistics, 17*, 60–73.

Jauregi, K., Canto, S., de Graaff, R., Koenraad, T., & Moonen, M. (2011). Verbal interaction in Second Life: Towards a pedagogic framework for task design. *Computer Assisted Language Learning, 24*(1), 77–101.

Jepson, K. (2005). Conversations and negotiated interactions in text and voice chat rooms. *Language Learning & Technology, 9*(3), 79–98.

Keck, C., Iberri-Shea, G., Tracy-Ventura, N., & Wa-Mbaleka, S. (2006). Investigating the empirical link between task-based interaction and acquisition: A meta-analysis. In J. M. Norris & L. Ortega (Eds.), *Synthesizing research on language learning and teaching* (pp. 91–131). Philadelphia: John Benjamins.

Kelm, O. R. (1992). The use of synchronous computer networks in second language instruction: A preliminary report. *Foreign Language Annals, 25*(5), 441–454.

Kern, R. G. (1995). Restructuring classroom interaction with networked computers: Effects on quantity and characteristics of language production. *Modern Language Journal, 79*(4), 457–476.

Kitade, K. (2000). L2 learners' discourse and SLA theories in CMC: Collaborative interaction in Internet chat. *Computer Assisted Language Learning, 13*(2), 143–166.

Lai, C., Fei, F., & Roots, R. (2008). The contingency of recasts and noticing. *CALICO Journal, 26*(1), 70–90.

Lai, C., & Li, G. (2011). Technology and task-based language teaching: A critical review. *CALICO Journal, 28*(2), 498–521.

Lai, C., & Zhao, Y. (2006). Noticing and text-based chat. *Language Learning & Technology, 10*(3), 102–120.

Lee, L. (2001). Online interaction: Negotiation of meaning and strategies used among learners of Spanish. *ReCALL, 13*(2), 232–244.

Lee, L. (2002). Synchronous online exchanges: A study of modification devices on non-native discourse. *System, 30*(3), 275–288.

Lee, L. (2006). A study of native and nonnative speakers' feedback and responses in Spanish-American networked collaborative interaction. In J. Belz & S. Thorne (Eds.), *Internet-mediated intercultural foreign language education* (pp. 147–176). Boston, MA: Thomson Heinle.

Lee, L. (2007). Fostering second language oral communication through constructivist interaction in desktop videoconferencing. *Foreign Language Annals, 40*(4), 635–649.

Leeman, J. (2003). Recasts and second language development. *Studies in Second Language Acquisition, 25*(1), 37–63.

Leeman, J. (2007). Feedback in L2 learning: Responding to errors during practice. In R. DeKeyser (Ed.), *Practice in a second language: Perspectives from linguistics and psychology* (pp. 111–137). Cambridge: Cambridge University Press.

Loewen, S., & Erlam, R. (2006). Corrective feedback in the chatroom: An experimental study. *Computer Assisted Language Learning, 19*(1), 1–14.

Long, M. H. (1983). Native speaker/non-native speaker conversation and the negotiation of comprehensible input. *Applied Linguistics, 4*(2), 126–141.

Long, M. H. (1996). The role of the linguistic environment in second language acquisition. In W. C. Ritchie & T. K. Bhatia (Eds.), *Handbook of language acquisition. Vol. 2: Second language acquisition* (Vol. 2, pp. 413–468). New York: Academic Press.

Long, M. H. (2007). *Problems in SLA*. Mahwah, NJ: Lawrence Erlbaum Associates.

McBride, K. (2009). Social-networking sites in foreign language classes: Opportunities for recreation. In L. Lomicka & G. Lord (Eds.), *The next generation: Social networking and online collaboration in foreign language learning* (pp. 35–58). San Marcos, TX: CALICO.

McDonough, K., & Mackey, A. (2006). Responses to recasts: Repetitions, primed production and linguistic development. *Language Learning, 56*(4), 693–720.

Mackey, A. (2012). *Input, interaction, and corrective feedback in L2 learning*. Oxford: Oxford University Press.

Mackey, A. (2012). Why (or why not), when, and how to replicate research. In G. Porte (Ed.), *Replication research in applied linguistics* (pp. 21–46). Cambridge: Cambridge University Press.

Mackey, A., Gass, S., & McDonough, K. (2000). How do learners perceive interactional feedback? *Studies in Second Language Acquisition, 22*(4), 471–498.

Mackey, A., & Goo, J. (2007). Interaction research in SLA: A meta-analysis and research synthesis. In A. Mackey (Ed.), *Conversational interaction in SLA: A collection of empirical studies* (pp. 408–452). New York: Oxford University Press.

Monteiro, K. (2014). An experimental study of corrective feedback during video-conferencing. *Language Learning & Technology, 18*(3), 56–79.

Murphy, L. (2011). I'm not giving up: Maintaining motivation in independent language learning. In B. Morrison (Ed.), *Independent language learning: Building on experience, seeking new perspectives* (pp. 73–85). Hong Kong: Hong Kong University Press.

Nabei, T., & Swain, M. (2002). Learner awareness of recasts in classroom interaction: A case study of an adult EFL student's second language learning. *Language Awareness, 11*(1), 43–63.

Nassaji, H. (2015). *The interactional feedback dimension in instructed second language learning: Linking theory, research, and practice.* London: Bloomsbury Publishing.

Nassaji, H. (2016). Anniversary article: Interactional feedback in second language teaching and learning: A synthesis and analysis of current research. *Language Teaching Research, 20*(4), 535–562.

Ortega, L. (2009). Interaction and attention to form in L2 text-based computer-mediated communication. In A. Mackey & C. Polio (Eds.), *Multiple perspectives on interaction* (pp. 226–253). New York: Routledge.

Parlak, O., & Ziegler, N. (2016). The impact of recasts on the acquisition of primary stress in a computer-mediated environment. *Studies in Second Language Acquisition, 0,* 1–29.

Payne, J. S., & Whitney, P. J. (2002). Developing L2 oral proficiency through synchronous CMC: Output, working memory, and interlanguage development. *CALICO Journal*, *20*(1), 7–32.

Pellettieri, J. (2000). Negotiation in cyberspace: The role of chatting in the development of grammatical competence in the virtual foreign language classroom. In M. Warschauer & R. Kern (Eds.), *Network-based language teaching: Concepts and practice* (pp. 59–86). Cambridge: Cambridge University Press.

Peterson, M. (2006). Learner interaction management in an avatar and chat-based virtual world. *Computer Assisted Language Learning*, *19*(1), 79–103.

Peterson, M. (2012). EFL learner collaborative interaction in Second Life. *ReCALL*, *24*(1), 20–39.

Pica, T. (1994). Research on negotiation: What does it reveal about second-language learning conditions, processes, and outcomes? *Language Learning*, *44*(3), 493–527.

Pica, T. (1996). Do second language learners need negotiation? *International Review of Applied Linguistics in Language Teaching*, *34*(1), 1–22.

Russell, J., & Spada, N. (2006). The effectiveness of corrective feedback for the acquisition of L2 grammar. In J. M. Norris & L. Ortega (Eds.), *Synthesizing research on language learning and teaching* (pp. 133–164). Philadelphia: John Benjamins.

Saito, K., & Akiyama, Y. (in press). Video-based interaction, negotiation for comprehensibility, and second language speech learning: A longitudinal study. *Language Learning*.

Salaberry, M. R. (2000). L2 morphosyntactic development in text-based computer-mediated communication. *Computer Assisted Language Learning*, *13*(1), 5–27.

Sauro, S. (2009). Computer-mediated corrective feedback and the development of L2 grammar. *Language Learning and Technology*, *13*(1), 96–120.

Sauro, S. (2011). SCMC for SLA: A research synthesis. *CALICO Journal*, *28*(2), 369–391.

Sauro, S. (2012). L2 performance in text-chat and spoken discourse. *System*, *40*(3), 335–348.

Sauro, S., & Smith, B. (2010). Investigating L2 performance in text chat. *Applied Linguistics*, *31*(4), 554–577.

Schmidt, R. (2001). Attention. In P. Robinson (Ed.), *Cognition and second language instruction* (pp. 3–32). Cambridge: Cambridge University Press.

Schwienhorst, K. (2004). Native-speaker/non-native-speaker discourse in the MOO: Topic negotiation and initiation in a synchronous text-based environment. *Computer Assisted Language Learning*, *17*(1), 35–50.

Shekary, M., & Tahririan, M. H. (2006). Negotiation of meaning and noticing in text-based online chat. *Modern Language Journal*, *90*(4), 557–573.

Smith, B. (2003). Computer-mediated negotiated interaction: An expanded model. *Modern Language Journal*, *87*(1), 38–57.

Smith, B. (2004). Computer-mediated negotiated interaction and lexical acquisition. *Studies in Second Language Acquisition*, *26*(3), 365–398.

Smith, B. (2005). The relationship between negotiated interaction, learner uptake, and lexical acquisition in task-based computer-mediated communication. *TESOL Quarterly*, *39*(1), 33–58.

Smith, B. (2009). The relationship between scrolling, negotiation, and self-initiated self-repair in a SCMC environment. *CALICO Journal*, *26*(2), 231–245.

Smith, B. (2010). Employing eye-tracking technology in researching the effectiveness of recasts in CMC. In F. M. Hult (Ed.), *Directions and prospects for educational linguistics* (pp. 79–97). Dordrecht, The Netherlands: Springer.

Smith, B. (2012). Eye tracking as a measure of noticing: A study of explicit recasts in SCMC. *Language Learning and Technology*, *16*(3), 53–81.

Smith, B., & Gorsuch, G. (2004). Synchronous computer-mediated communication captured by usability lab technologies: New interpretations. *System, 32*(4), 553–575.

Smith, B., & Renaud, C. (2013). Using eye tracking as a measure of foreign language learners' noticing of recasts during computer-mediated writing conferences. In K. McDonough & A. Mackey (Eds.), *Second language interaction in diverse educational contexts* (pp. 147–166). Amsterdam: John Benjamins.

Sotillo, S. M. (2000). Discourse functions and syntactic complexity in synchronous and asynchronous communication. *Language Learning & Technology, 4*(1), 82–119.

Sotillo, S. M. (2009). Learner noticing, negative feedback, and uptake in synchronous computer-mediated environments. In L. Abraham & L. Williams (Eds.), *Electronic discourse in language learning and language teaching* (pp. 87–110). Amsterdam: John Benjamins.

Swain, M. (2005). The output hypothesis: Theory and research. In E. Hinkel (Ed.), *Handbook of research in second language teaching and learning* (pp. 471–483). Mahwah, NJ: Lawrence Erlbaum Associates.

Sykes, J. M. (2005). Synchronous CMC and pragmatic development: Effects of oral and written chat. *CALICO Journal, 22*(3), 399–431.

Sykes, J. M. (2014). TBLT and synthetic immersive environments: What can in-game task restarts tell us about design and implementation? In M. Gonzalez-Lloret & L. Ortega (Eds.), *Technology-mediated TBLT: Researching technology and tasks* (pp. 149–182). Amsterdam: John Benjamins.

Toyoda, E., & Harrison, R. (2002). Categorization of text chat communication between learners and native speakers of Japanese. *Language Learning & Technology, 6*(1), 82–99.

Tudini, V. (2003). Using native speakers in chat. *Language Learning & Technology, 7*(3), 141–159.

Wang, Y. (2006). Negotiation of meaning in desktop videoconferencing-supported distance language learning. *ReCALL, 18*(1), 122–146.

Warschauer, M. (1995). Comparing face-to-face and electronic discussion in the second language classroom. *CALICO Journal, 13*(2–3), 7–25.

Warschauer, M. (1997). Computer-mediated collaborative learning: Theory and practice. *Modern Language Journal, 81*(4), 470–481.

Yanguas, Í. (2010). Oral computer-mediated interaction between L2 learners: It's about time. *Language Learning & Technology, 14*(3), 72–93.

Yanguas, Í. (2012). Task-based oral computer-mediated communication and L2 vocabulary acquisition. *CALICO Journal, 29*(3), 507–531.

Yilmaz, Y. (2012). The relative effects of explicit correction and recasts on two target structures via two communication modes. *Language Learning, 62*(4), 1134–1169.

Yilmaz, Y., & Yuksel, D. (2011). Effects of communication mode and salience on recasts: A first exposure study. *Language Teaching Research, 15*(4), 457–477.

Yuksel, D., & Inan, B. (2014). The effects of communication mode on negotiation of meaning and its noticing. *ReCALL, 26*(3), 333–354.

Zhao, Y. (2003). Recent developments in technology and language learning: A literature review and meta-analysis. *CALICO Journal, 21*(1), 7–27.

Zheng, D., Li, N., & Zhao, Y. (2008, March). *Learning Chinese in Second Life Chinese language school.* Paper presented at CALICO Annual Conference, San Francisco, US.

Ziegler, N. (2016a). Synchronous computer-mediated communication and interaction: A meta-analysis. *Studies in Second Language Acquisition, 38*, 553–586.

Ziegler, N. (2016b). Taking technology to task: Technology-mediated TBLT, performance, and production. *Annual Review of Applied Linguistics, 36*, 136–163.

Ziegler, N. (in press). The contingency of recasts, learners' noticing, and L2 development: Insights on saliency from multiple modalities. In S. Gass, P. Spinner, & J. Behney (Eds.). *Salience and SLA.* New York: Routledge.

PART III
Written Corrective Feedback

7

LANGUAGE-FOCUSED PEER CORRECTIVE FEEDBACK IN SECOND LANGUAGE WRITING

Magda Tigchelaar and Charlene Polio

Introduction

Two major areas of interest in second language (L2) writing are teacher-provided written corrective feedback on language and general peer review, as evidenced by the large number of studies in both areas. Few studies, however, have focused on how well peers can provide language-focused feedback. Traditionally, the literature describing peer review processes makes the distinction between two types of peer feedback. The first type is described as feedback on *macro* (Min, 2005), *rhetorical-level* (Berg, 1999a), *larger-level* (Berg, 1999b), *global* (Lundstrom & Baker, 2009), or *holistic* (Paulson, Alexander, & Armstrong, 2007) aspects of writing. For example, feedback of this type might address how well a piece of writing is organized or how adequately it addresses the writing prompt. The focus of the second feedback type is on *micro* (Min, 2005), *sentence-level* (Berg, 1999a), *local* (Lundstrom & Baker, 2009), *mechanical* (Ruecker, 2011), or *surface-level* (Paulson et al., 2007) aspects. Feedback of this second type generally targets grammar, vocabulary, and mechanical issues such as spelling and punctuation. In this chapter, we focus on the latter type of peer feedback, that is, feedback on language in L2 writing. In this review, we attempt to bring together a variety of studies that have discussed peer feedback on language in a variety of contexts. The ultimate aim is to provide guidance on the practice of language-focused peer feedback. To achieve this goal, we first deconstruct advice for L2 writing instructors in the pedagogical literature and then determine if those beliefs are supported by empirical studies. We conclude with a summary of what we do and do not know about peer feedback on language and provide our own suggestions based on the empirical research.

Guidelines for Writing Instructors on the Place of Language Feedback in Peer Review

Experts in the field of L2 writing have provided pedagogical recommendations and guidelines for using peer review in L2 writing contexts in language teaching journals (e.g., Hansen & Liu, 2005; Rollinson, 2005; Berg, 1999a) and teaching methods books (e.g., Ferris & Hedgcock, 2014; Weigle, 2014; Williams, 2005). Many of these guidelines provide specific instructions regarding the place of language-focused feedback in peer review, but do not cite empirical support for their suggestions. For example, Rollinson (2005) stated that without proper training, peer reviewers may provide inappropriate feedback that addresses "surface matters rather than meaning or content" (p. 26), which suggests that feedback on language is not appropriate during peer review. However, no references to any supporting research were provided.

Weigle (2014), in her chapter from an English as a second language (ESL) teaching methods book, raised a similar concern regarding language-focused feedback. She cited Williams (2005), another methods book aimed at L2 writing instructors, who said:

> Learners often tend to respond initially to surface features of the texts, largely grammatical accuracy. There is nothing inherently wrong with one student pointing out a grammatical error to a classmate. Discussions about what word/tense/preposition fits best in a specific context can be helpful for both parties. However, that should not be the focus of the peer activity. (p. 101)

Williams's suggestion is that although peer reviewers may notice language issues, their feedback should not focus on this aspect of writing. However, without empirical evidence it is unclear whether or not this recommendation is justified.

In contrast to the view that peer feedback on surface issues is inappropriate, Hansen and Liu (2005) suggested that peer review can be used in the language classroom to address all four areas of communicative competence *including* linguistic or grammatical competence. However, once again, the authors did not provide empirical evidence to support this claim. They stated that this can be accomplished by implementing proper training and by clearly defining what the focus of peers' feedback should be. They suggested that if students are to focus on language in their feedback, they should use feedback sheets that target specific grammatical or stylistic features that the class has already studied or that students are struggling with. This focus on language can also extend the peer feedback activity into a lesson or review on grammar. In contrast to the view that peer feedback should focus exclusively on the meaning of their peers' texts and avoid surface-level errors, these guidelines suggest that peer feedback can address both global and local aspects of writing, and that the focus of the review may depend on how students are trained and guided through the process.

A second issue regarding the place of language feedback in peer review addressed by some authors is the idea that language issues should be addressed *after* global issues during a response activity. In a survey of first language (L1) composition textbooks, Paulson et al. (2007) observed that there is a "widespread use of a global-to-local progression" (p. 307) in peer response activities. That is, students are typically guided to first consider global issues such as content and organization before considering local, language-focused issues. For example, Glenn, Goldthwaite and Connors (2003, cited in Paulson et al., 2007) give a series of questions guiding peer reviewers to first identify how well the text fulfills the task requirements and how well it is organized and to look for phrase- and word-level issues only at the end. This global-to-local progression is also observed in the L2 composition literature (Ferris & Hedgcock, 2014; Kroll, 2001; Weigle, 2014; Williams, 2005). For example, Kroll (2001) stated that "errors must be dealt with at an appropriate stage of the composing process, and this stage is best considered part of the final editing phase" (p. 229). In a sample peer response task, Ferris and Hedgcock (2014) instruct students not to focus on grammar or mechanical issues when they begin reviewing. Like Glenn et al. (2003), their guiding questions begin with a consideration of task fulfillment and overall clarity.

We end this section with a discussion of Berg (1999a), which is probably the most comprehensive piece in the literature with regard to suggestions for conducting peer review. In her guidelines, she addressed both the question of whether or not students should give language feedback as well as when and how. Berg encouraged teachers to instruct peer reviewers to direct their attention *away* from language issues and focus on "clarity and rhetorical-level aspects rather than sentence-level errors" (p. 21) in their feedback. In her guidelines for student preparation for peer response, students are directed to focus on the meaning of the texts they are reviewing and to "avoid getting stuck on minor spelling mistakes or grammar errors" (p. 22), unless they get in the way of meaning. She also stated that for shorter pieces of writing, "some type of peer editing activity could be conducted, where students could focus on one or more grammar points that have been introduced in class" (p. 25). Berg, in a footnote, cited five studies on which her guidelines are based. The three studies that were accessible (Hafernik, 1983; Nelson & Murphy, 1993; and Stanley, 1992) examined peer feedback, but did not investigate how well peers could give language feedback.

To summarize, the writing guides reviewed above suggest that second language peer reviewers might be able to attend to content and meaning as well as language use in writing if they are provided with proper training. However, there seems to be some sense that feedback targeting global issues should be prioritized over surface-level errors (e.g., Williams, 2005) or that global feedback should be provided before students attend to giving feedback on language (e.g., Ferris & Hedgcock, 2014). Much of the advice in the literature seems appropriate based on common sense. For example, it does not make sense to have students give language feedback before having them do global revisions. What remains unclear is whether these recommendations are supported by empirical evidence. The lack of empirical support provided by the authors of the above suggestions and the divergent opinions raises an important question: can peers give beneficial feedback on language and, if so, how and when should it be done?

Empirical Studies Related to Language-Focused Peer Feedback in L2 Writing

Research on Current Practices

The few recent studies available on teacher practices reveal that language teachers use peer feedback, but little information is available about the extent to which teachers have students provide feedback on language. For example, Ferris (2014) examined current practices in a study on teacher practices in response to student writing in which she surveyed 129 L1 and L2 writing instructors about their use of peer feedback in the classroom. Some instructors indicated that they provided a training sequence (32%) or an informal introduction to peer review (64%), but specific information about which aspects of writing students were trained to target in their feedback or the order in which they should address them was not provided. In response to the kind of structure or guidelines students receive to conduct peer review, Ferris (2014) found that the majority (57%) of instructors indicated that they provided peer reviewers with a detailed rubric or feedback form. However, no further details were provided about the contents of these rubrics or forms, namely whether they guided students to focus on language or not. A multiple case study of four Chinese university EFL teachers' writing practices (Yang & Gao, 2013) revealed divergent opinions from the instructors regarding peer review. While two did not believe it was useful, two found it important for aiding students' critical thinking skills and sense of audience, but they did not mention feedback on language. The only study that directly mentioned peer feedback on language was a study of 216 grade 4–8 Canadian writing teachers, who were not specifically L2 writing teachers (Peterson & McClay, 2010). Over half of the teachers thought that peer editing (as distinct from peer feedback on content) was a useful source of feedback.

We glean some information about current feedback guidelines from the studies discussed in the next section. Some of these classroom-based investigations provide descriptions of the feedback guidelines students used for peer review. For example, Ruecker (2011) used two feedback sheets: the first directed students' attention to content, while the second had them review mechanical issues. Specifically, the latter directed students to underline any grammatical issues and discuss any that were repeated in the writing or that prevented comprehension. Jegerski and Ponti (2014) used a two-page peer review guide that consisted of one and a half pages targeting content and organization and half a page targeting language use. These descriptions of classroom materials provide some evidence that writing instructors teach their students to focus on both meaning and language form in peer feedback in second language writing classrooms and that the global-to-local progression described earlier may be a standard practice.

Empirical Studies of Peer Response in L2 Writing

In this section of the chapter, we focus on discussions or brief mentions in the empirical literature related to language-focused peer feedback. The studies come from three areas: studies of what happens during peer review; studies of feedback training; and studies of students' perception of peer language feedback. We note that the majority of studies and reviews of peer feedback do not focus specifically on feedback targeting language, and references to language-related episodes in peer feedback are vague at best. For example, in their state-of-the-art review on feedback, K. Hyland and F. Hyland (2006), said, "Some researchers (Leki 1990; Nelson & Murphy 1992, 1993; Lockhart & Ng 1993; Mendoça [sic] & Johnson 1994; F. Hyland 2000) have found that students have problems detecting errors and providing quality feedback …" (p. 91). In fact, Leki focused only on teacher feedback, and there was no mention of peers' ability to give language feedback in F. Hyland (2000). The two Nelson and Murphy studies examined peer feedback in contexts in which students were told not to correct grammar errors, so they do not shed any light on how students provide language feedback. Mendonça and Johnson (1994) instructed the participants in their study to give feedback on the ideas in the paper and clarity, but they noted that there were two instances of grammar feedback. In the one example of grammar feedback that they provide, the peer actually accurately indicates the errors to his peer, which goes against K. Hyland and F. Hyland's (2006) assertion that students have problems detecting errors. Thus, we believe that none of these studies provide strong support for the idea that peers cannot give language feedback.

Studies of Peer Feedback Groups

A few studies have suggested that various factors might affect the type of feedback provided by peers. In their case study of two ESL writers, Zhu and Mitchell (2012) examined two students' stance as both writers (or receivers of feedback) and readers (or givers of feedback) during peer feedback in a low to advanced level English for academic purposes (EAP) writing class. Neither student focused on language in their peer response groups or in follow-up interviews, even though one student had the objective to make the ideas in the texts as clear as possible. The other student aimed to think critically about the writing process and to analyze peer texts on a global level. These findings show that the type of feedback peers give and wish to receive strongly depends on their goals and objectives for writing; if these goals do not relate to issues of language form, language may not be addressed in their feedback.

In contrast, Jegerski and Ponti (2014) conducted a study on heritage Spanish speakers in an advanced Spanish composition course, who participated in peer review. They classified the peer feedback that students gave as either addressing language meaning (content and organization) or language form (including punctuation and spelling, grammar, style and discourse). They found that the majority (78%) of peer comments focused on language form, while a smaller proportion (22%) discussed content and organization. Jegerksi and Ponti also considered the quality of the language feedback. Analysis of student revisions after receiving peer feedback revealed an accuracy rate of 86.4% for comments on language form, suggesting that heritage speakers are able to provide relevant feedback on language.

Paulson et al. (2007) used eye-tracking to investigate the allocation of attention during peer review in an L1 composition class. They found that participants spent more time looking at surface-level errors and returned to these words more than others when they first reviewed an essay, and their review typically began by addressing surface-level errors. It was not until midway through the process of providing feedback that peer reviewers' gazes moved back and forth between the prompt and the essay, which the authors interpreted as corresponding with global considerations in the writing. Global issues were addressed second in the peer review comments, following comments on local issues. This was despite the fact that the peer review questions for the participants to address began with a general question and did not ask the participants to first focus on local issues. We do not know if L2 writers behave in the same way, but if they do, it shows that they need to be instructed on the global-to-local progression suggested in L1 and L2 composition guides. These findings and observations raise the question of whether or not peer reviewers should be directed to avoid feedback targeting language in their feedback, since errors at the sentence level clearly stand out to them.

We found only one study that directly examined peer language feedback; however, the study could alternatively be framed as a study on collaborative revision. Baleghizadeh and Arab (2011) compared students who revised narratives in two different conditions. One group compared their narratives to a native speaker model. The other group "were asked to self-select a partner to collaborate with and provide each other with feedback on their written output …" (p. 68). The native speaker model group was recorded while comparing their narratives to the model, while the peer feedback dyads were recorded as they gave each other feedback. Baleghizadeh and Arab found that students in the native speaker model group produced more language-related episodes (i.e., any part of the verbal reports where students mention language, also called LREs) than the peer feedback group. The model group also retained the corrections to their writing on a subsequent narrative rewrite better than the peer group.

The study is very interesting in that it illustrates a somewhat novel method of feedback through models. It also suggests that while students in the peer feedback group do discuss their errors, the peer feedback was less likely to result in learning. Nevertheless, the authors concluded that "peer feedback was not very helpful in promoting awareness among the participants" (p. 72). We believe that this conclusion may be too hasty, however, because participants in the peer group did make changes for the better in their revisions. For LREs in which participants simply mentioned a problem, the LRE resulted in an improvement 13% of the time, but when a reason for the language problem was discussed, the LRE was resolved over 33% of time. (No examples of reasons are provided, but we assume a reason might be something like, "I see that I need to use the past tense here because the story took place in the past.") Baleghizadeh and Arab (2011) do not talk about errors missed by peers nor, with the exception of one example, incorrect feedback.

Of the four studies of peer feedback reviewed above, the majority documented evidence that peer reviewers can and do provide feedback on language issues. Given that the studies were very different in terms of focus and student population, we cannot generalize about what students want, the type of feedback they most commonly provide, or the quality of language feedback. However, we can observe that in general, students do notice language issues (Baleghizadeh & Arab, 2011; Jegerski & Ponti, 2014; Paulson et al., 2007) and that they can help each other to improve the accuracy of their texts (Baleghizadeh & Arab, 2011; Jegerski & Ponti, 2014). However, it is unclear whether peer feedback can help to promote language improvement over time or if it is better than other types of feedback

Peer Feedback Training

Peer feedback training is a relatively well-researched area in the L2 writing literature. We examined this literature to determine what the studies found regarding language feedback. For example, Min (2005) trained 18 Taiwanese English as a foreign language (EFL) students to provide each other with feedback on the final essay of their intermediate-level composition class. The training placed equal emphasis on feedback targeting global (idea development and organization) and local (grammar and mechanics) issues. The results showed that students provided more comments on global issues than on local issues before the training (though this difference was not statistically significant). However, there was a significantly greater number of comments on global issues after training. The author interpreted this finding to mean that students focused more on macro issues after training, even when they were trained to consider micro issues as well.

Levi Altstaedter (2016) found differences between the focus of trained and untrained students' feedback during a peer review activity in an L2 Spanish course. Students in both conditions received guidelines instructing them to focus "on global aspects, such as organization, transition of ideas, and exemplification, as well as local aspects, such as grammar or punctuation mistakes" (p. 6). Students who received peer review training provided significantly more global comments than local comments, whereas untrained reviewers focused more on local aspects. Rahimi (2013) also compared the type of review provided by trained versus untrained EFL peer reviewers and found similar results: "trained students shifted attention from mere focus on formal aspects of writing to global comments (comments on the content and organization of writing) after training, while the feedback provided by untrained students mainly addressed formal errors" (p. 67).

Berg (1999b), like Levi Altstaedter (2016) and Rahimi (2013), studied peer feedback training and argued that training in peer response can shape ESL students' revision types. Berg went a step further and looked at writing quality. In her study, peer reviewers were trained to avoid focusing on surface issues that were not related to the meaning of the text. A comparison of an untrained group with the trained peer reviewers revealed a significant main effect for training status: trained response resulted in more meaning-focused changes in student revisions. These findings demonstrate that students can be taught to provide specific types of feedback (in this case, global aspects that concern the meaning of the text) and that this feedback in turn shapes the way that peer reviewers revise their own texts. Berg's (1999b) second research question targeted the overall writing quality of texts that were produced by trained and untrained peer reviewers. She found that regardless of proficiency level, students who had received feedback training improved the scores of their own second drafts more than students in the untrained group. She concluded that training students to target global issues in their peer feedback could positively impact writing quality, but she was not able to tease apart the effects of training from the effects of the peer feedback itself, because students in the experimental group received both training and feedback from trained peers.

An important contribution to answering the question of whether and how peer review can improve L2 writing quality over time was made by Lundstrom and Baker (2009). This was the first study on peer feedback that teased apart the two key aspects involved in the activity of peer review: the act of reviewing peers' texts and that of utilizing peer feedback to make revisions. They found that students trained in providing peer review (the givers) saw greater improvements in their own writing than those trained to receive feedback to incorporate into subsequent revisions (the receivers). In terms of the aspects of writing that improved after giving or receiving peer feedback, the students in the beginner group made significant improvements on only global aspects (organization, development, and cohesion) of their writing. In the intermediate group, however, there were significant differences in ratings on organization, development and language structure from pretest to posttest. One interesting result that Lundstrom and Baker do not point out with respect to the impact of peer feedback on language is that in the receiver group, students made significant *improvements* on structural aspects of the writing, while in the giver group structure scores *decreased* significantly after the final writing. The lessons in their study targeted only global aspects of writing and they call for more research to be done on whether or not peer review and revision can result in improvement in structure, vocabulary, and mechanics as well. Taken together, these studies show that training for peer review can have a positive effect on both the givers or the receivers of the feedback. However, the training studies reveal a significant gap in what we know about peer review training, namely, its effects on language, since the majority of these studies aimed to shift peer reviewers' attention toward global feedback.

Students' Perceptions of Peer Language Feedback

Studies that have elicited student perceptions about giving and receiving peer feedback on language use in L2 writing also suggest that this activity can be appropriate for L2 writers in certain contexts. For example, Jegerski and Ponti (2014) distributed a questionnaire in their study and found that the Spanish heritage speakers in their study (n = 16) felt confident both giving and receiving peer review on written language use. In Ruecker's (2011) study on dual-language cross-cultural peer review, American students learning Spanish received peer review from their Chilean L1 Spanish L2 English peers on their Spanish texts and gave feedback on the Chileans' English writing. The American students expressed a preference for receiving feedback on form rather than on content, because they were less confident in their grammar than in their content. Students from both countries preferred receiving form-focused peer review from native speakers over other language learners because they could trust their advice.

In a similar vein, Yoshida (2008) found that learners in an EFL context did *not* always trust or understand feedback received from other EFL students. She studied three Japanese learners of English by observing them give peer feedback in class, audio-recording their interactions and conducting stimulated recall interviews. She analyzed instances in the data that focused on corrective feedback on language and found several instances where learners did not understand the feedback that they were given on incorrect language forms. Participants also expressed dissatisfaction with receiving corrective feedback from their peers, which the author noted influenced their willingness to incorporate their partner's suggestions.

Overall, without training or guidance students seem to focus on formal aspects of writing more naturally. This may be because while reviewing their peers' texts, their attention is drawn first to surface-level errors before they notice global issues relating to content (Paulson et al., 2007). It seems, however, that students can be trained to focus their review according to the guidelines they are given, such as those focusing on content (as in Berg, 1999b), form (e.g., Baleghizadeh & Arab, 2011), or both (e.g., Min, 2005). More research is required to determine whether the focus of the review results in differences in language quality for the students giving the review and those receiving it. What is interesting is that there is an assumption that instructors should divert students' attention from language problems by training them to look at more global issues, but no one has studied the effect of language-focused training on grammaticality in subsequent L2 written production.

Language-Focused Feedback in Collaborative Writing

Because we are interested in how well peers can give language feedback, we next turn to studies of collaborative writing, where peer feedback on language has been relatively well documented. Peer feedback and collaboration are supported by sociocultural theory because the opportunities exist for students to scaffold each other's learning (Vygotsky, 1978) and this view is often applied to the L2 collaborative writing research, most notably by Swain (e.g., Swain & Lapkin, 1998), Storch (e.g., Storch, 2013), and their colleagues. In addition to theoretical support that suggests that peers can provide each other with language-focused feedback during collaborative writing, empirical research has also demonstrated that this activity can draw L2 writers' attention to language use and that peers discuss and provide one another with feedback on language (e.g., Gutiérrez, 2008, discussed below). Furthermore, this feedback on language is immediate, which allows for students to interact and negotiate meaning in the context of writing. Thus, this type of feedback given to peers while writing together resembles oral feedback since they may correct each other's oral versions of what they suggest writing prior to producing any written text. We can also draw on interactionist perspectives of second language learning (e.g., Long, 1996; Gass, 1997; Mackey, Abbuhl, & Gass, 2012), which support the importance of immediate feedback in context. In other words, both sociocultural and interactionist approaches suggest the effectiveness of peer feedback as learners co-construct texts. We review below the research showing how learners provide each other with feedback while writing together, as well as research that addresses the effectiveness of collaborative writing with regard to language.

Language Focus in Peer Dialogue During Collaboration

Research on collaborative writing has considered language-related episodes (LREs, also called *form-focused episodes*). Broadly speaking, LREs are "any part of the dialogue where learners talk about the language they are producing, question their language use, or correct themselves or others" (Swain & Lapkin, 2002, p. 292). In the tradition of research on collaborative writing, LREs are used to analyze what collaborating writers talk about as they compose a text, either out loud (e.g., Swain & Lapin, 1998) or via online messaging (e.g., Kessler, Bikowski, & Boggs, 2012). This dialogue is coded according to the type of linguistic area of interest. For example, Storch (2013) provided categories of LREs focusing on grammatical form (e.g., verbal morphology), lexis (e.g., choice of adverb), discourse (e.g., linking words), and mechanics (e.g., the form of a Chinese character).

Considering which LREs are produced when peers write and discuss a text together allows us to consider what learners notice and attend to when they provide and receive feedback. Guttiérez (2008) described the various types of metalinguistic activity among Francophone peers in a Canadian ESL class as they wrote about poetry. He detailed the variety of types of interactions, but what is most striking and relevant to our discussion is that in four of the seven groups, reformulation of another student's proposed text was the most common type of linguistic feedback, which was sometimes accompanied by an explicit statement indicating a problem with the proposed language.

Other collaborative writing studies have detailed how students respond to feedback or a reformulated version of their writing. In their case study of Nina and Dara, Swain and Lapkin (2002) investigated the LREs produced during a collaborative writing activity (composing a jigsaw text), during the comparison of their text with a reformulated version and during a stimulated recall session. They observed that over half of the student writers' LREs focused on form (52%), while lexis and discourse received less of their attention (28% and 20%, respectively). Storch and Wigglesworth (2010) observed pairs during feedback processing in groups who had received either reformulations or edited versions of their co-authored texts (reports based on a graph giving statistics on rainfall) and during revising. During both phases, the two groups produced more lexis-focused LREs, but they also focused on form. These findings add further support to the idea that peers are able to point out and discuss both grammatical forms and lexical issues in their writing and do not seem to be hesitant about correcting each other in a collaborative context.

The number and type of LREs that learners produce during collaborative writing activities have been shown to be mediated by a number of factors, including task type, patterns of interaction, proficiency level, and group composition. Aldosari (2008, cited in Storch, 2012) illustrated how both task type and patterns of learner interaction influenced the number and type of LREs produced between collaborative writers. Tasks that were more meaning focused, such as writing a jigsaw text, produced more lexis-based LREs, while an editing task produced more grammar-based LREs. Collaborative interactions between pairs resulted in the generation of more LREs than expert-novice or dominant–passive peer interaction. Kim and McDonough (2008) observed that while intermediate-intermediate and intermediate-advanced student collaborators did not differ in the number of grammar-based LREs they produced, the intermediate-advanced group had a significantly higher number of lexis-based LREs. Dobao (2012) found that groups of four students writing a text together produced more LREs than pairs.

The Impact of Collaborative Writing on Language Learning

Research on the effect of collaborative writing has investigated the impact of peer collaboration on both writing quality and language learning (Dobao, 2012; Kim & McDonough, 2008; McDonough, Crawford, & De Vleeschauwer, 2016; Storch & Wigglesworth, 2010) and can shed some light on how well peers can give language feedback. Some studies have tried to address learning by looking at the resolution of specific LREs, which can be coded as unresolved, correctly resolved, or incorrectly resolved (Dobao, 2012; Kim & McDonough, 2008; Storch & Wigglesworth, 2010). This type of analysis provides a picture of the effectiveness of language-focused learner dialogue on individual pieces of writing.

The relationship between peer collaboration on overall writing improvement (e.g., McDonough et al., 2016) and use of language has also been considered. Both of these dependent variables have been operationalized in a number of ways, including improvement on tests targeting specific language features (e.g., Swain & Lapkin, 1998, 2002) and measures of complexity, accuracy, and fluency (Dobao, 2012; Storch, 2005; Storch & Wigglesworth, 2007; Wigglesworth & Storch, 2009).

Storch and Wigglesworth (2010) explored the effectiveness of the type of feedback that collaborative writing pairs received and how the learners engaged with the feedback. Some learners received direct feedback, where their original texts had been rewritten without any language errors. A second group received indirect feedback in the form of editing symbols. They found that while peers were processing the feedback by talking about it together and during the phase when they rewrote their text, writers in both conditions correctly resolved a similar number of LREs (78%). Fewer than 10% of the LREs were unresolved, and approximately 15% were incorrectly resolved. These findings suggest that the type of feedback that peers received did not have an impact on how they interacted with the language, and that the majority of the time peers were able to help each other resolve issues related to form, lexis, or mechanics in their writing. Kim and McDonough (2008) found that pair dynamics mattered in how LREs were resolved: students paired with more advanced interlocutors resolved significantly more LREs successfully.

Using the dependent variables of complexity, accuracy, and fluency in L2 writing, Storch (2005) compared collaborative and individual writing in terms of writing quality. She found that pairs produced texts that were slightly more accurate than individual writers. She also found that pairs wrote shorter texts than individuals. However, these differences were not significant. Wigglesworth and Storch (2009) also compared individual and peer writers and found that collaboration had a significant effect on accuracy, but not on complexity or fluency. Dobao (2012) found that pairs produced more accurate texts than individuals, and that students writing in groups produced significantly more grammatically accurate texts than pairs or individuals. These results point to peers being able to help each other to produce more accurate texts than when working on their own. Wigglesworth and Storch (2012) concluded that this holds true for learners who have at least an intermediate level of proficiency.

Henshaw (2015) took a different approach and assessed gains by determining if information from the collaborative, form-focused episodes was used by writers in an individual task immediately after writing and two weeks later. Henshaw studied pairs of heritage and nonheritage learners of Spanish to determine who benefited more from the collaboration. She found, first, that the two types of learners differed in the types of problems that they resolved. Most notably, heritage learners were better able to resolve problems related to lexis and morphosyntax, while the nonheritage learners were better at correcting problems related to spelling and Spanish accent marks. Furthermore, even when provided with correct linguistic information by their peers, heritage learners were less likely to incorporate the information in their writing. Taken together, these studies suggest some language benefits of collaborative writing, but that individual learner differences might have an effect.

Pedagogical Implications and Further Research

In the first part of this chapter, we reviewed some of the available pedagogical guidelines related to peer feedback on language, sparse though they were. The consensus, based on common sense, was that global feedback should be given first, which is common sense. We agree with Berg (1999a) that "to make editing the focus of peer response to a first draft when students are not even sure of their main idea or how to support it may not be productive" (p. 25). A second issue addressed in the guidelines for writing instructors is whether or not peers can or should focus their feedback on language. We agree with Berg (1999a) and Hansen and Liu (2005) that if language is the focus of peer response, students should focus on only a few grammar points because this provides students with a structure for the language feedback activity. However, there is no evidence to suggest that this procedure will be more effective than extensive, or unfocused, peer language feedback. Because there is evidence from the studies reviewed above on peer review and collaborative writing that peers can help each other to focus on language problems, we feel that we can infer the following implications from the empirical research. There is, however, much we do not know, so we conclude with suggestions for further research.

Teach Students How and When to Give Language Feedback

The studies discussed earlier all point to the fact that peer feedback training can be helpful in terms of influencing the types of feedback that students give. It is possible, as suggested by Lundstrom and Baker (2009), that the training itself, as opposed to the feedback, may result in improved writing. Furthermore, the studies suggested that students can give more global feedback after training. In addition, individual differences among the participants might affect their preferences and goals related to peer feedback, as seen in Zhu and Mitchell (2012), and teaching students how to give feedback might result in both an appropriate progression of feedback (i.e., global to local) as well as an increase in both global and local feedback. The studies did not address the next step, namely language feedback, however, so it is unclear how well teaching students to give language feedback might work in terms of getting them to provide more accurate language feedback.

Provide a Setting in Which Students Can Seek Clarification When Giving or Evaluating Language Feedback

A number of the studies we have reviewed have shown that students may not trust their peers' feedback on language-related issues (Yoshida, 2008), particularly if they are receiving feedback from non-native speakers (Ruecker, 2011) or nonheritage language learners (Henshaw, 2015). One way to mediate these reservations is to provide a setting where students can seek clarification with their teacher or a language user whom they trust when giving or receiving feedback. Baleghizadeh and Arab (2011) suggested that if the students in their study had had access to more advanced learners or teachers, they may have received more effective corrective feedback. This is directly in line with Kim and McDonough's (2008) finding that students paired with more advanced peers were able to resolve more language issues.

Have Students Write Collaboratively

More is known about how students focus on language during collaborative writing, and it is well documented that this activity promotes focus on language. In fact, it is likely that students give more language feedback when writing together than when giving feedback on a draft individually. Although there is no empirical evidence on such a comparison, students were found, particularly in Guttiérez (2008), to directly correct their peers' formulations of sentences in collaborative writing. It is perhaps less face-threatening to correct someone as they are composing as opposed to once a sentence has been committed to paper. In addition, as Storch (this volume) suggests, students may take more ownership over writing produced *with* a peer as opposed to writing produced *by* a peer. There is certainly a wide variety of benefits to collaborative writing tasks with few reasons to not use them (e.g., time constraints), so we highly recommend collaborative writing activities. What we do not know is how best to structure the sessions so as to maximize helpful language feedback (but see Storch, this volume, for a more general discussion of pairing during collaboration) or whether collaboration is best used during the draft stage or as students interpret feedback together.

Future Directions

The most basic issue—how well students can give language feedback and whether or not such feedback improves peers' or one's own writing—has not been resolved and has rarely been addressed. We greatly suspect that like when giving global feedback, students should be given clear instructions, perhaps limiting them to certain features so as not to make the task overwhelming, but this is an issue that could be investigated by giving different students different instructions and examining the quality of the feedback. A related option would be to adapt self-editing guidelines such as those suggested by Ferris (1995). It would be interesting to have students use such a guide for training students to give language feedback to their peers. We don't know if these guidelines would result in more accurate feedback, so this is an area that could be empirically studied.

Another pedagogical concern is helping students to deal with incorrect feedback. Before we can address this, however, we need to better understand what happens when students are provided with incorrect feedback. The only related study we know is Lavolette, Polio, and Kahng (2015), who investigated how students revised for language when given incorrect feedback from an automated feedback program. They found that students ignored a correct sentence that was coded as containing an error about half the time, whereas if the sentence included an error that was coded either correctly or incorrectly, the students made changes about three-quarters of the time. Thus, they were somewhat discriminating in applying the feedback, but still tried to correct sentences that were already correct half the time. A follow-up study would be useful to determine if students responded in the same way to incorrect peer feedback.

Student–student language feedback is theoretically supported by both sociocultural and interactionist approaches to language learning. Furthermore, if peer feedback and collaborative writing increase student interaction and decrease the amount of teacher feedback needed, we should certainly encourage it. Although we do not have evidence to suggest that peer language feedback is as effective as other types of feedback, we hope that this chapter has dispelled the myth that peer language feedback is ill advised.

References

Baleghizadeh, S., & Arab, F. (2011). Comparing native models and peer feedback in promoting noticing through written output. *Innovation in Language Learning and Teaching*, *5*(1), 63–79.

Berg, E. C. (1999a). Preparing ESL students for peer response. *TESOL Journal*, *8*(2), 20–25.

Berg, E. C. (1999b). The effects of trained peer response on ESL students' revision types and writing quality. *Journal of Second Language Writing*, *8*(3), 215–241.

Dobao, A. F. (2012). Collaborative writing tasks in the L2 classroom: Comparing group, pair, and individual work. *Journal of Second Language Writing*, *21*(1), 40–58.

Ferris, D. (1995). Teaching students to self-edit. *TESOL Journal*, *4*(4), 18–22.

Ferris, D. (2014). Responding to student writing: Teachers' philosophies and practices. *Assessing Writing*, *19*(1), 6–23.

Ferris, D., & Hedgcock, J. S. (2014). *Teaching L2 composition: Purpose, process and practice, third edition*. New York: Routledge.

Gass, S. M. (1997). *Input, interaction, and the second language learner*. Mahwah, NJ: Lawrence Erlbaum Associates.

Glenn, C., Goldthwaite, M. A., & Connors, R. (2003). *The St. Martin's guide to teaching writing*. Boston, MA: Bedford/St. Martin's.

Gutiérrez, X. (2008). What does metalinguistic activity in learners' interaction during a collaborative L2 writing task look like? *The Modern Language Journal*, *92*(4), 519–537.

Hafernik, J. J. (1983). The how and why of peer editing in the ESL writing class. Paper presented at the State Meeting of the California Association of TESOL, Los Angeles (ERIC Document Reproduction Service No. ED 253 064).

Hansen, J., & Liu, J. (2005). Guiding principles for effective peer response. *ELT Journal*, *59*(1), 31–38.

Henshaw, F. G. (2015). Learning outcomes of L2-heritage learner interaction: The proof is in the posttests. *Heritage Language Journal*, *12*(3), 245–270.

Hyland, F. (2000). ESL writers and feedback: Giving more autonomy to students. *Language Teaching Research*, *4*(1), 33–54.

Hyland, K., & Hyland, F. (2006). Contexts and issues in feedback on L2 writing: An introduction. In K. Hyland & F. Hyland (Eds.), *Feedback in second language writing: Contexts and issues* (pp. 1–19). Cambridge: Cambridge University Press.

Jegerski, J., & Ponti, E. (2014). Peer review among students of Spanish as a heritage language: The effectiveness of a metalinguistic literacy task. *Linguistics and Education*, *26*(1), 70–82.

Kessler, G., Bikowski, D., & Boggs, J. (2012). Collaborative writing among second language learners in academic web-based projects. *Language Learning & Technology*, *16*(1), 91–109.

Kim, Y., & McDonough, K. (2008). The effect of interlocutor proficiency on the collaborative dialogue between Korean as a second language learners. *Language Teaching Research*, *12*(2), 211–234.

Kroll, B. (2001). Considerations for teaching an ESL/EFL writing course. In M. Celce-Murcia (Ed.), *Teaching English as a second or foreign language, third edition* (pp. 219–232). Boston, MA: Heinle & Heinle.

Lavolette, B., Polio, C., & Kahng, J. (2015). The accuracy of computer-assisted feedback and students' responses to it. *Language Learning and Technology*, *19*(2), 50–68.

Leki, I. (1990). Coaching from the margins: Issues in written response. In B. Kroll (Ed.), *Second language writing* (pp. 57–68). Cambridge: Cambridge University Press.

Levi Altstaedter, L. (2016). Investigating the impact of peer feedback in foreign language writing. *Innovation in Language Learning and Teaching*, 1–15.

Lockhart, C., & Ng, P. (1995). Analyzing talk in ESL peer response groups: Stances, functions, and content. *Language Learning*, *45*, 605–655.

Long, M. (1996). The role of the linguistic environment in second language acquisition. In W.C. Ritchie & T.K. Bhatia (Eds.), *Handbook of second language acquisition*, (pp. 413–468). San Diego, CA: Academic Press.

Lundstrom, K., & Baker, W. (2009). To give is better than to receive: The benefits of peer review to the reviewer's own writing. *Journal of Second Language Writing*, *18*(1), 30–43.

McDonough, K., Crawford, W. J., & De Vleeschauwer, J. (2016). Thai EFL learners' interaction during collaborative writing tasks and its relationship to text quality. In M. Sato & S. Ballinger (Eds.), *Peer interaction and second language learning: Pedagogical potential and research agenda* (pp. 185–208). Philadelphia: John Benjamins.

Mackey, A., Abbuhl, R., & Gass, S. (2012). Interactionist approach. In S. Gass & A. Mackey (Eds.), *The Routledge handbook of second language acquisition* (pp. 7–23). New York: Routledge.

Mendonça, C., & Johnson K. (1994). Peer review negotiations: Revision activities in ESL writing instruction. *TESOL Quarterly*, *28*(4), 745–768.

Min, H. T. (2005). Training students to become successful peer reviewers. *System*, *33*(2), 293–308.

Nelson, G., & Murphy, J. (1992). An L2 writing group: Task and social dimensions. *Journal of Second Language Writing*, *1*(3), 171–193.

Nelson, G., & Murphy, J. (1993). Peer response groups: Do L2 writers use peer comments in revising their drafts? *TESOL Quarterly*, *27*(1), 135–141.

Paulson, E. J., Alexander, J., & Armstrong, S. (2007). Peer review re-viewed: Investigating the juxtaposition of composition students' eye movements and peer-review processes. *Research in the Teaching of English, 41*(3), 304–335.

Peterson, S. S., & McClay, J. (2010). Assessing and providing feedback for student writing in Canadian classrooms. *Assessing Writing,* 15(2), 86–90.

Rahimi, M. (2013). Is training student reviewers worth its while? A study of how training influences the quality of students' feedback and writing. *Language Teaching Research, 17*(1), 67–89.

Rollinson, P. (2005). Using peer feedback in the ESL writing class. *ELT Journal, 59*(1), 23–30.

Ruecker, T. (2011). The potential of dual-language cross-cultural peer review. *ELT Journal, 65*(4), 398–407.

Stanley, J. (1992). Coaching student writers to be effective peer evaluators. *Journal of Second Language Writing, 1,* 217–233.

Storch, N. (2005). Collaborative writing: Product, process, and students' reflections. *Journal of Second Language Writing, 14*(3), 153–173.

Storch, N. (2011). Collaborative writing in L2 contexts: Processes, outcomes, and future directions. *Annual Review of Applied Linguistics, 31*(1), 275–288.

Storch, N. (2013). *Collaborative writing in L2 classrooms.* Bristol, UK: Multilingual Matters.

Storch, N., & Wigglesworth, G. (2007). Writing tasks: The effects of collaboration. In M. P. García Mayo (Ed.), *Investigating tasks in formal language learning* (pp. 157–177). Clevedon, UK: Multilingual Matters.

Storch, N., & Wigglesworth, G. (2010). Learners' processing, uptake, and retention of corrective feedback on writing. *Studies in Second Language Acquisition, 32*(2), 303–334.

Swain, M., & Lapkin, S. (1998). Interaction and second language learning: Two adolescent French immersion students working together. *The Modern Language Journal, 82*(3), 320–337.

Swain, M., & Lapkin, S. (2002). Talking it through: Two French immersion learners' response to reformulation. *International Journal of Educational Research, 37*(3), 285–304.

Vygotsky, L. S. (1978). *Mind in society: The development of higher psychological processes.* Cambridge, MA: Harvard University Press.

Weigle, S. (2014). Considerations for teaching second language writing. In M. Celce-Murcia, D. M. Brinton, & M. A. Snow (Eds.), *Teaching English as a second or foreign language* (pp. 222–237). Boston, MA: National Geographic Learning.

Wigglesworth, G., & Storch, N. (2009). Pairs versus individual writing: Effects on fluency, complexity and accuracy. *Language Testing, 26*(3), 445–466.

Williams, J. (2005). *Teaching writing in second and foreign language classrooms.* New York: McGraw-Hill.

Yang, L., & Gao, S. (2013). Beliefs and practices of Chinese university teachers in EFL writing instruction. *Language, Culture and Curriculum, 26*(2), 128–145

Yoshida, R. (2008). Learners' perception of corrective feedback in pair work. *Foreign Language Annals, 41*(3), 525–541.

Zhu, W., & Mitchell, D. A. (2012). Participation in peer response as activity: An examination of peer response stances from an activity theory perspective. *TESOL Quarterly, 46*(2), 362–386.

8

NEGOTIATED ORAL FEEDBACK IN RESPONSE TO WRITTEN ERRORS

Hossein Nassaji

Introduction

The past two decades have witnessed considerable debate and discussion on the value of error correction in promoting L2 writing accuracy. Many L2 writing researchers are familiar with the debate initiated by Truscott and his opposing view on the usefulness of error correction. Truscott (1996, p. 328) pointed out that error correction "has significant harmful effects" and that "the various arguments offered for continuing it all lack merit." Therefore, it "should be abandoned" in L2 classrooms. He also provided evidence from a number of studies (e.g., Kepner, 1991; Robb, Ross, & Shortreed, 1986; Semke, 1984; Sheppard, 1992) to support his claim. Several L2 researchers have strongly reacted to Truscott's position, expressing their disagreement with his critiques (Chandler, 2003, 2004; Ferris, 1999, 2004; Ferris & Helt, 2000; Lyster, Lightbown, & Spada, 1999). Ferris (1999), for example, described Truscott's conclusion as "premature" and based on an inadequate database. She argued that, although Truscott's observation regarding the complexity of corrective feedback should be taken into consideration, his dismissal of grammar correction is unfounded. Ferris also pointed out that although some early studies demonstrated that corrective feedback was ineffective, many subsequent studies provided evidence that written corrective feedback could have facilitative effects on L2 learning.

The position taken by Truscott seems too strong. However, although substantial evidence currently exists regarding the effectiveness of corrective feedback, there are still many studies in which the results are inconclusive. Therefore, Hyland and Hyland (2006) pointed out that it is hard "to draw any clear conclusions and generalizations from the literature" on L2 error correction (p. 84). They further stated that "there are ... still uncertainties concerning the most effective ways of responding to different text features." (p. 96).

Given the growing research evidence both for and against the effectiveness of corrective feedback, researchers have looked for ways to explain such discrepancies. A number of reasons have been discussed in the literature for the non-significant or inconclusive findings of many error correction studies, including inconsistencies in research methodologies, problems with sample size, and the ways feedback effects are measured, as well as the lack of adequate control for a number of extraneous variables (Bitchener & Knoch, 2008; Ferris, 2004; Guenette, 2007; Karim & Nassaji, 2015; Truscott, 2007). There are also other factors that may influence the impact of error correction, including the context in which the feedback is used, as well as various individual learner needs and differences.

In addition to these factors, however, another important reason for the inconsistent or negative results could be the nature of the feedback itself, as well as how and when it is provided. In most studies of written corrective feedback, the feedback has often involved unidirectional feedback with no student–teacher interaction and negotiation. In such feedback, the teacher has always been the provider of the information and the learner has been the receiver. Truscott (1996) pointed out that one reason for the failure of error correction is that the teacher does not understand the cause of the error, that is, the teacher may not know exactly why a learner has made a particular mistake. Clearly, there is a relationship between understanding the source of an error and the provision of effective feedback. When the feedback is unidirectional, the teacher may not be able to find out why the learner has made an error and therefore may not be able to provide appropriate feedback. Without negotiation, the student does not have a chance to clarify any misunderstanding or confusion that they may have regarding the feedback either.

In recent years, a considerable body of research has examined and provided evidence for the effectiveness of various forms of negotiation in addressing L2 learners' errors (e.g., Braidi, 2002; Doughty, 1994; Doughty & Varela, 1998; Gass & Varonis, 1989, 1994; Mackey & Gass, 2006; Mackey, Gass, & McDonough, 2000; Mackey, Oliver, & Leeman, 2003; Mackey & Philp, 1998; Nassaji, 2007, 2009; Oliver, 1995, 2000, 2002; Oliver & Mackey, 2003; Pica, 1992, 2002; Pica, Young, & Doughty, 1987; Ross-Feldman, 2007; Van den Branden, 1997). However, this research has mainly focused on oral errors taking place in spoken conversations. In this chapter, I will examine the role of negotiation in addressing L2 written errors. I begin with an overview of some of the key concepts associated with feedback negotiation, including its theoretical underpinnings and the different ways in which it may contribute to language learning. I then present and discuss the research that has explored the effects of such feedback in improving L2 writing accuracy. I conclude by discussing some of the implications of such research for classroom teaching and learning.

What is Negotiation?

Negotiation is a process that takes place during student–teacher interaction and is delivered through the back and forth interactional strategies used to reach a solution to a problem in the course of communication. More specifically, it refers to various modification strategies such as repetition, clarification requests, confirmation checks, and the like, which are made by the teacher or the learner to facilitate understanding (Pica, 1994). Two types of negotiation have been distinguished and discussed in the literature: meaning negotiation and form negotiation (Ellis, Basturkmen, & Loewen, 2001; Lyster, 1994, 2001; Nassaji, 2015, 2016; Pica, 1996, 2002; Van den Branden, 1997). Meaning negotiation refers to the side sequences to the conversational interaction in order to deal with communication problems and to make input more comprehensible (Pica, 1994, 1996; Van den Branden, 1997). Form negotiation, on the other hand, is triggered by an attention to form and occurs when "one interlocutor tries to push the other towards producing a formally more correct and/or appropriate utterance" (Van den Branden, 1997, p. 592). In the case of negotiation of meaning, the interlocutor, either the learner or the interlocutor, has not understood the message and the role of negotiation is, therefore, to clarify meaning. In the case of negotiation of form, the message is often clear and the feedback is used with the intention of alerting the learner to his or her language problems. Negotiation of form can also occur to negotiate how a language system works and thus can provide a useful means for promoting metalinguistic understanding about the form–meaning relationship that must be developed for successful language learning (Nassaji, 2015). Since negotiation of form is mainly triggered by a focus on accuracy, feedback on written errors can be considered to be an instance of negotiation of form, particularly when the aim is to promote learner accuracy rather than resolve a communicative problem. In what follows, I provide an overview of the theoretical underpinnings that support the use of negotiated feedback in treating learner errors in language production.

Theoretical Arguments for the Role of Negotiation

Arguments for the role of negotiation link closely with the theoretical significance attributed to the importance of interaction for L2 learning. In this context, one supportive perspective is Long's interaction hypothesis (1996), which emphasizes negotiated interaction as an essential source of L2 learning (e.g., Gass, 2003; Gass & Varonis, 1994; Long, 1996; Mackey & Gass, 2006; Pica, 1994; Pica, et al., 1987). In this framework, negotiation refers to the interactional adjustments that occur in conversational discourse to repair communication breakdowns (Gass, 1997, 2003; Long, 1996; Pica, 1988, 1994). Negotiation is assumed to contribute to L2 development by enhancing message comprehensibility and encouraging attention to form (Pica, 1994). It also provides opportunities for negative feedback through various forms of interactional adjustments that occur in the course of communication (Gass, 2003; Long, 1996).

The value of negotiation also links with the notion of focus on form (Doughty, 2001; Long, 1991; Long & Robinson, 1998). Focus on form refers to instruction that occurs in the context of meaning-focused interaction (Doughty &

Varela, 1998; Doughty & Williams, 1998; Long & Robinson, 1998). Within a focus on form perspective, the effectiveness of feedback depends to a large extent on the degree to which it is negotiated and also integrated within a meaning-focused context (Doughty, 2001; Long, 1991; Long & Robinson, 1998). When feedback is negotiated, it helps learners to interact with the teacher and also be pushed to focus on form.

A further perspective on the role of negotiation comes from the Vygotskian sociocultural theory (e.g., Appel & Lantolf, 1994; Donato, 1994; Lantolf & Appel, 1994; Lantolf & Thorne, 2006; Nassaji & Cumming, 2000; Nassaji & Swain, 2000). The sociocultural perspective views language learning as essentially a socially mediated process, which is highly "dependent on face to face interaction and shared processes, such as joint problem solving and discussion" (Mitchell & Myles, 2004, p. 195). This perspective places particular emphasis on the dialogic nature of feedback and suggests that the effectiveness of feedback depends to a large extent on the "joint participation and meaningful transactions between the learner and the teacher" (Nassaji & Swain, 2000, p. 35).

A number of concepts are central to the sociocultural theory, which have important implications for how to provide effective feedback. One is the notion of the ZPD (Zone of Proximal Development), which refers to "the distance between the actual developmental level as determined by independent problem solving and the level of potential development as determined through problem solving under adult guidance or in collaboration with more capable peers" (Vygotsky, 1978, p. 86). The concept of ZPD highlights the importance of negotiation in the process of language learning as it is based on the idea that when learners collaborate within their ZPD, they can use their existing linguistic knowledge to develop what they have not yet mastered independently (Appel & Lantolf, 1994; Donato, 1994; Lantolf & Appel, 1994; Nassaji & Cumming, 2000; Nassaji & Swain, 2000; Rahimi, Kushki, & Nassaji, 2015). Also, when feedback is provided through negotiation, it is possible to discover learners' developmental level or ZPD and provide feedback in ways that can be appropriate to the learner's language level (Nassaji & Cumming, 2000).

Another central concept is the notion of scaffolding, which refers to the guided support learners receive during interaction (Donato, 1994). Scaffolding is not random support, but it is support that is negotiated within the learner's ZPD and jointly constructed on the basis of the learner's developmental needs and capacity (Nassaji & Swain, 2000). It is through such support that feedback becomes effective and thus can further the learners' interlanguage growth and development (Aljaafreh & Lantolf, 1994).

A third concept central to a Vygotskian framework is the notion of regulation, which refers to how an individual is capable of managing and regulating his or her own learning (Wertsch, 1985). In the Vygotskian view, learning is not only a social process but also a process of moving from other-regulation to self-regulation. Other-regulation refers to a situation where learners have not yet gained control over their learning and still need the help or guidance of others. Self-regulation occurs when the learner becomes skilled and able enough to act autonomously. The notion of regulation highlights the importance of negotiation as a tool to help other-regulated learners become self-regulated by acquiring and internalizing knowledge through interaction and feedback.

Negotiation in Response to Written Errors

Although the role of negotiation in the effectiveness of corrective feedback has attracted much theoretical and empirical attention in the field of L2 error correction, the bulk of the literature on negotiated feedback has been on oral errors, namely errors that occur during conversational interaction. Negotiated feedback, however, can also be used to address written errors. That is, when students make errors in their written work, the teacher can address these errors through oral interaction and negotiation.

The following illustrates an example of negotiated feedback on written errors. The example comes from Nassaji (2007), which documented the occurrence of such feedback in the context of a routine classroom activity in an adult English as a second language (ESL) classroom. In the class observed, students wrote weekly journals on topics of their choice. The teacher reviewed the journals, identified samples of the erroneous utterances that included common errors, and then conducted follow-up oral feedback sessions in response to those utterances in the next class session. To address the errors, the teacher frequently used negotiated feedback. That is, he often began the feedback episode with indirect help and gradually moved towards more direct help as needed.

> Example (1):
>
> Student's erroneous sentence: *Teachers in class like our friend*.
> Teacher: So who can make a correction? Who's got an idea to correct this? Mitny what would you do to correct this? Any idea?
> Student: I don't know. I don't know.
> Teacher: Just try. Just try. Just try your best.
> Student: Okay, okay. Their.
> Teacher: OK so there is 'their'?
> Student: Their teachers?
> Teacher: How about I'll help here. How about 'our teachers'?
> Student: Our teachers?
> Teacher: Can you start with that?
> Student: Our teachers?
> Teacher: Yeah.
> Student: Hm. Hm. They are?
> Teacher: OK. So we have 'teachers', so we don't need 'their'. We just need 'teachers are.'

In the above example, the feedback is triggered by the problem in the sentence *Teachers in class like our friend.* The teacher begins by redirecting the correction to all students in the class, asking if anyone knows how to make a correction. He then asks the student who had made the error to correct it. As can be seen, the teacher has started the exchange by eliciting the correct form from the learner, but upon the learner's initial failure, he has pushed the learner further, providing the learner with opportunities for negotiation and scaffolding. The negotiation continues until the error becomes resolved. The progression seen in this feedback episode is in line with the notion of scaffolding reviewed earlier and the idea of feedback provided within the ZPD.

When L2 learners are acquiring a language form, the form may either be completely new or the learner may already have some knowledge of the form (Ellis, 2008). There may also be cases where the learner has full declarative knowledge but has not yet fully internalized the language form. The length of negotiation thus depends on the type of the error or the degree of the learners' knowledge about the form. In the above example, the negotiated feedback took quite a number of turns, which suggests that the learner did not have sufficient prior knowledge of the target form and thus required a great deal of assistance before being able to discover the error.

Studies of Oral Negotiation on Written Errors

Although a considerable body of research has examined the role of oral negotiation, this has been mainly in response to oral errors. Only a few studies have investigated the role of negotiation in response to written errors. One of the first studies was Aljaafreh and Lantolf (1994), which explored the role of negotiation in oral interactions between three ESL learners and a tutor. Within a Vygotskian framework, Aljaafreh and Lantolf developed and used a "regulatory scale" to provide feedback within the learner's ZPD. The scale consisted of feedback moves, starting with indirect help and gradually moving toward more direct help if needed. The analysis of the dialogic interactions between the learner and the tutor revealed that error treatment was effective when it was negotiated and provided with sufficient support. It also found that negotiation helped learners to gain increasingly more control over their L2 production, and thus, the need for direct feedback to correct an error decreased over time.

Aljaafreh and Lantolf's study provided important insights into the nature of negotiated feedback and its impact on learners' interlanguage development. However, the study was descriptive, with no systematic comparison between feedback provided within the ZPD and feedback provided regardless of the ZPD. Nassaji and Swain (2000) used a comparative design that examined the efficacy of feedback within the ZPD and feedback that was provided irrespective of the ZPD. The data were collected in tutorial sessions between a tutor and two intermediate ESL learners who received feedback on their compositions. One of the learners received feedback in a random manner, and the other one within her ZPD using Aljaafreh and Lantolf's regulatory scale. The results showed that providing feedback within the learner's ZPD was more effective than random feedback. In addition, the examination of the degree of assistance required within the same session and in subsequent sessions revealed that when learners received feedback within their ZPD, they needed less and less assistance in correcting their errors across sessions.

Both Aljaafreh and Lantolf's study and Nassaji and Swain's study were laboratory studies conducted outside the classroom. Therefore, their results cannot be generalized to classroom contexts. Thus, in a more recent study, Nassaji (2007) investigated the role of oral negotiation in response to written errors in an L2 classroom setting. In this classroom, students wrote weekly journals on topics of their interest. Initial observations of this classroom revealed a frequent use of negotiated oral feedback by the teacher in response to students' written errors. The study then analyzed the nature and the degree of such feedback and their effects. Three types of feedback were identified and compared: non-negotiated feedback, feedback with limited negotiation, and feedback with extended negotiation. Non-negotiated feedback was feedback in which the error was resolved by the teacher unidirectionally and without any negotiation. Feedback with limited negotiation involved some negotiation, but the teacher corrected the error after a few interactional turns. Feedback with extended negotiation involved encouraging and guiding the learner to discover the correct form by first providing the learner with indirect help and then moving progressively towards more direct help as needed. The results revealed a significant effect for negotiation by showing that feedback with negotiation resulted in more successful correction of the error than feedback with no negotiation. Also, feedback with negotiation resulted in quicker correction of the same errors in subsequent sessions than feedback with no negotiation.

Nassaji's (2007) study was observational and the feedback occurred incidentally on any error. As a follow-up, Nassaji (2011) investigated the role of oral negotiation further in a more controlled, experimental, classroom-based study. The aim was twofold: to find out whether (1) previous findings can be confirmed and (2) whether the effectiveness of feedback and negotiation would differ depending on the nature of the target form. Three types of feedback were compared: direct reformulation with no negotiation, prompt plus reformulation, and feedback with negotiation. The linguistic targets were English articles and prepositions. Data were collected over a four-week period in two ESL classes and involved five cyclic phases of data collection: a journal-writing phase, a pretest phase, a feedback phase, an immediate post-test phase, and a delayed post-test phase. The tests were tailor-made, learner-specific error identification/correction tasks that asked learners to identity and correct their own erroneous sentences in subsequent sessions. The results showed a clear advantage for negotiated feedback overall. However, a comparison of the data per error types showed that the effect of negotiation was more apparent for article errors than for preposition errors. This finding was explained in terms of the opaqueness of the rules involved in English articles (Kiparsky, 1971) and the amount of feedback needed to resolve article errors versus prepositions errors.

Finally, Erlam, Ellis and Batstone (2013) compared the effects of explicit direct feedback with that of negotiated feedback that occurred between a teacher and 15 low-intermediate L2 writers. The learners were divided into two groups, with one group receiving negotiated feedback and another group receiving explicit feedback. The target structures were past tense verb forms and English articles. The analysis of the data showed an important effect of negotiated feedback in promoting self-correction, with the resolution of the error being much more likely to occur in the negotiated feedback group than in the explicit group. There was no evidence of the reduction of the degree of assistance over time, which could be due to the new context in which the target structure was used each time.

Negotiated Feedback in Oral Conferencing

In addition to the above studies, several studies have also examined negotiated feedback alone or in combination with other feedback types in teacher–student oral conferencing, that is, when the teacher and the student review and discuss the student's writing in individualized sessions (Bitchener, Young, & Cameron, 2005; Goldstein & Conrad, 1990; Saito, 1994; Sze, 2002; Weissberg, 2006; Williams, 2004). These studies have shown a significant effect for negotiated feedback. Bitchener et al. (2005), for example, investigated the effect of oral negotiation (five-minute individual conferences) in combination with direct written feedback. The target forms were prepositions, the past simple tense, and the definite articles. The study found a significant effect for written feedback when it was combined with oral conferencing on the accuracy of the past simple tense and the definite article, but not the accuracy of prepositions. The researchers explained these differences in terms of Ferris' distinction between treatable and less treatable errors. Ferris (1999, p. 6) defined treatable errors as those that are rule based and "occur in a patterned, rule governed way," and untreatable errors as those that do not follow certain rules such as the choice of lexical forms. Bitchener et al. argued that oral feedback on prepositions was less effective because prepositions are less treatable than past tense and articles. This study provides important insights into the role of oral negotiation when combined with written feedback.

Sze (2002) examined the role of oral conferencing in a case study with an ESL student who received feedback on his writing in one-on-one oral conferencing. The results showed that negotiated feedback had a positive effect on both the degree and types of revision learners made to their writing. Similarly, Goldstein and Conrad (1990) examined the degree of negotiation in oral conferencing between one teacher and three students in an advanced ESL composition course and its effects on students' revisions. The study found differences among the students in terms of their participation in interaction and negotiation. However, those students who participated in negotiation were more successful in revising their texts than those who did not. Similar findings were reported by Williams (2004), who examined the nature of oral conferencing in tutor–student sessions and found more successful revisions when students participated in negotiation. These findings provide clear evidence for the significant effect of oral conferencing. They also suggest that it is not just the act of conferencing that may be helpful, but it is the quality of the negotiation that makes a difference.

Students' Perceptions about Negotiated Feedback

An important area of research in L2 corrective feedback concerns learners' perception and attitudes towards feedback. Teachers often provide feedback on students' writings, believing that it helps students to restructure their interlanguage. But it is not always clear whether and how students perceive the usefulness of corrective feedback provided. Also, when teachers use a particular type of feedback, they often do so according to what they think would be effective (Amrhein & Nassaji, 2010). However, research has at times shown mismatches between the teachers' intention and the learners' interpretation of the feedback (Ferris, 1995).

Due to the importance of learners' beliefs and their possible effects on the efficacy of feedback, a number of studies have investigated students' perceptions and preferences for corrective feedback (e.g., Amrhein & Nassaji, 2010; Anderson, Benson, & Lynch, 2001; Brandl, 1995; Chen, Nassaji, & Liu (2016); Karim & Nassaji, 2015; Leki, 1991; Li, this volume, Loewen, et al., 2009; Schulz, 2001). These studies have demonstrated that in general students have very positive views about corrective feedback. They have also shown a relationship between learners' perceptions and the effectiveness of feedback (Karim & Nassaji, 2015).

However, although previous research has explored students' perceptions and opinions about corrective feedback in L2 writing, much of this research has focused on written feedback rather than oral negotiation in response to written errors. One of the very few studies that investigated this issue is Saito (1994), which examined students' attitudes towards oral conferencing. Participants were three ESL writing teachers and their students in four classes. After receiving various forms of feedback on their writings (including a combination of both oral and written as well as peer feedback), students completed a questionnaire regarding their opinions and preferences about the feedback. The study found that in general the students had very positive attitudes towards error correction and preferred teacher feedback to peer feedback. It also found that the majority of students (80%) who took part in conferencing and negotiation expressed a highly positive attitude towards negotiation, believing that negotiation between them and the teacher was very helpful. One of the students, for example, commented, "It helped me a lot to understand the unclear points about my writing." (Saito, 1994, p. 59). These findings provide some evidence for the learners' preference for negotiated feedback. However, more studies of this kind, and in particular, studies comparing learners' perceptions of negotiated versus non-negotiated feedback are needed.

Conclusions and Implications for Classroom Teaching

The questions of whether second language learning can be promoted through feedback and also what particular type of feedback is more effective have always been controversial issues among second language researchers. Even if many studies have shown an advantage for feedback in general, the results of studies that have compared different types of feedback remain quite mixed. The perspective presented in this paper has important implications for how to provide effective feedback in L2 writing instruction.

Almost all studies reviewed in this paper support the role of negotiation in feedback, with the majority revealing an advantage for negotiated feedback over non-negotiated feedback. Studies on the role of oral conferencing have also shown that students prefer to discuss their errors with the teacher rather than receive feedback with no interaction and discussion. An implication of these findings is that teachers should try to use negotiated feedback and engage learners in the process of feedback as much as possible. When students obtain feedback through negotiation, they take a more active part in the feedback process and hence, have more opportunities to attend to and process the feedback provided in response to their error. Also, when feedback is negotiated, the act of negotiation pushes learners towards stretching their language and hence reaching higher levels of development, enabling them to learn what they are capable of learning (Nassaji & Swain, 2000). Negotiated feedback can also provide learners with the time and attention needed to process and learn from feedback.

Research has shown that instruction and feedback are effective if feedback targets forms for which learners are developmentally ready (Pienemann, 1984, 1995, 2005; Pienemann & Keßler, 2012). This suggests that teachers should take into account learners' developmental readiness and provide feedback that matches learners' ability level. However, it is not always easy to determine developmental readiness of individual learners. To address this issue, some researchers have suggested that teachers should be flexible and use a combination of different feedback types, so that learners can be exposed to a variety of feedback forms (Ellis, 2009). Certainly, by using a variety of feedback strategies, teachers can address a wider group of learners with more varied linguistic abilities and feedback preferences. However, using a variety of feedback types does not necessarily guarantee that individual learners would receive the kind and amount of the feedback they need. Another possibility would be to provide feedback through negotiation. One characteristic of negotiated feedback is that it involves feedback moves that are guided and scaffolded based on the learners' ongoing needs. Since the feedback is negotiated, the teacher would be able to discover the cause of the error more effectively and, at the same time, fine-tune the feedback to the learner's level of interlanguage competence (Nassaji, 2011).

The production of modified output, which refers to learners' revision of their errors following feedback, has been suggested to be an important process that contributes significantly to L2 learning (McDonough, 2005; Swain, 1995). As reviewed earlier, research comparing negotiated with non-negotiated feedback has shown that negotiated feedback provides more opportunities for learner revisions of their own text than unidirectional, non-negotiated feedback. An important implication of this, then, is that teachers should try to incorporate negotiated feedback in their teaching if they want their learners to be able to make effective revisions of their erroneous utterances following feedback.

One disadvantage of negotiated feedback is that it is more time-consuming than non-negotiated feedback. However, if negotiated feedback helps acquisition more successfully than non-negotiated feedback, the time spent on negotiation is justified. Furthermore, although an effective way of assisting learners would be through feedback that is conducted in one-on-one sessions, as shown in Nassaji (2007), negotiated feedback does not need to be necessarily conducted in individual sessions. The teacher can also review students' written compositions and then provide whole-class interaction around common errors. This provides an efficient way of providing negotiated feedback on learner errors within the classroom.

References

Aljaafreh, A., & Lantolf, J. (1994). Negative feedback as regulation and second language learning in the zone of proximal development. *The Modern Language Journal, 78*, 465–483.

Amrhein, H., & Nassaji, H. (2010). Written corrective feedback: What do students and teachers prefer and why? *Canadian Journal of Applied Linguistics, 13*, 95–127.

Anderson, K., Benson, C., & Lynch, T. (2001). Feedback on writing: Attitudes and uptake. *Edinburgh Working Papers in Applied Linguistics*, 1–20.

Appel, G., & Lantolf, J. (1994). *Vygotskian approaches to second language research*. Norwood, NJ: Ablex Pub. Corp.

Bitchener, J., & Knoch, U. (2008). The value of written corrective feedback for migrant and international students. *Language Teaching Research, 12*, 409–431.

Bitchener, J., Young, S., & Cameron, D. (2005). The effect of different types of corrective feedback on esl student writing. *Journal of Second Language Writing, 14*, 191–205.

Braidi, S. M. (2002). Reexamining the role of recasts in native-speaker/nonnative-speaker interactions. *Language Learning, 52*, 1–42.

Brandl, K. (1995). Strong and weak students' preferences for error feedback options and responses. *Modern Language Journal, 79*, 194–211.

Chandler, J. (2003). The efficacy of various kinds of error feedback for improvement in the accuracy and fluency of L2 student writing. *Journal of Second Language Writing, 12*, 267–296.

Chandler, J. (2004). A response to Truscott. *Journal of Second Language Writing, 13*, 345–348.

Chen, S., Nassaji, H., & Liu, Q. (2016). EFL learners' perceptions and preferences of written corrective feedback: A case study of university students from Mainland China. *Asian-Pacific Journal of Second and Foreign Language Education, 1*(1), 1–5.

Donato, R. (1994). Collective scaffolding in second language learning. In J. Lantolf & G. Appel (Eds.), *Vygotskian approaches to second language research* (pp. 33–59). Norwood, NJ: Ablex Pub. Corp.

Doughty, C. (1994). Fine-tuning of feedback by competent speakers to language learners. In J. Alatis (Ed.), *Georgetown University round table 1993: Strategic interaction and language acquisition* (pp. 96–108). Washington, DC: Georgetown University Press.

Doughty, C. (2001). Cognitive underpinning of focus on form. In P. Robinson (Ed.), *Cognition and second language instruction* (pp. 206–257). Cambridge: Cambridge University Press.

Doughty, C., & Varela, E. (1998). Communicative focus on form. In C. Doughty & J. Williams (Eds.), *Focus on form in classroom second language acquisition* (pp. 114–138). Cambridge: Cambridge University Press.

Doughty, C., & Williams, J. (1998). Pedagogical choices in focus on form. In C. Doughty & J. Williams (Eds.), *Focus on form in classroom second language acquisition* (pp. 197–261). Cambridge: Cambridge University Press.

Ellis, R. (2008). *The study of second language acquisition, second edition*. Oxford: Oxford University Press.

Ellis, R. (2009). Corrective feedback and teacher development. *L2 journal, 1*, 3–18.

Ellis, R., Basturkmen, H., & Loewen, S. (2001). Learner uptake in communicative esl lessons. *Language Learning, 51*, 281–318.

Erlam, R., Ellis, R., & Batstone, R. (2013). Oral corrective feedback on L2 writing: Two approaches compared. *System, 41*, 257–268.

Ferris, D. (1995). Student reactions to teacher response in multiple-draft composition classrooms. *TESOL Quarterly, 29*, 33–53.

Ferris, D. (1999). The case for grammar correction in L2 writing classes: A response to truscott (1996). *Journal of Second Language Writing, 8*(1), 1–11.

Ferris, D. (2004). The "grammar correction" debate in L2 writing: Where are we, and where do we go from here? (and what do we do in the meantime …?). *Journal of Second Language Writing, 13*(1), 49–62.

Ferris, D., & Helt, M. (2000). Was Truscott right? New evidence on the effects of error correction in L2 writing classes. Paper presented at the at the American Association for Applied Linguistics.

Gass, S. (1997). *Input, interaction, and the second language learner*. Mahwah, NJ: Erlbaum.

Gass, S. (2003). Input and interaction. In C. Doughty & M. Long (Eds.), *The handbook of second language acquisition* (pp. 224–255). Oxford: Blackwell.

Gass, S., & Varonis, E. (1989). Incorporated repairs in nonnative discourse. In M. Eisenstein (Ed.), *Variation and second language acquisition* (pp. 71–86). New York: Plenum.

Gass, S., & Varonis, E. (1994). Input, interaction, and second language production. *Studies in Second Language Acquisition, 16*, 283–302.

Goldstein, L., & Conrad, S. (1990). Student input and negotiation of meaning in esl writing conferences. *TESOL Quarterly, 24*, 443–460.

Guenette, D. (2007). Is feedback pedagogically correct?: Research design issues in studies of feedback on writing. *Journal of Second Language Writing, 16*, 40–53.

Hyland, K., & Hyland, F. (2006). Feedback on second language students' writing. *Language Teaching, 39*(2), 83–101.

Karim, K., & Nassaji, H. (2015). ESL students' perceptions of written corrective feedback: What type of feedback do they prefer and why? *The European Jorunal of Applied Linguistics and TEFL, 4*, 5–25.

Kepner, C. G. (1991). An experiment in the relationship of types of written feedback to the development of second-language writing skills. *The Modern Language Journal*, *75*, 305–313.

Kiparsky, P. (1971). Historical linguistics. In W. O. Dingwall (Ed.), *A survey of linguistic science*. (pp. 577–649). College Park, MA: University of Maryland Press.

Lantolf, J., & Appel, G. (1994). *Vygotskian approaches to second language research*. Norwood, N. J.: Ablex Pub. Corp.

Lantolf, J., & Thorne, S. L. (2006). *Sociocultural theory and the genesis of second language development*. Oxford: Oxford University Press.

Leki, I. (1991). The preferences of esl students for error correction in college-level writing classes. *Foreign Language Annals*, *24*, 203–218.

Loewen, S., Li, S., Fei, F., Thompson, A., Nakatsukasa, K., Ahn, S., et al. (2009). Second language learners' beliefs about grammar instruction and error correction. *The Modern Language Journal*, *93*, 91–104.

Long, M. (1991). Focus on form: A design feature in language teaching methodology. In K. DeBot, R. Ginsberge & C. Kramsch (Eds.), *Foreign language research in cross-cultural perspective* (pp. 39–52). Amsterdam: John Benjamins.

Long, M. (1996). The role of the linguistic environment in second language acquisition. In W. Ritchie & T. Bhatia (Eds.), *Handbook of second language acquisition* (pp. 413–468). San Diego, CA: Academic Press.

Long, M., & Robinson, P. (1998). Focus on form: Theory, research and practice. In C. Doughty & J. Williams (Eds.), *Focus on form in classroom language acquisition* (pp. 15–41). Cambridge: Cambridge University Press.

Lyster, R. (1994). Negotiation of form: analytic strategy in the immersion classroom. *Canadian Modern Language Review*, *50*, 446–465.

Lyster, R. (2001). Negotiation of form, recasts, and explicit correction in relation to error types and learner repair in immersion classrooms. *Language Learning*, *51*, 265–301.

Lyster, R., Lightbown, P., & Spada, N. (1999). A response to Truscott's 'What's wrong with oral grammar correction.' *Canadian Modern Language Review*, *55*, 457–467.

McDonough, K. (2005). Identifying the impact of negative feedback and learners' responses on ESL question development. *Studies in Second Language Acquisition*, *27*, 79–103.

Mackey, A., & Gass, S. (2006). Pushing the methodological boundaries in interaction research: An introduction to the special issue. *Studies in Second Language Acquistion*, *28*, 169–178.

Mackey, A., Gass, S., & McDonough, K. (2000). How do learners perceive interactional feedback? *Studies in Second Language Acquisition*, *22*, 471–497.

Mackey, A., Oliver, R., & Leeman, J. (2003). Interactional input and the incorporation of feedback: An exploration of NS-NNS and NNS-NNS adult and child dyads. *Language Learning*, *53*, 35–66.

Mackey, A., & Philp, J. (1998). Conversational interaction and second language development: Recasts, responses, and red herrings? *Modern Language Journal*, *82*, 338–356.

Mitchell, R., & Myles, F. (2004). *Second language learning theories, second edition*. London: Arnold.

Nassaji, H. (2007). Elicitation and reformulation and their relationship with learner repair in dyadic interaction. *Language Learning*, *57*, 511–548.

Nassaji, H. (2009). Effects of recasts and elicitations in dyadic interaction and the role of feedback explicitness. *Language Learning*, *59*, 411–452.

Nassaji, H. (2011). Correcting students' written grammatical errors: The effects of negotiated versus nonnegotiated feedback. *Studies in Second Language Learning and Teaching*, *1*, 315–334.

Nassaji, H. (2015). *Interactional feedback dimension in instructed second language learning.* London: Bloomsbury Publishing.

Nassaji, H. (2016). Anniversary article: Interactional feedback in second language teaching and learning: A synthesis and analysis of current research. *Language Teaching Research, 20,* 535–562.

Nassaji, H., & Cumming, A. (2000). What's in a ZPD? A case study of a young ESL student and teacher interacting through dialogue journals. *Language Teaching Research, 4,* 95–121.

Nassaji, H., & Swain, M. (2000). A Vygotskian perspective on corrective feedback in L2: The effect of random versus negotiated help on the learning of English articles. *Language Awareness, 9,* 34–51.

Oliver, R. (1995). Negative feedback in child NS-NNS conversation. *Studies in Second Language Acquisition, 17,* 459–481.

Oliver, R. (2000). Age differences in negotiation and feedback in classroom and pairwork. *Language Learning, 50,* 119–151.

Oliver, R. (2002). The patterns of negotiation for meaning in child interactions. *Modern Language Journal, 86,* 97–111.

Oliver, R., & Mackey, A. (2003). Interactional context and feedback in child ESL classrooms. *Modern Language Journal, 87,* 519–533.

Pica, T. (1988). Interlanguage adjustments as an outcome of NS-NNS negotiated interaction. *Language Learning, 38,* 45–73.

Pica, T. (1992). The textual outcomes of native speaker-non-native speaker negotiation: What do they reveal about second language learning? In C. Kramsch & S. McConnell-Ginet (Eds.), *Text and context* (pp. 198–237). Cambridge, MA: D. C. Heath.

Pica, T. (1994). Research on negotiation: What does it reveal about second-language learning conditions, processes, and outcomes? *Language Learning, 44,* 493–527.

Pica, T. (1996). Do second language learners need negotiation? *International Review of Applied Linguistics in Language Teaching, 34,* 1–21.

Pica, T. (2002). Subject-matter content: How does it assist the interactional and linguistic needs of classroom language learners? *Modern Language Journal, 86,* 1–19.

Pica, T., Young, R., & Doughty, C. (1987). The impact of interaction on comprehension. *TESOL Quarterly, 21,* 737–758.

Pienemann, M. (1984). Psychological constraints on the teachability of languages. *Studies in Second Language Acquisition, 6,* 186–214.

Pienemann, M. (1995). Second language acquisition: A first introduction. *Australian Studies in Language Acquisition, 2,* 3–27.

Pienemann, M. (2005). Discussing PT. In M. Pienemann (Ed.), *Cross-linguistic aspects of processability theory* (pp. 61–83). Amsterdam: John Benjamins.

Pienemann, M., & Keßler, J. U. (2012). Processability theory. In A. Gass & A. Mackey (Eds.), *Handbook of second language acquisition* (pp. 228–247). New York: Routledge.

Rahimi, M., Kushki, A., & Nassaji, H. (2015). Diagnostic and developmental potentials of dynamic assessment for L2 writing. *Language and Sociocultural Theory, 2,* 185–208.

Robb, T., Ross, S., & Shortreed, I. (1986). Salience of feedback on error and its effect on EFL writing quality. *TESOL Quarterly, 20,* 83–93.

Ross-Feldman, L. (2007). Interaction in the L2 classroom: Does gender influence learning opportunities? In A. Mackey (Ed.), *Conversational interaction in second language acquisition: A collection of empirical studies* (pp. 53–77). Oxford: Oxford University Press.

Saito, H. (1994). Teachers' practices and students' preferences for feedback on second language writing: A case study of adult ESL learners. *TESL Canada Journal, 11,* 46–70.

Schulz, R. (2001). Cultural differences in student and teacher perceptions concerning the role of grammar instruction and corrective feedback: USA-Colombia. *The Modern Language Journal, 85*, 244–258.

Semke, H. (1984). The effects of the red pen. *Foreign Language Annals, 17*, 195–202.

Sheppard, K. (1992). Two feedback types: Do they make a difference? *RELC Journal: A Journal of Language Teaching and Research in Southeast Asia, 23*, 103–110.

Swain, M. (1995). Three functions of output in second language learning. In G. Cook & B. Seidlhofer (Eds.), *Principle and practice in applied linguistics: Studies in honour of H. G. Widdowson* (pp. 125–144). Oxford: Oxford University Press.

Sze, C. (2002). A case study of the revision process of a reluctant ESL student writer. *TESL Canada journal, 19*, 21–36.

Truscott, J. (1996). The case against grammar correction in L2 writing classes. *Language Learning, 46*, 327–369.

Truscott, J. (2007). The effect of error correction on learners' ability to write accurately. *Journal of Second Language Writing, 16*, 255–272.

Van den Branden, K. (1997). Effects of negotiation on language learners' output. *Language Learning, 47*, 589–636.

Vygotsky, L. S. (1978). *Mind in society: The development of higher psychological processes.* Cambridge, MA: Harvard University Press.

Weissberg, R. (2006). Conversations about writing: Building oral scaffolds with advanced L2 writers. In K. Hyland & F. Hyland (Eds.), *Feedback in second language writing: Contexts and issues* (pp. 246–264). New York: Cambridge University Press.

Wertsch, J. V. (1985). *Vygotsky and the social formation of mind.* Cambridge, MA: Harvard University Press.

Williams, J. (2004). Tutoring and revision: Second language writers in the writing center. *Journal of Second Language Writing, 13*, 173–201.

9

WHY SOME L2 LEARNERS FAIL TO BENEFIT FROM WRITTEN CORRECTIVE FEEDBACK

John Bitchener

Introduction

A considerable body of theoretical and empirical literature on the role of input, including corrective feedback (CF), in second language (L2) development has been published over the past 30–40 years. Although more attention has been given in this literature to learning that occurs in the oral context, a growing body of research in the written context, especially in the last 15–20 years, has revealed that written CF also has the potential to facilitate L2 development (see overview in Bitchener & Storch, 2016). While most of the studies have reported that a single written CF episode results in at least a short-term benefit (immediate improved accuracy and retention over one or two weeks), some have also revealed more durable effects over a longer period of time. The findings in the majority of these studies are group findings and, as such, do not focus on individual learners within these groups who may have failed to benefit immediately from the feedback. Because the focus of these studies has been on output accuracy (that is, improved written accuracy in revised texts and new pieces of writing) and not on the cognitive processing that is required to produce modified output, little attention has been given to factors that may explain why learners have not been successful in producing such output. Thus, little attempt has been made to explain why some learners fail to either engage with the feedback and/or successfully process it across the various cognitive stages that have been hypothesized as essential for text modification and the ongoing production of accuracy in new pieces of writing.

This chapter aims, therefore, to do three things. First, it outlines the research evidence on the role that written CF can play in facilitating the L2 development process. Second, it considers from a theoretical perspective the conditions that have been considered necessary for the cognitive processing of input, like written CF, so that accurate output may be produced. In doing so, it advances a number of reasons why a learner may fail to move from one cognitive processing stage to the next. Third, it considers the types of individual and contextual factors that may have a moderating effect on the progress that learners make when processing the feedback. Consequently, it identifies additional reasons why a learner may fail to benefit from written CF. This discussion focuses on the development that occurs in a single written CF episode, that is, the development in the learner's knowledge and understanding of accurate L2 form and structure that results in an accurate modification of an erroneous use of a particular form or structure. Arising from this discussion, the chapter will close with some recommendations for further work and some pedagogical implications for classroom practitioners.

Research Evidence on the Contribution of Written CF to L2 Development

The research evidence presented in this section refers only to that which has specifically investigated the potential of written CF, targeting specific linguistic error categories, to facilitate L2 development. Adopting a pretest, treatment, post-test design, studies in recent years have consistently shown that written CF as input has the potential to be effectively used, as a result of cognitive processing, to produce accurate output and be the first manifestation of L2 development (Bitchener, Young, & Cameron, 2005; Bitchener, 2008; Bitchener & Knoch, 2008, 2010a, 2010b; Ellis, Sheen, Murakami, & Takashima, 2008; Frear, 2012; Guo, 2015; Rummel, 2014; Sheen, 2007; Sheen, Wright, & Moldawa, 2009; Shintani & Ellis, 2013; Shintani, Ellis, & Suzuki, 2014; Stefanou, 2014). Crucially, these studies have included control groups and tested the effect of written CF in the revision of linguistic errors and/or the writing of new texts immediately after the feedback has been provided, thereby enabling researchers to claim that it is the feedback, rather than any other factor (e.g., instruction), that has facilitated the change. These studies have also revealed that the feedback provided had a durable effect over different periods of time (e.g., one or two weeks to ten months). Readers interested in a detailed discussion of these studies may refer to two recent books on the subject (Bitchener & Ferris, 2012; Bitchener & Storch, 2016). Readers who wish to consult the journal articles in which the studies were first published and read the findings sections of the articles will see that not all learners in the groups who outperformed the control group of learners (that is, those who did not receive written CF) were successful in producing accurate output after one feedback episode. A recent study by Guo (2015) found, however, that with additional written CF (especially feedback which was more explicit than that which had initially been received) the learners who had failed to accurately modify their output immediately after receiving feedback were successful after they had received an additional feedback opportunity.

In these studies, the focus was on the learners' output (that is, a product-oriented focus). In order to understand why some learners failed to either engage with the feedback provided or to fully and successfully process the feedback so that their erroneous output may be modified and used accurately on subsequent occasions, it is necessary to consider the various stages and conditions that theorists have identified as essential for effective cognitive processing and see what factors might have contributed to a breakdown in this processing and at which stages. In the next section, consideration is given to the stages and conditions that have been identified by theorists as essential for the effective processing of input (including CF), namely, that which results in modified, accurate output. Then, a range of individual and contextual factors that might explain why a learner is unable to progress beyond any one of these stages are discussed.

Stages and Conditions in the Cognitive Processing of a Single Written CF Episode

In order to understand why some learners fail to effectively process the feedback they are given and therefore fail to produce accurate output, it is necessary to know what theorists have proposed as the necessary processing stages. The framework proposed by Gass (1997) brought together a range of theoretical proposals about the cognitive processing stages considered essential for output modification and the conditions that need to be met by learners if they are to move from one processing stage to the next. Thus, if any of these stages and conditions are not reached or not met by learners, it would be possible to understand why they may have failed to benefit from the feedback provided.

Although the five-stage framework (comprising attention to and noticing/apperception of input, comprehended input, intake, integration and output) was designed to explain the cognitive processing of oral input (including oral CF), the same stages in the cognitive processing of written input (including written CF) are also required even though the conditions associated with each stage in the oral context may differ in some respects to those associated with the written context. Some of these differences have been discussed in earlier literature (e.g., Bitchener & Storch, 2016; Williams, 2012).

The first stage of the Gass (1997) framework explains the types of input learners may be exposed to, including negative evidence or negative feedback, and that they need to notice or apperceive. This can be applied to situations in which learners receive written CF as input; they need to notice the gap between the written CF input and their erroneous use of the target language in order to accurately modify it. However, for this to occur, second language acquisition (SLA) researchers (e.g., Schmidt, 2001; Sharwood Smith, 1993; Swain, 1985, 1995) suggest that learners may benefit more if they *consciously attend* to the input that has been provided. Explaining what this involves, Schmidt refers to the three stages of attention proposed by Tomlin and Villa (1994). The lowest level of attention, *alertness*, means that learners need to be motivated and ready to learn from the task or activity before them. Applying this to learners who have received written CF, they need to be motivated when they are given the feedback, that is, they need to have a desire to (1) find out what errors they have made and (2) learn from the feedback they are given so that the errors can be accurately modified. Thus, the corollary would be that if learners are not motivated in this sense when receiving feedback, they may not be able to successfully modify their output. The next level of attention, *orientation*, refers to the need for the learners' attention to be orientated toward 'some type or class of sensory information at the exclusion of others' (Tomlin & Villa, 1994, p. 191) such as form (that is, linguistic accuracy) rather than meaning. The highest level of attention referred to by Tomlin and Villa is *detection* and this refers to the cognitive recognition of a stimulus being present for the processing of information (e.g., in this case, written CF). Schmidt (1995) explains that if these conditions are met, learners will be (1) ready to *notice/ apperceive* that some aspect of linguistic information has been provided and, if in the form of corrective feedback, (2) *notice that there is a mismatch or gap* between their output and the target language input that has been provided in the feedback. He adds that in addition to *noticing-with-awareness* (that new information has been provided), *noticing-with-understanding* is necessary to some extent if the informa-tion is to help learners modify their erroneous output. In the strong version of his Noticing Hypothesis, Schmidt (2001) explains that learners *only* learn what they attend to in the input/CF they receive but, in the weak version of the hypothesis, he suggests that individuals learn about the things they attend to and do *not learn much* about the things they do not attend to. It may be that *noticing-with-awareness* and *noticing-with-understanding* can be enhanced in the written context given the permanence of the feedback and the time that is available for learners to refer back to the feedback as many times as they choose. Oral CF, on the other hand, given its fleeting presence, may be a less rich environment in which learners can notice and benefit from CF.

So what deductions can be made from the proposals associated with stage one of the framework about why learners may fail to benefit from written CF? From the three stages of attentional readiness proposed by Tomlin and Villa (1994), it would seem that if learners fail to meet these preconditions for noticing or apper-ceiving that CF has been provided, they may not be ready then to notice that there is, in fact, a mismatch or gap between what they have written and what the feedback is saying. Thus, either of these conditions may be the reason learners fail to benefit from the feedback and fail to produce modified output.

The second stage of the Gass (1997) framework explains that if learners are to *notice-with-understanding*, the input/CF needs to be *comprehended* by the learner. There are a number of factors that may determine whether or not learners com-prehend/understand the feedback they have been given. First and foremost, it is likely that the explicitness or the inexplicitness of the feedback may be a critical factor (Bitchener, 2012; Polio, 2012). The type of feedback that is provided may not, in its most indirect form (e.g., the underlining of errors), tell some learners anything about the nature and cause of the errors or what is needed for an accurate modification, whereas, in its more direct form (e.g., error correction and/or meta-linguistic explanations and examples of accurate usage), it may be more informative in both of these respects. Secondly, the extent to which the explicitness of the feedback is a critical factor may also depend on the proficiency level of learners. Learners at a higher level of proficiency are more likely to have a more developed long-term memory store than learners at a lower level of proficiency (Ortega, 2009). It may be that when more advanced learners receive feedback on particular forms and structures, a certain level of knowledge about them is already stored in their long-term memory and be drawn upon for understanding the feedback that is given. It can be seen, then, that the type of feedback given to learners and the depth of knowledge in their long-term memory may be factors that prevent them from comprehending the feedback and moving to the next stage in their cognitive processing. In addition, a range of individual and contextual factors may further facilitate or prevent learners from comprehending the feedback they have been given. These are discussed in the next section of this chapter.

The third stage of the Gass (1997) framework, *intake*, explains that learners need to match the input/CF they have received with their existing knowledge in their long-term memory. This process involves different levels of analysis and reanalysis in the *working memory* as comparisons are made between their existing knowledge and the feedback provided. Such comparisons enable learners to make hypotheses about what is accurate target linguistic form. It is likely that lower proficiency learners (those with more limited information in their long-term memory) or those with a limited processing capacity may struggle sometimes to successfully complete the amount of analysis required to frame a hypothesis for accuracy testing. In the following section, consideration will be given to indi-vidual difference factors (e.g., processing capacity, language learning aptitude) that may moderate the extent to which learners progress at this stage of matching new and existing information and hypothesizing the form/structure to use.

As each modification hypothesis is tested, any one of three outcomes is pos-sible in the process of *integration*, the fourth stage of the Gass (1997) framework: the learners' existing L2 hypotheses, drawn from their long-term memory, may be accepted or rejected; the information may be stored until learners receive more evidence about the acceptability of their hypotheses; or the hypotheses may exit from the processing system when learners realise they are incorrect. As Williams (2012, p. 328) speculates, it may be that "the cognitive window is open somewhat wider and that learners have a richer opportunity to test their hypotheses when they write than when they speak." Thus, the potential for a successful processing of feedback at this stage may be greater and learners may be less likely to fail to complete the cognitive process when the feedback is written.

Producing modified output, stage five of the framework, is the overt manifesta-tion that learners have begun the process of developing new explicit knowledge.

It may be a development from no knowledge to some knowledge or it may be a development from one level of partial knowledge to another level of knowledge consolidation. If the modified output is not accurate, the learning process will need to be repeated when new feedback is provided. However, as Gass (1997) explains and as Guo (2015) found, learning may have actually begun but may require further feedback episodes before it is overtly manifested.

In presenting this cognitive processing framework, it can be seen that learners may fail at a number of stages in their response to and processing of written CF. However, the framework does not consider the wide range of individual and contextual factors that may further moderate how successful learners are in reaching each stage and in accurately modifying their written output. This, then, is the focus of the next section of this chapter.

Individual and Contextual Factors that May Moderate The Cognitive Processing of Written CF in a Single Feedback Episode

Realizing the potential of individual difference and contextual factors to impact positively or negatively on a learner's cognitive processing of input and, therefore, on the outcome of that processing, the call for theoretical proposals and empirical investigations into this possibility has led to a quite extensive amount of theorizing and research on the issue in the wider SLA literature (Dörnyei, 2010; Ellis, 2008). However, very little consideration has been given to the effect of these factors on the cognitive processing of written CF input. In this section, an outline is presented of some of the factors that have so far been identified for their moderating potential and it is these that might also explain why some learners fail to benefit from written CF.

Individual *learner-internal cognitive factors* that have been shown to have an effect on the cognitive processing of written CF include the learner's working memory, processing capacity, and language learning aptitude. Compared with the long-term memory, the working memory has a limited capacity and is therefore constrained by the amount of information it can process at any one time. Thus, as Skehan (1998) explains, learners with larger working memory capacities are better equipped to process the input they receive. It may be, for example, that if learners receive written CF on the passive voice, those with smaller working memory capacities may struggle to process all the elements of its formation and therefore not be able to produce an accurate modification. As Skehan's model proposes, lower proficiency learners may have difficulty attending to more than one aspect of language (e.g., form and meaning). They may only choose to engage with meaning-focused feedback.

Robinson (2005) and Sawyer and Ranta (2001) have suggested (in relation to the processing of oral input, including oral CF) that there is a relationship between learners' working memory capacity and their language learning aptitude. In terms of two of the characteristics of language aptitude defined by Carroll (1981), grammatical sensitivity and inductive ability, learners with high language analytic ability may be more successful than learners with less language analytic ability in processing the feedback they receive. They may be more likely in both the oral and written contexts (1) to notice the grammatical difference or gap between their output and the new feedback input, (2) to make connections between the new input and their existing knowledge, (3) to process the feedback more deeply (that is, notice with awareness-as-understanding), and (4) to engage in problem-solving activity when writing a new text (e.g., deciding the correct form/structure when they are momentarily uncertain about what is required). Learners with less aptitude may be more likely to not complete these cognitive processes and therefore fail to produce modified accurate output. But, as Dörnyei (2010) explains, one factor alone may not be why the reason a learner's behavior or performance is affected. Two or more factors may interact with one another and moderate their behavior. In this context, there may be an interactional effect between aptitude and the type of feedback given. For example, it may be that learners with high language analytic ability who receive metalinguistic feedback are able to produce modified, accurate output, whereas learners with low analytic ability may be less able to make the same use of the metalinguistic feedback and therefore fail to modify their output accurately.

Given the extent to which individual *learner-internal motivational and affective factors* have been found in the wider SLA research to impact upon the learning process and its outcomes, it is just as likely that these factors will have an effect to some extent on the learner's engagement with and processing of written CF. Motivation explains why people select a particular activity, how long they are willing to persist with it, and what effort they are willing to invest in it (Dörnyei, 2010; Dörnyei & Ushioda, 2009). *Selection* is often associated with a person's goals (for example, instrumental goals, integrative goals or international posture goals). Deci and Ryan (1985) explain that these goals may only have a motivational influence on behavior if they are sufficiently internalized. Thus, learners who have well-established goals and a high level of interest in learning a language might be expected to exhibit a higher level of motivation across the cognitive processing stages, whereas those who are less motivated may not always want to engage with written CF when it is given. If this is the case, the latter may be less likely to attend to the feedback and carry out the cognitive processing required for a modification of their erroneous output. However, some demotivated learners may still use the feedback they are given and modify their erroneous output. Motivated learners, on the other hand, would be expected to exhibit the three levels of attention described earlier by Tomlin and Villa (1994), make every effort to notice the difference between their output and the feedback they have been given, and persevere with hypothesis-testing beyond an initial feedback episode if it fails to result in accurate output.

A range of additional internal factors (for example, *attitudes and beliefs*) may also interact with the level of motivation a learner gives to written CF. A learner's *attitude* to language learning in general, to target language communities, to the learning of a particular language, to a focus on form and/or meaning, and to written CF and particular types of written CF may influence whether he/she responds to and attends to the feedback that has been provided. Because attitudes tend to operate on an emotional level, they alone may be sufficient for a learner to not respond to, attend to, or process the feedback. For instance, if learners are given a particular type of written CF and do not believe it is helpful, they may decide to ignore it (Storch & Wigglesworth, 2010; Rummel, 2014). The strength of their feeling against the feedback type may be the result of unsuccessful prior experiences in using such feedback. In other words, they may have formed a belief that such feedback is unlikely to ever help them. Thus, the interaction of beliefs (especially self-efficacy beliefs, concerned with a learner's capacity to carry out a particular learning activity) and attitudes may alone neutralize the presence of other individual and/or contextual factors and mean that the learner fails to attend to the feedback and attempt a modification (Bandura, 1997; Pajares, 2003). Motivation in its various manifestations would seem to be essential if learners are to be successful at the first hurdle, that is, of attending to and cognitively processing the feedback given in a single episode.

As well as learner-internal factors having the potential to affect a learner's cognitive processing of written CF, mention was made earlier in this chapter that *learner-external factors* may also have a moderating effect with internal factors, separately or interactionally. It has been argued that macro-contextual factors such as the educational context may play a role in shaping the L2 learning process. Referring to foreign language learning, Hedgecock and Lefkowitz (1994) have suggested that some learners in this context may be less motivated, be less orientated to focusing on form/accuracy, and therefore be less likely to attend to written CF if their learning goal is only the receipt of a qualification. On the other hand, it has been argued that other foreign language learners may be more focused on accuracy because their instructional activities are more accuracy oriented than communicatively oriented. However, even if the majority of foreign language learners are influenced by the dominant instructional focus of their educational context, it is also possible that individual learners within it may have goals, attitudes and processing orientations that are different from those of the majority (Bitchener & Storch, 2016; Rummel, 2014). Thus, within a single context (like the foreign language learning context), there may be a complex interaction of external and internal motivational factors and while these may determine whether or not a learner is likely to respond positively or negatively to written CF, there is no certainty about whether, or the extent to which, any of these factors may prevent the learner from processing the feedback and producing modified accurate output. They may or may not be the reason why a learner fails to benefit from written CF.

While the instructional focus of a language learning context may foster positive or negative attitudes and beliefs about focusing on accuracy and on certain types of written CF, the social environment of the classroom may exert equally positive or negative behaviors toward the provision of written CF. *Social setting factors*, such as those between teacher and learner and between learner and learner, have been shown in the SLA literature to play a role in the type of interaction that occurs or fails to occur (Dörnyei, 2005; Ellis, 2008). However, little consideration has been given to the effect that social relationships in the classroom might have on a learner's response to and processing of written CF as input. Learners who have a positive attitude toward their teacher and respect their knowledge and feedback decisions may be more responsive to the feedback delivery choices that their teacher makes (e.g., about what to focus on, when to provide the feedback, and the types of feedback to be employed) than those who, for one reason or another, do not respect their teacher or the decisions that are made about giving written CF. Learners in the first category may be more likely to attend to and process the feedback than those in the second category who may refuse to respond to feedback when it is provided.

Further Work Recommended

Several recommendations can be given to extend our understanding of why some learners may fail to benefit from a single written CF episode. First, a more extensive mapping is needed of potential individual and contextual factors that may moderate the progress that learners make as they meet or fail to meet the conditions considered essential at key processing stages. Such a mapping would do well to draw upon insights and proposals from the wider SLA literature on classroom-based learning and from those offered in sociocultural accounts of the learning process. Empirical research that seeks to validate and extend theoretical proposals should include self-report studies in which learners are asked to (1) think out loud as they process the feedback they have been given and (2) reflect on this data in follow-up interviews (immediately after the processing). Interviews could also tap into their 'state-of-being' before they were given feedback on their writing to see whether or not they met the preconditions referred to by Tomlin and Villa (1994). Research of this type, for example, may reveal more about (1) why learners respond to or fail to engage with the feedback when they receive it and (2) why there may be a breakdown at certain points in their processing of the feedback.

Conclusion and Pedagogical Implications

Drawing on theoretical insights and proposals from the SLA literature that are applicable to L2 development occurring within a single written CF episode, this chapter has identified a number of stages when a learner's cognitive processing may break down and not result in modified output. It has also identified a number of conditions that learners may fail to meet as they progress from one stage to another. The potential effect of several individual differences and contextual factors to moderate negatively as well as positively at different points in the process has also been discussed. Presented as a sample of factors that may lead to a break-down in processing, this outline is far from exhaustive. However, hopefully, it opens the door for further work.

Understanding that there is a range of reasons why learners may sometimes fail to modify their output, even when written CF has been provided, should help teachers reflect on whether they are providing the most helpful type of feedback and whether it is being provided at the most optimal time. It may be that the lin-guistic focus of the feedback that is given to some learners is inappropriate given their level of proficiency and the likely capacity of their long-term memory store. If learners have insufficient knowledge in store, they may not *notice-with-understanding* the gap between their output and that which is being provided in the feedback. It may also be that the type of feedback given (that is, its level of explicitness) is inap-propriate for some learners and prevents them from understanding or comprehend-ing what it says. Teachers would also do well to think carefully about the timing of their feedback, bearing in mind that certain times of the day, for example, may not be conducive to learners meeting the preconditions (of Tomlin and Villa, 1994) for a positive response to feedback. Selecting types of written CF that align with what teachers perceive to be their students' level of L2 knowledge on specific forms and structures (based, for example, on their knowledge of earlier and recent instructional syllabi and resources) may mean that learners receive input that can be analyzed and compared more effectively with knowledge stored in their long-term memory and assist with making successful hypotheses about accurate uses of forms and structures. Teachers could discuss with their students the factors that they (the students) think may help them or not help them benefit from written CF. They could also ask their students if they think that any of the factors referred to in this chapter and in the wider literature (especially those which their students have not referred to in discus-sion) are helpful or unhelpful. This may help to motivate any demotivated learners and help all learners to understand their teachers' priorities and practices. Again, this is not an exhaustive list of possible implications, but hopefully it is one that might stimulate the reflective thinking of teachers as they consider their current and future practices involving the provision of written CF.

References

Bandura, A. (1997). *Self-efficacy: The exercise of control.* New York: W. H. Freeman.

Bitchener, J. (2008). Evidence in support of written corrective feedback. *Journal of Second Language Writing, 17*(2), 102–118.

Bitchener, J. (2012). A reflection on 'the language learning component' of written CF. *Journal of Second Language Writing, 21*(4), 348–363.

Bitchener, J., & Ferris, D. (2012). *Written corrective feedback in second language acquisition and writing.* London: Routledge.

Bitchener, J., & Knoch, U. (2008). The value of written corrective feedback for migrant and international students. *Language Teaching Research, 12*(3), 409–431.

Bitchener, J., & Knoch, U. (2010a). The contribution of written corrective feedback to language development: A ten month investigation. *Applied Linguistics*, *31*(2), 193–214.

Bitchener, J., & Storch, N. (2016). *Written corrective feedback for L2 development*. Bristol, UK: Multilingual Matters.

Bitchener, J., & Knoch, U. (2010b). Raising the linguistic accuracy level of advanced L2 writers with written corrective feedback. *Journal of Second Language Writing*, *19*(4), 207–217.

Bitchener, J., Young, S., & Cameron, D. (2005). The effect of different types of corrective feedback on ESL student writing. *Journal of Second Language Writing*, *14*(3), 191–205.

Carroll, J. (1981). Twenty-five years of research on foreign language aptitude. In K. Diller (Ed.), *Individual differences and universals in language learning aptitude* (pp. 83–118). Rowley, MA: Newbury House.

Deci, E. L., & Ryan, R. M. (1985). *Intrinsic motivation and self-determination in human behaviour*. New York: Plenum.

Dörnyei, Z. (2005). *The psychology of the language learner*. Mahwah, NJ: Lawrence Erlbaum Associates.

Dörnyei, Z. (2010). The relationship between language aptitude and language learning motivation. In E. Macaro (Ed.), *Continuum companion to second language acquisition* (pp. 247–267). London: Continuum.

Dörnyei, Z., & Ushioda, E. (Eds.) (2009). *Motivation, language identity and the L2 self*. Bristol, UK: Multilingual Matters.

Ellis, R. (2008). *The study of second language acquisition* (2nd ed.). New York: Oxford University Press.

Ellis, R., Sheen, Y., Murakami, M., & Takashima, H. (2008). The effects of focused and unfocused written corrective feedback in an English as a foreign language context. *System*, *36*(3), 353–371.

Frear, D. (2012). *The effect of written CF and revision on intermediate Chinese learners' acquisition of English*. Unpublished doctoral thesis, University of Auckland, New Zealand.

Gass, S. (1997). *Input, interaction, and the second language learner*. Mahwah, NJ: Lawrence Erlbaum Associates.

Guo, Q, (2015). *The effectiveness of written CF for L2 development: A mixed method study of written CF types, error categories and proficiency levels*. Unpublished doctoral thesis, AUT University, Auckland, New Zealand.

Hedgecock, J., & Lefkowitz, N. (1994). Feedback on feedback: Assessing learner receptivity in second language writing. *Journal of Second Language Writing*, *3*, 141–163.

Ortega, L. (2009). *Understanding second language acquisition*. London: Hodder Eduation.

Pajares, F. (2003). Self-efficacy beliefs, motivation and achievement in writing: A review of the literature. *Reading and Writing Quarterly*, *19*, 139–158.

Polio, C. (2012). The relevance of second language acquisition theory to the written error correction debate. *Journal of Second Language Writing*, *21*(4), 375–389.

Robinson, P. (2005). Aptitude and second language acquisition. *Annual Review of Applied Linguistics*, *25*, 46–73.

Rummel, S. (2014). *Student and teacher beliefs about written CF and the effect these bliefs have on uptake: A multiple case study of Laos and Kuwait*. Unpublished doctoral thesis, AUT University, Auckland, New Zealand.

Sawyer, M., & Ranta, L. (2001). Aptitude, individual differences, and instructional design. In P. Robinson (Ed.), *Cognition and second language instruction* (pp. 319–353). New York: Cambridge University Press.

Schmidt, R. (1995). *Attention and awareness in foreign language learning* (Vol. 9). Honolulu: University of Hawai'i Press.

Schmidt, R. (2001). Attention. In P. Robinson (Ed.), *Cognition and second lanugage instruction* (pp. 3–32). Cambridge: Cambridge University Press.

Sharwood Smith, M. (1993). Input enhancement in instructed SLA: Theoretical bases. *Studies in Second Language Acquisition, 15*(2), 165–179.

Sheen, Y. (2007). The effect of focused written corrective feedback and language aptitude on ESL learners' acquisition of articles. *Tesol Quarterly, 41*(2), 255–283.

Sheen, Y., Wright, D., & Moldawa, A. (2009). Differential effects of focused and unfocused written correction on the accurate use of grammatical forms by adult ESL learners. *System, 37*(4), 556–569.

Shintani, N., & Ellis, R. (2013). The comparative effect of direct written corrective feedback and metalinguistic explanation on learners' explicit and implicit knowledge of the English indefinite article. *Journal of Second Language Writing, 22*(3), 286–306.

Shintani, N., Ellis, R., & Suzuki, W. (2014). Effects of written feedback and revision on learners' accuracy in using two English grammatical structures. *Language Learning, 64*(1), 103–131.

Skehan, P. (1998). *A cognitive approach to language learning.* Oxford: Oxford University Press.

Stefanou, C. (2014). *L2 article use for generic and specific plural reference: The role of written CF, learner factors and awareness.* Unpublished doctoral thesis, Lancaster University, UK.

Storch, N., & Wigglesworth, G. (2010). Students' engagement with feedback on writing: The role of learner agency/beliefs. In R. Batstone (Ed.), *Sociocognitive Perspectives on Language Use and Language Learning* (pp. 166–185). Oxford: Oxford University Press.

Swain, M. (1985). Communicative competence: Some roles of comprehensible input and comprehensible output in its development. In S. Gass & C. Madden (Eds.), *Input in second language acquisition* (pp. 235–253). Rowley, MA: Newbury House.

Swain, M. (1995). Three functions of output in second language learning. In G. Cook & B. Seidlhofer (Eds.), *Principle and practice in applied linguistics: Studies in honour of H.G. Widdowson* (pp. 125–144). Oxford: Oxford University Press.

Tomlin, R. S., & Villa, V. (1994). Attention in cognitive science and second language acquisition. *Studies in Second Language Acquisition, 16*(2), 183–203.

Williams, J. (2012). The potential role(s) of writing in second language development. *Journal of Second Language Writing, 21*(4), 321–331.

PART IV
Student and Teacher Issues in Corrective Feedback

10

STUDENT AND TEACHER BELIEFS AND ATTITUDES ABOUT ORAL CORRECTIVE FEEDBACK

Shaofeng Li

Introduction

Beliefs about corrective feedback (CF) refer to the attitudes, views, opinions, or stances learners and teachers hold about the utility of CF in second language (L2) learning and teaching and how it should be implemented in the classroom. There are several reasons why it is important to examine CF-related beliefs. First, the effectiveness of CF may depend upon learners' receptivity of CF, which is evidenced by Sheen's (2007) finding that learners who were more positive about CF benefited more from metalinguistic feedback. Second, it is important to compare student and teacher beliefs about CF because mismatches between learners' expectations and teachers' beliefs may have a great impact on students' satisfaction with the class and their motivation to learn the language. Third, as an integral piece of the puzzle of CF, knowledge about the stakeholders' beliefs affords valuable information about the extent to which their views on CF are congruent with or deviant from what has been demonstrated about its effectiveness and occurrence in the classroom. Finally, the importance of investigating CF beliefs also lies in the fact that it is an independent construct that is distinct from beliefs about other aspects of language learning. For example, Loewen et al.'s (2009) large-scale survey showed that learners' responses to CF-related questions loaded on a different factor than their responses to questions relating to grammar learning, leading the authors to conclude that "learners viewed error correction and grammar instruction as distinct categories" (p. 101) and suggest that future research incorporate the distinction.

This chapter seeks to provide a systematic and comprehensive synthesis of the empirical research on learners' and teachers' beliefs about CF. Given that there are fundamental differences between oral and written CF and that the bulk of the research on CF beliefs concerns oral CF, studies on beliefs about written CF are beyond the scope of this review. This synthetic review deviates from a traditional literature review in that (1) it is based on an exhaustive search of the literature and transparent selection criteria, rather than a small set of studies that are selected based on unknown criteria and are therefore subject to biased conclusions and false claims; (2) it integrates meta-analysis and narrative review, using the former approach to aggregate quantitative results and the latter to synthesize themes and patterns that emerge in the literature.

This synthesis provides an inductive review of all themes about CF beliefs, which relate to four dimensions of the topic. The first and most important dimension concerns how learners and teachers view CF, which can be approached by answering the five questions Hendrickson (1978) formulated: (1) Should errors be corrected? (2) How should errors be corrected? (3) When should errors be corrected? (4) Who should provide CF? and (5) Which errors should be corrected? The second dimension is whether training or instructional treatment can affect learners' and teachers' beliefs about CF. The third dimension relates to the congruence and incongruence between teachers' CF beliefs and their CF practice. The fourth dimension pertains to whether learners' attitude toward CF has an effect on their learning gains after receiving CF.

Methods

In order to identify all related studies, a comprehensive literature search was conducted by using domain-general and domain-specific electronic databases such as *Google Scholar* and *LLBA*, checking the reference sections of related articles, and consulting state-of-the-art articles about CF such as Nassaji (2016). This synthesis included any published studies and unpublished PhD dissertations and MA theses investigating learners' or teachers' beliefs about oral CF exclusively or along with beliefs about other aspects of L2 learning. The synthesis did not include studies published in non-peer-reviewed journals, conference proceedings, studies on beliefs about CF provided in other modalities such as in written form or via the computer, and studies on learners' uptake and noticing of feedback.

Two types of analysis were conducted: meta-analysis and narrative review. Meta-analysis was conducted for quantitative data with more than three effect sizes. Effect sizes were operationalized as agreement rates for survey items on teachers' and learners' attitudes toward CF. The results for "agree" and "strongly agree" were collapsed as one category in the meta-analysis. Each data point was weighted by the related sample size such that the results associated with larger samples carried more weight. Where necessary, Q_b tests—a meta-analytic procedure for detecting group differences—were performed to ascertain whether there were systematic differences between subgroups (e.g., teachers vs. students).

A narrative approach was utilized for synthesizing the bulk of the retrieved data, and was applied to (1) quantitative studies conducted using methods that were incompatible with the meta-analyzed studies, such as survey studies based on a four-point rather than five-point Likert scale, (2) quantitative data that were not meta-analyzable, either because there were few effect sizes ($k < 4$) or there were no statistical procedures for effect size calculation (e.g., the results of factor analysis), and (3) results of qualitative studies, which were reported by primary researchers as themes and patterns.

Results and Discussion

Twenty-six studies were identified that met the inclusion criteria. Among them, four investigated student beliefs about CF, three examined teacher beliefs, and six compared student and teacher beliefs. The remaining studies explored other aspects of CF beliefs, including six on the congruence and incongruence between teachers' beliefs and practices, one on the influence of teachers' individual differences on their beliefs and practices, four on whether CF beliefs can be changed through some type of training, and two on whether CF beliefs had an impact on CF effectiveness. However, some studies investigated multiple research questions and reported results that relate to several dimensions of the topic, which made it difficult to categorize them in a straightforward manner. The findings of these studies and more methodological details follow.

Beliefs about CF

Should Errors be Corrected?

Seven survey studies contributed data on students' views on the importance of receiving CF (Agudo, 2015; Davis 2003; Lee, 2013; Loewen et al., 2009; Oladejo, 1993; Schulz, 1996, 2001). Aggregation of the results of the four studies using the same scale showed that learners were overwhelmingly positive about CF: the mean agreement rate for the importance of CF was 89%. Lee (2013) and Loewen et al. (2009) coded learners' answers to Likert scale items as continuous data, which were incompatible with the percentage agreement rates reported by other studies and were therefore not included in the aggregation. However, these two studies also showed learners' overall positive attitude toward CF. Lee (2013) reported that the mean score for the item regarding CF importance was 4.43 out of 5 and Loewen et al. (2009) reported that the mean score was 5.1 out of 6.

While students were keen to receive CF, teachers were not enthusiastic about providing CF. Aggregation of the results of the seven related studies (Agudo, 2014; Bell, 2005; Davis, 2003; Gurzynski-Weiss, 2010; Rahimi & Zhang, 2015; Schulz, 1996, 2001) showed that only 39% of the teachers agreed that CF was important. A Q_b test was conducted to determine whether there was a significant difference between students' and teachers' overall attitudes toward CF, and the result showed that there was: $Q(1, 9) = 501, p < .00$, in favor of students. However, a closer inspection of the results for teachers showed much variation among the studies, with the agreement rates ranging from 30% (Schulz, 1996) to 83% (Gurzynski-Weiss, 2010; Rahimi & Zhang, 2015). It is unclear why the teachers in Gurzynski-Weiss's and Rahimi & Zhang's studies were more supportive of CF, but one possible explanation is that these two studies were exclusively about CF, which may have raised the teachers' awareness of CF, whereas in the other studies, CF was examined as one aspect of language learning and teaching.

The identified studies also showed that students' and teachers' attitudes toward CF may vary as a function of their experience and the instructional context. For example, Loewen et al. (2009) found that ESL learners who received more grammar instruction and error correction in their previous learning experience were less supportive of receiving CF than other learner groups. In Schulz's study (1996), only 11% of the ESL teachers agreed with providing CF on students' speaking errors, which stood in contrast with other teacher groups, whose agreement rates were between 26% and 50%, suggesting these two groups of teachers had distinct beliefs. There is also evidence that more experienced teachers were more positive about feedback than less experienced teachers (90% vs. 75% in Rahimi & Zhang, 2015), with the latter expressing more concern over the harmful effects of CF on students' motivation and self-esteem (Vásquez & Harvey, 2010). Teachers' attitudes may also be affected by the nature of the class they teach. For example, Junqueira and Kim (2013) and Kamiya (2014) found that teachers of oral communication classes dismissed the need for CF in classes focusing on fluency rather than accuracy.

How Should Errors be Corrected?

There has been very little research on students' preferred feedback types. Lee (2013) is perhaps the only study in the data set that reported results on students' views on some major feedback types identified in classroom CF research. The respondents in this survey study were 60 international teaching assistants enrolled in an ESL speaking program at a large U.S. university. The survey showed that the mean score for the item "When my teacher corrects me, I want him/her to tell me what I got wrong and provide the correct form immediately" was 4.43 out of 5, which suggests strong preference for explicit correction. The mean score for the item asking the students' opinion on self-correction was 3.60. The author also included a figure displaying the students' rankings of different CF types, which showed a clear pattern: their rankings for explicit correction and recasts were substantially higher than prompts—elicitation, repetition, clarification, and metalinguistic feedback. The results seemed to suggest that overall these students wanted to be told, either implicitly or explicitly, what the correct form was. However, the participants were a special group who may not represent the whole learner population.

There are more studies, however, on the types of CF that teachers favor. The results for the three survey studies are displayed according to feedback type in

TABLE 10.1 Teachers' Preferences Regarding Different CF Types

Feedback	% Agree	Respondents	Source
Recasts	56.9	55 student teachers	Agudo, 2014
	70	20 novice teachers	Rahimi & Zhang, 2015
	75	20 experienced teachers	
	80	475 experienced teachers	Bell, 2005
Explicit correction	68.6	55 student teachers	Agudo, 2014
	75	20 experienced teachers	Rahimi & Zhang, 2015
	15	20 novice teachers	
Metalinguistic feedback	64.7	55 student teachers	Agudo, 2014
	60	20 experienced teachers	Rahimi & Zhang, 2015
	15	20 novice teachers	
Clarification	49	55 student teachers	Agudo, 2014
	70	20 experienced teachers	Rahimi & Zhang, 2015
	60	20 novice teachers	
Indirect feedback	70.5	475 experienced teachers	Bell, 2005
Direct feedback	48	475 experienced teachers	Bell, 2005

Table 10.1. The aggregated weighted mean agreement rate for recasts was 76.7%, suggesting that overall teachers were positive about recasts, with the caveat that the student teachers in Agudo (2014) had less faith in this CF type. The number of effect sizes for other feedback types were all below four and were therefore not aggregated. Overall the results on those feedback types seem to show that (1) teachers, especially novice teachers, were less certain about explicit correction, metalinguistic feedback, clarification, and direct feedback and (2) teachers were in favor of indirect feedback. Rahimi and Zhang's study (2015) suggested that teachers' views were affected by their experience: Novice teachers disagreed with the provision of explicit CF and experienced teachers advocated a more balanced approach to CF provision. This finding is consistent with Junqueira and Kim's (2013) observation about two teachers' CF practices in the classroom: the novice teacher almost always used recasts and clarification requests (both were implicit) while the experienced teacher's CF use was more varied.

Some small-scale qualitative studies confirmed the findings of the above larger-scale, quantitative studies. Several (Dong, 2012; Junqueira & Kim, 2013; Kamiya, 2014) reported that teachers seemed to resist explicit feedback and favor implicit feedback. Roothooft (2014) administered a survey using a questionnaire, including 11 open-ended questions to 10 English as a foreign language (EFL) teachers asking the teachers' opinions about the best method of error correction. Four of the teachers indicated that the best way was to integrate different types of feedback. Roothooft's study suggests that close-ended questions with mutually exclusive choices are not always effective in eliciting respondents' opinions.

To sum up, there is only one study on students' preferences, which found that they liked to receive explicit correction and recasts—two types of input-providing feedback. The studies on teachers' preferences, except for Bell (2005) (N = 479), were mostly small scaled and the findings were varied. Overall, teachers were positive about recasts and indirect feedback and novice teachers seemed to be more concerned about the debilitative effects of CF on students' motivation and self-esteem.

When Should Errors be Corrected?

The timing of CF involves at least two distinctions: immediate versus delayed and online versus offline, with the former referring to whether errors should be corrected immediately after learners receive instruction on a certain linguistic structure or some time after the instruction, and the latter referring to whether errors should be corrected during an oral activity or after it is completed. Unfortunately, these distinctions are not unequivocally defined in the research on CF beliefs and in CF research in general. In fact, to date there has been no published research investigating the impact of timing on the effectiveness of CF (but see Li, Zhu, & Ellis, 2016).

Two studies investigated whether students preferred immediate correction. Davis (2003) found that 86.6% of the 97 EFL students in his study agreed with the statement that errors should be corrected as soon as possible in order to prevent the formation of bad habits. Brown (2009) asked 1,409 foreign language learners whether they agreed with the statement that effective teachers should not correct errors immediately and the mean score was 2.12 out of 4, suggesting a somewhat favorable opinion about immediate correction. Based on the results of these two studies, a claim can be made that students want their errors to be corrected immediately. However, the questions included in the survey studies regarding the 'immediate versus delayed' distinction only focused on the first, but not the second, part of the distinction, such as "The effective foreign language teacher corrects errors as soon as they occur" (Bell, 2005). Therefore, while learners were in favor of immediate correction, it is unclear whether they also endorsed delayed correction.

As for online and offline feedback, Harmer (2007) described a survey conducted at a language school in London revealing that 62% of the students (sample size not reported) liked being corrected at the moment errors were made and 38% preferred to receive CF after finishing the task. Lynch (2009) extended the scope of CF to include providing a sample performance (audio recording or transcript) to learners after an activity to help them notice the gap between their own performance and the provided model. The majority of the 60 international postgraduate students at a British university he surveyed preferred to receive the model after a role-play activity instead of before the activity.

Six studies (Bell, 2005; Brown, 2009; Davis, 2003; Kartchava, 2006; Rahimi & Zhang, 2015; Roothooft, 2014) contributed data on teachers' beliefs about CF timing. The average percentage of teachers agreeing with immediate CF based on the four effect sizes extracted from three survey studies was 40%. Brown (2009) found that the mean score for the item stating teachers should not perform immediate correction was 3.13 out of 4, which the author said was significantly different from the student respondents' ratings (mean score: 2.12). These studies suggest that overall teachers are hesitant about performing immediate correction of students' errors. Teachers' convictions on CF timing, however, may be influenced by their backgrounds, as shown by Kartchava (2006), who found that preservice teachers who had not taken a language acquisition course were more likely to object to immediate correction than those who had. However, as with the studies on students' beliefs, these studies only tapped teachers' views on immediate CF and failed to ask their opinions about delayed CF.

Two studies contributed data on whether teachers favored online or offline feedback. Roothooft (2014) revealed that in their responses to some open-ended questions, two of the 10 teachers considered it important to distinguish error types when it comes to feedback timing: Errors interfering with communication need to be addressed immediately, while other errors can wait. Rahimi and Zhang (2015) reported that in the follow-up interview of their survey study, one teacher indicated that he/she would perform immediate corrections for errors impeding communication or relating to the target structure of the lesson or for recurrent errors. These studies demonstrate that teachers' opinions about the ideal time to provide CF are likely more complicated than the online–offline dichotomy and that there is a need for survey studies to include questions that tap alternative positions on this topic.

Who Should Provide CF?

This question concerns the source of feedback, which could be the teacher, peers, or the learner him/herself. According to Schulz's (1996, 2001) studies, only 15% of the 824 Colombian EFL students and 13% of the 607 U.S. foreign language students preferred to be corrected by their fellow students in small group work rather than by their teachers in front of the entire class. Similarly, Agudo (2015) found that only 42% of the 173 Spanish EFL students agreed or strongly agreed with receiving feedback from their classmates in small group work. Sato (2013) identified four belief factors relating to peer interaction and peer feedback based on 167 Japanese EFL learners' responses to a 27-item questionnaire. Different from other studies which showed learners' unwillingness to receive peer CF, Sato found that the learners responded positively to the questions on the factor about receiving peer CF, with a mean factor score of 4.16 (maximum 6); however, they were less confident about providing CF to others, the mean score being 3.92. The disparity between Sato's and other studies in terms of learners' receptivity toward peer CF is perhaps due to the different ways in which the statements were phrased. Schulz and Agudo asked about receiving peer CF in group work and the questions were therefore more restrictive, and the related items in Schulz's study even dismissed the importance of teacher feedback. The statements in Sato's study, however, were broader in scope in that they were mainly related to whether the students felt comfortable if their grammar errors were pointed out by their classmates and whether they would trust their classmates' corrections.

There is scant attention to teachers' beliefs about the source of CF, with Agudo (2014) being the only study (N = 55) in the data set that included items about teachers' stances on peer correction and self-correction. The student teacher respondents did not show strong support for the two related items for peer correction—only 33% agreed that peer correction is more effective than teacher correction and 37% agreed that peer correction causes less anxiety than teacher correction. The teachers believed in the value of self-correction: 78% agreed that students should be prompted to self-correct.

To sum up, although students were not satisfied with receiving feedback only from their peers and only during group work, they did not mind their peers pointing out their errors. Preservice teachers rejected the claim that student CF is superior to teacher CF and that student CF causes less anxiety than teacher CF. They acknowledged the importance of pushing learners to self-correct. More research on beliefs about the source of CF is needed, however, to reach firmer conclusions.

Which Errors Should be Corrected?

To answer this question, the primary researchers have asked learners and teachers to comment on (1) the extent to which errors should be corrected (e.g., all or some errors), (2) whether CF should only target errors impeding communication, and (3) whether correction should target only those errors that are the focus of the lesson. In terms of the extent of error correction, Jean and Simard's large-scale study (2011) on high school learners' beliefs showed that 30% of the 990 learners of French as a second language (FSL) and 54% of the 1,314 learners of EFL thought that grammar errors should be corrected all the time during speaking. The authors further pointed out that the gap between the percentage rates for the two groups of learners were attributable to their first language learning experience—whereas the FSL learners had limited grammar instruction in the language arts classes in their first language (English), the EFL learners received more grammar training in their L1 (French) language arts classes. In Lee (2013), the 60 international teaching assistants indicated that they would like the errors that occurred most often in their speaking to be corrected (mean score being 4.42 out of 5). In terms of whether only errors impeding communication should be corrected, the endorsement rates for the FSL and EFL learners were 51% and 41% respectively in Jean and Simard (2011), and 87% of the 500 university EFL learners in Oladejo (1993) rejected the statement. In terms of whether CF should only target grammar points that are the foci of the lesson, only 32% of the FSL and 23% of the EFL learners in Jean and Simard (2011) concurred.

On the teacher's side, regarding the extent of error correction, only 33% of the 55 teachers in Agudo (2014) entertained the idea of correcting all grammar errors, and 31% of the 26 FSL and 16% of the 19 high school EFL teachers in Jean and Simard (2011) thought it necessary to correct errors all of the time. Only 19% of the 457 teachers in Bell's study considered it essential to correct most errors, and 63% of the teachers Agudo (2014) surveyed approved of correcting only some errors so as not to discourage students. When it comes to only correcting errors impeding communication, only 33% of the 92 foreign language teachers in Schulz (1996) agreed and 54% of the FSL and 68% of the ESL teachers in Jean and Simard (2011) agreed. Concerning whether to only target errors relating to the foci of the lesson, Jean and Simard reported an endorsement rate of 46% for FSL teachers and 52% for EFL teachers.

In a nutshell, neither learners nor teachers considered it necessary to correct all errors and teachers seemed more negative about this practice. The idea of only correcting errors impeding communication did not receive strong support either, but the high school respondents in Jean and Simard's study seemed to be more supportive of this idea. Finally, there appeared to be some discrepancy between teachers and students in terms of whether CF should only focus on preselected linguistic structures: students declined the idea but teachers tended to be less dismissive. As can be seen, none of the three aspects of the question of what errors should receive CF was strongly supported by the respondents in the available studies; this is perhaps to large extent due to the extremeness or absoluteness of the assertions of the related survey items, which contained such words as "only," "all", or "every". Extreme statements are, then, less likely to be supported by respondents.

The Effects of Training on the Change of CF Beliefs

One important question is whether learners' and teachers' beliefs about CF can be changed. Sato (2013) conducted a 10-week experimental study to ascertain the influence of peer feedback and peer interaction on learners' attitudes toward feedback and interaction. One hundred and sixty-seven Japanese university EFL learners were assigned to four conditions: prompts, recasts, interaction, and control. The two feedback groups provided prompts and recasts on their partners' speech errors while engaged in communicative tasks, the interaction group only performed communicative tasks, and the control group did not receive any treatment. The results revealed that the two feedback groups became significantly more positive about providing CF to their classmates and participating in communicative activities after receiving feedback treatments.

Three studies have explored whether teachers' thoughts can be changed through some type of training. Vásquez and Harvey (2010) reported a case study examining the changes brought about by replicating a research study in the beliefs and awareness about CF of nine postgraduate (MA and PhD) students enrolled in a master's level second language acquisition (SLA) course. The teacher trainees recorded a lesson, transcribed the data, coded CF episodes, and wrote a report of their findings. The authors observed that at the beginning of the semester, the trainees had little knowledge about CF and were concerned about the affective aspects of CF, that is, that learners might be discouraged or demotivated by receiving CF. However, after conducting the study, they focused on other aspects of CF, such as students' noticing of CF, uptake, and CF types, demonstrating "a more nuanced and sophisticated understanding of its role and function, and its interaction with student uptake" (p. 430). The teachers also indicated that this project made them change the way they provided feedback and would lead to changes in their future teaching practice as well.

A similar study by Busch (2010) confirmed the effects of teacher training on teacher beliefs. This study involved 381 student teachers enrolled in a course to meet the requirement for K-12 certification. The assignments of the course included tutoring an ESL learner, analyzing language samples collected from the learner, reflecting on their personal language learning experience, and analyzing the changes and non-changes of their beliefs as a result of taking the course. The teachers' responses to a 23-item questionnaire administered before and after taking the course underwent significant changes.

Kamiya and Loewen (2014) investigated whether reading academic articles on CF had an effect on a teacher's beliefs. The participant was an experienced ESL teacher, who was asked to read two articles on CF effectiveness and the noticing of CF. A semi-structured interview conducted before and after reading the articles showed no change in the teacher's beliefs. The disparities between this study and the two studies reviewed above testify to Busch's (2010) observation that "professional coursework which includes experiential and reflective activities seems to have a stronger effect on the development of beliefs systems than declarative knowledge" (p. 319). Declarative knowledge obtained through reading the related literature must be processed and consolidated through reflective activities and proceduralized through hands-on practice activities such as tutoring a learner or conducting a replication study in order for systematic and substantial changes to occur in teacher trainees' belief systems.

Teachers' Beliefs about CF and Their CF Practice

There has been a relatively large amount of research on whether teachers are consistent in their preferences about CF and the way they use CF in their teaching. These studies (Table 10.2) fall into the qualitative paradigm, where a small number of teacher participants were (1) asked to report their beliefs through interview or other self-reporting procedures such as stimulated recall and cued response, and (2) observed in the classroom to see whether and how they corrected students' errors. As Table 10.2 shows, the studies showed both congruence and incongruence between teachers' beliefs and practices. It would seem that teachers were consistent about implicit CF, that is, they preferred to use recasts and had qualms over

TABLE 10.2 Congruence and Incongruence Between Teachers' CF Beliefs and CF Practices

Study	Participants	Congruence	Incongruence
Basturkmen, Loewen, & Ellis, 2004	3 ESL teachers at a private language school in Auckland		All three teachers said CF should be meaning-oriented but the CF they provided was all code(language)-related; two teachers said they would use prompts but they used recasts; one teacher said he would provide feedback after an oral activity but he did during oral tasks
Dong, 2012	2 teachers of Chinese at a U.S. university	Both teachers said they preferred implicit feedback and they did provide recasts the most; one teacher said he would not provide explicit feedback and he followed what he said in practice	Both said they would encourage self-repair but they used recasts the most; one teacher said he would not interrupt students' speech but he constantly jumped in to correct
Junqueira & Kim, 2013	2 teachers in an intensive English program at a U.S. university	One teacher said her CF would be about pronunciation and the other said he preferred to correct grammar errors; they did what they said they would do	Both teachers said CF was not effective but they provided lots of recasts
Kameiya, 2014	4 teachers in an intensive English program at a U.S. university	Different from previous findings, most teachers were consistent in their beliefs and practice; they all disliked explicit correction and in reality they did not provide any such feedback	On teacher dismissed the value of CF but he provided lots of recasts
Kartchava, 2006	10 (selected) pre-service ESL teachers in Montreal	The teachers said they would use recasts and they did	They promised to correct more errors than they actually did

the "humiliating" nature of explicit feedback, and in their teaching practice, the most frequently used feedback type was indeed recasts (Dong, 2012; Kamiya, 2014; Kartchava, 2006). Inconsistency mainly occurs in two aspects: (1) some teachers did not acknowledge the value of CF but provided a lot of CF in their teaching, mainly in the form of recasts (Junqueira & Kim, 2013; Kamiya, 2014); (2) while some thought it a good idea to encourage self-correction through prompts, they used recasts instead (Basturkmen, Loewen, & Ellis, 2004; Dong, 2012).

The inconsistency between teachers' beliefs and practices is likely due to several factors. First, most of these studies only involved a few teachers and were based on a limited amount of data (e.g., observation of one or a few hours of teaching), which compromises the generalizability of the results. Second, the teachers who did not believe in the effects of CF but provided lots of recasts may have discounted recasts as CF, assuming that CF means explicit correction. For example, Kamiya reported that one novice teacher did not have a clear idea about the concept of CF, but out of the nine CF episodes in her lesson, eight involved recasts and one was a clarification request. Therefore, the inconsistency may to some extent result from the gap between teachers' perceptions and researchers' interpretations.

The Effect of Beliefs about CF on Learning Outcomes

To date, there have been only several studies investigating the putative links between learners' attitude toward feedback and the effects of feedback. Sheen (2007) investigated the comparative effectiveness of two types of feedback and the correlations between the effects of feedback and learners' willingness to receive feedback. The experimental groups partook in two treatment sessions, during which they performed narrative tasks and received metalinguistic correction or recasts on their wrong use of English articles *a/the*. It was found that metalinguistic correction was more effective than recasts and no feedback, but recasts were not effective. The gain scores of the metalinguistic group were significantly correlated with their attitudes toward feedback, but there were no significant correlations for recasts and control.

Kartchava (2012) reported a complicated study on the relationships between CF type, noticing of CF, CF beliefs, and learning outcomes. One hundred and ninety-seven francophone college EFL learners were divided into four groups: recasts, prompts, mixed (recasts + prompts), and control, and the experimental groups attended two two-hour treatment sessions. It was found that (1) the CF groups did not outperform the control group, (2) beliefs about CF importance were significantly correlated with the noticing of feedback, (3) beliefs about prompts and about the negative consequences of CF had no significant correlations with noticing, and (4) CF beliefs had no significant associations with the gains of the treatment groups.

These two studies suggest that the relationships between learners' attitudes toward CF and the effects of CF are contingent. It was correlated with the effects of explicit feedback, but not implicit feedback, and it was correlated with the noticing of feedback. It would seem that learners who were more enthusiastic about feedback did benefit more from feedback when the corrective intention was salient, and that these learners were also more sensitive to the corrective force of feedback. It can also be concluded that learners' attitudes toward feedback were predictive of L2 achievements when the feedback was effective, as in the case of metalinguistic correction in Sheen (2007), and that their attitudes were not correlated with learning outcomes when feedback had no effect, as in the case of recasts in Sheen's study and in the case of all three treatment types in Kartchava's study.

Pedagogical Implications

This chapter provided a summative review of the research on learner and teacher beliefs about CF and the findings have valuable implications for teachers and practitioners. First, it is important for teachers to recognize that students are keen to receive CF and that they prefer immediate, explicit correction of their errors. Therefore, teachers' concern over the deleterious effects of CF on students' self-esteem and motivation is unfounded and they should reconsider their own preference for delayed and indirect feedback. The need for a change in teachers' attitudes and preferences is also justifiable on the basis of what has been found in experimental CF research about the overall facilitative effects of CF on L2 development and the superior effects of explicit and immediate feedback (Li, 2010; Li et al., 2016).

Second, given that students' CF beliefs are predictive of the effects of CF and their noticing of CF, it is necessary for teachers to actively seek students' opinions and provide activities that change students' attitudes. As Sato's (2013) study showed, engaging in activities where students consistently provide CF on each other's speech errors may improve their attitudes toward both CF and participation in group work. Sato's study also provides specific information about a training package teachers can utilize, which consists of activities raising students' awareness of interaction, teachers' modelling of CF, students' practice of CF, and students' use of CF in communicative contexts.

Third, teachers should recognize that they may hold incorrect beliefs about CF, such as their overall negative attitudes toward CF. There is also evidence that teachers may equate CF with explicit correction and may not consider other CF strategies as CF. Fortunately, research (Busch, 2010; Vásquez & Harvey, 2010) shows that teachers' beliefs about CF are changeable. The studies suggest that hands-on activities requiring trainees to engage in the experience of conducting a replication study or tutoring a learner are particularly effective and that activities that aim only to enhance their explicit/declarative knowledge such as by reading academic articles may not have substantial effects (Kamiya & Loewen, 2014). The studies also suggest that the experiential activities are probably more effective when combined with reflective activities such as group discussions or retrospective reports of the trainee's own beliefs, the changes and non-changes in their beliefs during, and so on. Teachers, therefore, are encouraged to conduct action research where their beliefs or assumptions that deviate from what has been found in the research can be changed by solving problems that they come across in the classroom.

References (*Studies Included in This Synthesis)

*Agudo, J. (2014). Beliefs in learning to teach: EFL student teachers' beliefs about corrective feedback. *Utrecht Studies in Language and Communication, 27,* 209–362.

*Agudo, J. (2015). How do Spanish EFL learners perceive grammar instruction and corrective feedback? *Southern African Linguistics and Applied Language Studies, 33*(4), 411–425.

*Basturkmen, H., Loewen, S., & Ellis, R. (2004). Teachers' stated beliefs about incidental focus on form and their classroom practices. *Applied Linguistics, 25*(2), 243–272.

*Bell, T. (2005). Behaviors and attitudes of effective foreign language teachers: Results of a questionnaire study. *Foreign Language Annals, 38*(2), 259–270.

*Brown, A. V. (2009). Students' and teachers' perceptions of effective foreign language teaching: A comparison of ideals. *The Modern Language Journal, 93*(1), 46–60.

*Busch, D. (2010). Pre-service teacher beliefs about language learning: The second language acquisition course as an agent for change. *Language Teaching Research, 14*(3), 318–337.

*Davis, A. (2003). Teachers' and students' beliefs regarding aspects of language learning. *Evaluation & Research in Education, 17*(4), 207–222.

*Dong, Z. (2012). *Beliefs and practices: A case study on oral corrective feedback in the teaching Chinese as a foreign language (TCFL) classroom.* MA thesis, Arizona State University, US.

*Gurzynski-Weiss, L. K. (2010). *Factors influencing oral corrective feedback provision in the Spanish foreign language classroom: Investigating instructor native/nonnative speaker status, second language acquisition education, & teaching experience.* PhD dissertation, Georgetown University, US.

Harmer, J. (2007). *The practice of English language teaching.* Harlow, UK: Pearson.

Hendrickson, J. M. (1978). Error correction in foreign language teaching: Recent theory, research, and practice. *The Modern Language Journal, 62*(8), 387–398.

*Jean, G., & Simard, D. (2011). Grammar teaching and learning in L2: Necessary, but boring? *Foreign Language Annals, 44*(3), 467–494.

*Junqueira, L., & Kim, Y. (2013). Exploring the relationship between training, beliefs, and teachers' corrective feedback practices: A case study of a novice and an experienced ESL teacher. *Canadian Modern Language Review, 69*(2), 181–206.

*Kamiya, N. (2014). The relationship between stated beliefs and classroom practices of oral corrective feedback. *Innovation in Language Learning and Teaching, 10*(3), 206–219.

*Kamiya, N., & Loewen, S. (2014). The influence of academic articles on an ESL teacher's stated beliefs. *Innovation in Language Learning and Teaching, 8*(3), 205–218.

Kartchava, E. (2006). *Corrective feedback: Novice ESL teachers' beliefs and practices.* MA thesis, Concordia University, Canada.

*Kartchava, E. (2012). *Noticeability of corrective feedback, L2 development and learner beliefs.* PhD dissertation, Université de Montréal, Canada.

*Lee, E. (2013). Corrective feedback preferences and learner repair among advanced ESL students. *System, 41*(2), 217–230.

Li, S. (2010). The effectiveness of corrective feedback in SLA: A meta-analysis. *Language Learning, 60*(2), 309–365.

Li, S., Zhu, Y., & Ellis, R. (2016). The effects of the timing of corrective feedback on the acquisition of a new linguistic structure. *Modern Language Journal, 100*(1), 276–295.

*Loewen, S., Li, S., Fei, F., Thompson, A., Nakatsukasa, K., Ahn, S., & Chen, X. (2009). Second language learners' beliefs about grammar instruction and error correction. *The Modern Language Journal, 93*(1), 91–104.

*Lynch, T. (2009). Responding to learners' perceptions of feedback: The use of comparators in second language speaking courses. *International Journal of Innovation in Language Learning and Teaching, 3*(2), 191–203.

Nassaji, H. (2016). Interactional feedback in second language teaching and learning: A synthesis and analysis of current research. *Language Teaching Research, 20*(4), 535–562.

*Oladejo, J. A. (1993). Error correction in ESL: Learners' preferences. *TESL Canada Journal, 10*(2), 71–89.

*Rahimi, M., & Zhang, L. (2015). Exploring non-native English-speaking teachers' cognitions about corrective feedback in teaching English oral communication. *System, 55*, 111–122.

*Roothooft, H. (2014). The relationship between adult EFL teachers' oral feedback practices and their beliefs. *System, 46*, 65–79.

*Sato, M. (2013). Beliefs about peer interaction and peer corrective feedback: Efficacy of classroom intervention. *The Modern Language Journal, 97*(3), 611–633.

*Schulz, R. A. (1996). Focus on form in the foreign language classroom: Students' and teachers' views on error correction and the role of grammar. *Foreign Language Annals, 29*, 343–364.

*Schulz, R. A. (2001). Cultural differences in student and teacher perceptions concerning the role of grammar instruction and corrective feedback: USA–Colombia. *The Modern Language Journal, 85*(2), 244–258.

*Sheen, Y. (2007). The effects of corrective feedback, language aptitude, and learner attitudes on the acquisition of English articles. In A. Mackey (Ed.), *Conversational interaction in second language acquisition* (pp. 301–322). New York: Oxford University Press.

*Vásquez, C., & Harvey, J. (2010). Raising teachers' awareness about corrective feedback through research replication. *Language Teaching Research, 14*(4), 421–443.

11

NON-VERBAL FEEDBACK

Kimi Nakatsukasa and Shawn Loewen

Introduction

In this chapter, we present how non-verbal features, such as gestures, play an integral role in classroom interaction, including corrective feedback. First, we discuss the benefits of corrective feedback in general and introduce some characteristics of corrective feedback that may impact its effectiveness. Then, we review some descriptive and interventionist gestural studies in the field of second language acquisition (SLA) to present how gestures have been used by teachers and students in the language classroom, as well as to show whether or not such gestures have any impact on various domains of second language (L2) learning. Next, we review some gestural studies which were conducted in relation to corrective feedback. Finally, we conclude this chapter with suggestions for future studies and pedagogical implications.

Corrective Feedback

Corrective feedback during meaning-focused L2 interaction has proven to be an effective mechanism for increasing both noticing of linguistic structures and L2 development (e.g., Li, 2010; Lyster & Saito, 2010; Lyster, Saito, & Sato, 2013; Russell & Spada, 2006). Studies of noticing have relied on a variety of measures such as online and retrospective reports to determine learners' attentional focus. But most importantly, quasi-experimental studies have found that in general, learners who are provided with corrective feedback perform significantly better on subsequent measures of linguistic performance than do learners who have not received corrective feedback.

In addition to investigating the overall benefits of corrective feedback, researchers have also examined the characteristics of corrective feedback that may influence its effectiveness. Several corrective feedback characteristics in particular have received attention, including its input-providing or output-prompting qualities (e.g., Goo & Mackey, 2013; Lyster & Ranta, 2013), its degree of implicitness (e.g., Ellis, Loewen, & Erlam, 2006), and its linguistic targets (e.g., Brown, 2016). A seminal study into the characteristics of corrective feedback is Lyster and Ranta's (1997) description of corrective feedback in high school French immersion classes in Canada, in which they identified six different types of feedback, namely recasts, elicitations, explicit correction, clarification requests, metalinguistic cues, and repetition. In a recent meta-analysis, Brown (2016) found that recasts accounted for 57% of corrective feedback in descriptive studies, while prompts occurred 30% of the time.

Additionally, studies have conducted fine-grained analyses of discoursal features that accompany corrective feedback. For example, Loewen and Philp (2006) investigated the prosody that teachers used when providing recasts. They found that recasts accompanied by declarative intonation were more likely to be followed by uptake, but the linguistic targets that received recasts with interrogative intonation, as in Example 1, were more likely to be produced accurately by L2 learners on a subsequent posttest.

> Example 1: Recast with interrogative intonation (Loewen & Philp, 2006, p. 556)
>
> Student: somebody steal my paper (.) stolen
> Teacher: someone stole your paper?

In spite of numerous previous studies, many of which are reviewed in this volume, there are still aspects of corrective feedback that remain relatively under-investigated. One such area is the issue of non-verbal feedback that either accompanies oral corrective feedback or is provided by itself without any oral component. In order to better situate the few studies that have examined non-verbal feedback, a review of several of the more general aspects of non-verbal communication and SLA is necessary.

Non-Verbal Behavior and L2 Learning

Non-verbal behavior is an overarching term which has been used to refer to various behavioral elements of communication that play an integral role in human interaction, such as facial expressions, eye movements, and body postures (e.g., Hall, Coats, & Labeau, 2005; Jungheim, 2001). For example, during a phase of corrective feedback, an instructor may keep maintaining eye contact with a learner even after the learner responded to the feedback. This could indicate that the turn is still the learner's because the response was still incorrect. Similarly, tilted head and pursed lips may indicate a problem with the learner's response. Among various types of non-verbal behavior, gesture is a type of non-verbal behavior that is used for communication and it can occur either by itself or it can accompany verbal discourse, in which case it is considered co-expressive with speech.

Gestural Studies and Education

Gesture has been investigated using several different frameworks, but one of the more common ones is McNeill's (1992) classifications, who has identified the following categories. *Emblems* are gestures that have specific meanings that are culturally determined and do not need to be accompanied by speech to convey their meaning. The gesture of the thumb and index finger making a circle with the other fingers extended upward is an example that means 'okay' in the United States, but signifies 'money' in Japan. *Iconic* gestures are those that present images of concrete entities and/or actions (Example: Thumbs and index fingers of both hands create a circle while saying, "Please shape the dough into *a round shape*."). *Metaphoric* gestures also present an image, but of abstract concepts (Example: Right and left arms are extended outwards slightly and moved vertically repeatedly. Palms are held upwards as if they are holding something inside while saying, "We discussed two options. Which one is better—*Option A or B*?"). *Deictic* gestures are pointing with the finger or other body parts and they are used to indicate both concrete and abstract entities (Example: An index finger points to two types of cat food one by one while saying, "Which one is better for our cat? *This one or that one?*"). *Beats* gestures refer to vertical or horizontal hand movements which are made with the rhythm of speech (Example: Extended right arm moves in accordance with the emphasis of a sentence, "First, I will describe the procedure. *Then*, you will make your own sauce.") (McNeill, 1992, except for the examples).

The use of gestures has received significant attention in the field of psychology, education, and communication studies. Education researchers have conducted observational studies in classrooms and found that teachers frequently incorporate gestures while teaching (Alibali, Flevares, & Goldin-Meadow, 1997; Goldin-Meadow, Cook, & Mitchell, 2009; Crowder, 1996; Perry, Birch, & Singleton, 1995; Roth, 2001; Roth & Lawless, 2002a, 2002b) and that gestures are often used to obtain students' attention in class (e.g., Flevares & Perry, 1995). Some studies further examined if gestures impact learning in general (e.g., Cook, Yip, & Goldin-Meadow, 2010; Goldin-Meadow, Cook, & Mitchell, 2009; Goldin-Meadow & Sandhofer, 1999; Goldin-Meadow & Singer, 2003). For instance, Goldin-Meadow and her colleagues examined how seeing and producing gestures facilitate the learning of mathematical concepts. In Goldin-Meadow et al. (2009), one group of children was directed to point out the relevant numbers (4 and 5) of a math equation (e.g., $4 + 5 + 7 =$ ___ $+ 7$), whereas the second group was told to point at partially relevant numbers (4 and 7 or 5 and 7) and the third group was told not to use any gestures. The researchers found that the first condition surpassed the remaining groups on a subsequent math test. Overall, their findings suggested that seeing the adult's or instructor's gestures and producing appropriate gestures are beneficial for student learning.

Observational Gesture Studies in SLA

Extending this line of research, studies in the field of SLA have also investigated the relevance of gestures in relation to L2 learning. Since 2000, several observational studies have been conducted in language classrooms (e.g., Allen, 2000; Faraco & Kida, 2008; Hudson, 2011; Inceoglu, 2015; Lazaraton, 2004; Smotrova 2014; Smotrova & Lantolf, 2013; Tellier, 2006; Wang, 2009; Zhao, 2007).

Several researchers have observed language classrooms to understand how gestures and other non-verbal features are used in a language classroom. Allen (2000), for example, videotaped six 55-minute Spanish as a foreign language classes and identified what types of gestures the instructor incorporated. She found several functions of gestures, including: (a) use of culture-specific emblematic gestures such as pointing to one's eye to indicate "Watch out!", (b) to accent a particular word or phrase, (c) to describe the meaning of vocabulary words (e.g., *close the textbook*), (d) to indicate a referent point such as people or objects, and (e) to maintain turn-taking. Furthermore, she found that the teacher's facial expressions that revealed emotions also played a significant role in classroom interaction.

One of the notable function of gestures in Allen's study is how gestures were used to convey meaning in a language classroom. Similarly, Lazaraton (2004) also reported how gestures served as another type of input to L2 learners. She observed three English as a second language (ESL) classrooms in the United States taught by a Japanese ESL graduate student. The class involved several instances of incidental vocabulary lessons and Lazaraton's gestural analysis showed that the instructor's gestures illustrated the meaning of the verbs without verbal explanations. For instance, when introducing the word *weave*, the instructor moved her hands close to each other to show a knitting motion while saying *What does weave mean?* simultaneously. This study included detailed description of gestures which were used to describe the meaning of verbs.

Another descriptive study is Faraco and Kida's (2008) exploration of the non-verbal features, including gestures and gaze, that accompanied the negotiation of meaning during native/non-native interaction in L2 French. The authors conducted a close analysis of the discourse and non-verbal actions that occurred during specific negotiation sequences, finding that non-verbal behavior could have a positive impact on negotiation for meaning. For example, teachers used gaze to indicate the recipient(s) of verbal feedback, while hand and body gestures were used, either by themselves or accompanying verbal feedback, as a 'meta-linguistic gloss' (p. 292). However, Faraco and Kida also identified negative impacts of non-verbal behavior. Specifically, the abandonment of mutual gaze by the teacher created ambiguity regarding the function of the verbal negotiation, and the teacher's provision of similar gestures on both corrections (i.e., recasts) and repetitions of learner utterances created misunderstanding of the teacher's corrective intent.

Although Allen (2000), Lazaraton (2004), and Faraco and Kida (2008) illustrated when and how gestures were used in L2 instructional contexts, the frequency of occurrence of such gestures had not yet been investigated. However, Inceoglu (2015) added another layer to the existing studies by showing to what extent gestures were used during focus on form episodes (FFEs) targeting lexical items. She observed 10 hours of intermediate French as a foreign language classrooms and identified 110 FFEs and found that close to half of the FFEs were accompanied by gestures. Furthermore, gestures accompanied the majority of FFEs targeting verbs (15 out of 18) and collocations (14 out of 15), whereas the use of gestures was considerably less frequent for nouns (28 out of 71) and adjectives (2 out of 6). Inceoglu also found that iconic gestures were most frequently used during lexical FFEs. Another notable distinction that she observed was that when the FFEs were initiated by the learners, about 90% of the FFEs were accompanied by gestures, even though it was only about 50% when initiated by the teachers. Collectively, these studies indicate that language instructors often incorporate gestures with pedagogical purposes to facilitate learners' L2 understandings.

In addition to teacher's gestures, some researchers have used a sociocultural framework to examine how gestures were used between teachers and students (e.g., McCafferty & Rosborough, 2014, Smotrova & Lantolf, 2013; Smotrova, 2014). For example, Smotrova and Lantolf (2013) examined a two-hour-long video recording of an EFL classroom in Eastern Ukraine. They identified that some gestures that the instructor used to describe the meaning of a phrasal verb (e.g., [a plane] takes off) were reused when describing the same phrasal verb but in a different context (e.g., [a train] takes off). They found that these gestures were later used by the EFL learners as well and argued that the recurring images illustrated by gestures served as a reference point in verbal utterances.

These descriptive studies are rich in nature and have demonstrated how teachers and students use gestures in language classrooms. Had the studies solely relied on the oral data, we would not have known the various functions of gestures in a language classroom: (1) introduction of a culture-specific gesture, (2) facilitating learners' understanding of important vocabulary words and phrasal verbs, and (3) impacting the student–teacher interaction negatively and positively. However, to argue for its impact on L2 learning, intervention studies, as described in the next section, are needed.

Experimental Gesture Studies in SLA

In addition to observational studies, some SLA researchers have conducted intervention studies in order to examine whether or not being exposed to gestures and/ or producing appropriate gestures may facilitate L2 learning. The studies which are introduced here are not necessarily related to corrective feedback; however, they are important studies to refer back to when we discuss the effectiveness of gestures in corrective feedback later in this chapter, because the studies illustrate whether or not exposure to gestures helps L2 learning. Specifically, studies have investigated the areas of L2 comprehension, vocabulary learning, and pronunciation learning and, as a result, researchers have identified the facilitative functions of gestures in most, but not all, pedagogical areas (e.g., Macedonia & Kliemesch, 2014; Sueyoshi & Hardison, 2005; Kelly & Lee, 2012).

When considering the effectiveness of gestures for L2 comprehension and learning, it is important to consider their compensatory nature in relation to L2 comprehension. When L2 learners' proficiency levels are not high enough or when they are listening to a conversation in a loud setting, it is natural to rely on the interlocutor's gestural cues to understand the interlocutor. Likewise, the existing studies suggest that seeing a speaker's gestures is indeed helpful for some learners (e.g., Allen, 1995; Church, Ayman-Nolley, & Mahootian, 2004; Sime, 2006; Sueyoshi & Hardison, 2005). For example, Sime (2006) observed a total of five 90-minute classes and conducted a stimulated recall session with the learners about the teachers' non-verbal behaviors. One of the major functions that the learners reported was how they actively tried to make sense of teachers' gestures, and they reported that some gestures were helpful for meaning-making. The intervention studies seem to support this argument as well. For example, Dahl and Ludvigsen (2014) conducted a study with L1 and L2 English speaking children. Half of the children in each group were given the description of a cartoon in English in a video in which the speaker's gestures were visible. The other half saw a video where gestures were invisible. After watching the video, the participants were asked to draw a picture that matched the given description. The researchers found that the presence of gestures did not affect the comprehension by L1 English speaking children; furthermore, the drawings by the L2 English speaking children were identical to those by L1 English speaking children when gestures were visible. But the pictures drawn by L2 children who did not see gestures were not as accurate as those who saw gestures. In another study, Sueyoshi and Hardison (2005) investigated whether or not low-intermediate and advanced L2 learners' comprehension benefited from seeing a speaker's facial expressions and gestures. Learners watched a video in one of three conditions: (1) audio-visual lecture with facial expressions and co-speech gestures, (2) audio-visual lecture with facial expressions only, and (3) audio-only lecture. The results obtained from the comprehension questions showed that the low-intermediate learners performed the best under the gesture and facial expressions conditions; however, the advanced learners from the facial expressions only condition received the highest score. The study indicated that non-verbal features such as gestures and facial expressions are indeed helpful for L2 comprehension. However, their effectiveness seems to depend on learners' level of proficiency.

In the domain of vocabulary teaching, it has been reported that teachers often incorporate gestures when describing the meaning of new vocabulary words and expressions (Tellier, 2008). This seems to be in line with a teacher's use of 'foreigner talk,' which is used to aid students' comprehension (Adams, 1998). As for learning of vocabulary items, generally the studies have indicated that seeing gestures and repeating gestures facilitate the memorization of vocabulary items. Tellier (2008) investigated whether or not seeing and repeating the instructor's gestures impacted the L2 English vocabulary learning by L1 French children. She introduced eight English vocabulary items related to animals. The researcher verbally presented the first group of children with the vocabulary items using gestures and directed the children to repeat the gestures. As for the second group, she showed the pictures of the relevant animals. Her results indicated the positive impact of seeing and repeating gestures when teaching new vocabulary items. Macedonia, Müller, and Friederici (2011) and Macedonia and Klimesch (2014) conducted similar studies with adult learners. They found that learners who saw gestures were better able to retain the vocabulary items long-term. The researchers argued that being provided with the information in multiple modalities allowed the learners to remember the vocabulary items better because learners' neural networks were reinforced.

Although gestures have been found to have a facilitative effect for comprehension and vocabulary learning, researchers have not found a similar effect for gestures and pronunciation instruction, even though language instructors often incorporate gestures during pronunciation instructions (e.g., Hudson, 2011). Kelly and his colleagues have extensively investigated whether or not using gestures during phonological instruction can help L1 English speakers learn difficult phonetic systems. Their linguistic targets included contrasting long and short vowels (Hirata & Kelly, 2010; Hirata, Kelly, Huang, & Manansala, 2014), moraic and syllabic system (Kelly, Hirata, Manansala, & Huang, 2014), and single and double consonants (Kelly & Lee, 2012). Kelly and Lee (2012), for example, examined if seeing gestures during pronunciation instructions can help learners distinguish short and long vowels in Japanese. A total of 60 learners viewed one of the four following videos: (a) audio only; (b) audio and mouth movement; (c) audio and gesture that indicated the sound pattern; and (d) audio, mouth movement, and gestures. Their results indicated that the learners who saw mouth movement surpassed the audio-only condition. However, the researchers did not find effects for the presence of gestures in developing L2 phonological awareness. Similarly, other studies also reported the lack of significance of seeing gestures in pronunciation instruction. Despite these findings, it may be premature to conclude that gestures are not helpful for pronunciation teaching. In these previous studies, the participants were not necessarily actual L2 Japanese learners. In other words, participants were not ready to distinguish these phonetic contrasts because it was the first time that they were exposed to Japanese phonology. Consequently, further studies with real L2 learners are needed to better examine the effects of gesture on pronunciation learning.

As for L2 grammar teaching, most studies are descriptive in nature except for Nakatsukasa (2016), which we introduce in a later section. The descriptive studies collectively reported that instructors used gestures and other non-verbal features such as body positioning when teaching some grammatical features such as tense and aspect (e.g., Hudson, 2011). Taking all these findings together, it appears that non-verbal features play an integral role in L2 instruction and development overall.

Although these studies have not involved corrective feedback directly, they are informative for understanding the impact of exposure to gestures on L2 learning in various linguistic domains. As a result of these studies, researchers can identify the types and uses of gestures in order to consider linking such gestures with feedback. For example, Nakatsukasa (2016) drew on descriptions of teachers' gestures pertaining to verb tense and incorporated specific gestures into a corrective feedback study.

Corrective Feedback and Gestures

Recently, researchers have begun to investigate the relationship between classroom interaction and the instructors' and students' use of non-verbal features. Some researchers have used the interactionist approach to examine how non-verbal features, including gestures, are embedded during corrective feedback episodes (Wang, 2009; Wang & Loewen, 2016) and some also investigated whether or not the presence of non-verbal features contributes to L2 development (Davies, 2006; Nakatsukasa, 2016; Wang, 2009).

Davies (2006) was one of the first studies to incorporate paralinguistic features in interaction research, when he compared the ratio of uptake in relation to the corrective feedback that incorporated paralinguistic features. Davies did not specifically define 'paralinguistic features' in his manuscript; however, the results showed that corrective feedback which was provided purely paralinguistically resulted in 100% successful uptake. Furthermore, the ratio of learner uptake was substantially higher when following feedback that incorporated paralinguistic features compared to feedback that did not involve any paralinguistic features.

In a more detailed study based on Wang's (2009) dissertation data, Wang and Loewen (2016) took a further step in identifying and describing the ways in which English L2 teachers used non-verbal features during the provision of corrective feedback. The researchers observed and video-recorded 65 hours of classroom interaction from nine different classes at an English language center in North America. From the video recordings, the researchers used McNeill's (1992) framework to identify various gestural cues (iconics, metaphorics, and beats) and also non-gestural cues (e.g., head movements, affect displays, kinetographs) that accompanied corrective feedback. Results of the analysis indicated that, on average, 60% of teachers' corrective feedback was accompanied by non-verbal behavior; however, teachers varied considerably in their use, ranging from 43% to 85%. As for the types of non-verbal behavior, Wang and Loewen found that head movements were most frequent (32%), followed by deictics (27%), iconics

(12%), and beats (11%). Affect displays, kinetographs, and emblems accounted for the remaining non-verbal behaviors. In terms of head movements, there were two different types: nodding and shaking. Example 1 (Wang & Loewen, 2016, p. 8) illustrates both of these behaviors, with the teacher shaking her head when she provides an explicit evaluation of the student's incorrect utterance and then nodding when she provides the correct form.

Example 1

Mato:	Is it rain tomorrow?
T:	Is it rain tomorrow? Your grammar [is not good]. Is it– *Shakes head*
Nass:	Is it may?
T:	Future future future
Mato:	Is it going to rain tomorrow?
T:	Is it [going to rain tomorrow]? Future, be going to. Is it going to rain tomorrow *Nods*

Note: Transcription key

Italicizing	Description of non-verbal behavior
[	Onset of non-verbal behavior
]	Offset of non-verbal behavior
RPF	Right pointing finger

In terms of deictics, the second most frequent non-verbal behavior to accompany feedback, there were also two main types: pointing at an artifact and pointing at a person. In the first instance, the teachers used non-verbal behavior to indicate an object, such as a blackboard or textbook, that might be helpful in correcting the learners' errors. In the second case, deictics were used to point at individuals, either to nominate them to respond to the discourse in some way or to "increas[e] the chances that a specific student might notice the correction provided" (p. 16). Example 2 illustrates this latter function, with the teacher pointing at herself and then the student to emphasize that it is the teacher, not the student, who may use an imperative verb in a pragmatically appropriate manner.

Example 2

Bia:	Tell me the homework.
T:	Just tell me the homework? Not if you want to be polite. Like [I] can say to *RPF points to self* [you] tell me the homework. You can't say to me tell me the homework. *RPF points at Bia*
Bia:	(Writes in book)

Wang and Loewen conclude that due to the pervasiveness of non-verbal behavior during feedback, it is important to gain a better understanding of how teachers use non-verbal behavior and, perhaps more importantly, its potential impact on L2 development.

To the best of our knowledge, there have not been many studies which have examined the effectiveness of gestures used during corrective feedback. Two exceptions are Wang (2009), who used individualized post hoc tests to investigate the effects of non-verbal behavior during naturally occurring classroom feedback, and Nakatsukasa (2016), who conducted a quasi-experimental study of gestures and corrective feedback.

In a non-interventionist study, Wang (2009) compared the effects of verbal and non-verbal corrective feedback on L2 development. Using the feedback episodes from the 65 hours of classroom interaction that were also analyzed in Wang and Loewen (2015), she administered tailor-made, individualized post hoc tests to the students who had been the recipients of corrective feedback. Overall, students had an accuracy rate of 59% on the immediate posttest and 47% on a delayed posttest two weeks later. When non-verbal behavior accompanied the verbal feedback, student accuracy was 73% and 61% on the immediate and delayed posttests, respectively; however, when non-verbal feedback was not included, the accuracy rates were statistically lower at 56% and 47%. Based on these results, Wang argues that non-verbal behavior can enhance the effectiveness of verbal feedback, and she calls for additional studies, both descriptive and quasi-experimental, to further explore these effects.

One study that has responded to this call is Nakatsukasa (2016), who examined whether instructors' recasts accompanied by gestures illustrating English locative prepositions affected learners' subsequent spontaneous oral production of the target structure. One group of ESL students received verbal recasts with gestures during 30 minutes of communicative tasks that were designed to elicit locative prepositions. The second group also received verbal recasts, but without gestures, and the third group received no feedback. Her results showed that the groups who received recasts regardless of the presence of gestures improved equally in the immediate posttest, whereas the no feedback group did not improve. However, in the delayed posttest, only the group who received the verbal and gestural recasts maintained the development which was observed in the immediate posttest. Based on these results, it seems that seeing gestures during corrective feedback improved the durability of the learners' gains in knowledge.

These studies indicate that incorporating gestures and other non-verbal behaviors during corrective feedback is helpful for L2 development because learners are better able to understand the linguistic target of feedback and because learning is better retained. These findings call for further studies to understand what kind of linguistic structures or what types of non-verbal behavior benefit L2 development.

Uptake and Gestures

Uptake has been described as the student's discoursal response that follows corrective feedback (e.g., Loewen, 2004; Lyster & Ranta, 1997). As such, it is an optional move; students are not obligated to respond to corrective feedback. Furthermore, sometimes students do not have the opportunity to verbally respond to feedback because the teacher continues to hold the floor after the provision of feedback and it would be conversationally inappropriate for the student to respond to the teacher. In terms of verbal responses, learners have several options. Learners may simply repeat the incorrect utterance, without modifying their output. Alternatively, learners may acknowledge the feedback with an ambiguous token such as *yeah* or *okay*, in which case it is difficult to know if the learner is acknowledging the semantic content of the teacher's feedback or if they are acknowledging the corrective intent. Finally, learners can successfully incorporate the correct linguistic form into their production, in an instance of successful uptake.

Until recently, all studies of corrective feedback that have investigated uptake have examined it verbally. Any non-verbal responses have not been documented, even though it is possible that learners might respond non-verbally. However, Wang (2009) examined the occurrence of verbal and non-verbal uptake. Specifically, she noted if a learner's verbal response to feedback was accompanied by a gesture or nodding of the head. Additionally, she noted if such non-verbal behavior occurred without any verbal expression. In coding the successfulness of the uptake, she took into account the non-verbal response. Thus, if a learner responded with a gesture that indicated their understanding of the feedback, it was coded as successful uptake. If a learner nodded without responding verbally, this was coded as an acknowledgement and not as a lack of uptake. Wang also coded student writing as a type of non-verbal response to feedback. However, Wang did not differentiate between uptake that did or did not contain non-verbal behavior, so it is not possible to know how much student uptake was only verbal, was verbal accompanied by non-verbal behavior, or was non-verbal only. Yet, this study suggests the importance of incorporating non-verbal aspects in the descriptive interaction studies.

Directions for Future Studies

To sum up, the aforementioned studies have identified the following points: (1) corrective feedback helps L2 development overall; however, its effectiveness depends on the characteristics of feedback, including non-verbal features; (2) language instructors often use gestures in a classroom to facilitate L2 comprehension, particularly for the vocabulary items that the learners may not know; (3) some gestures are shared by both instructor and learners and become a part of the discourse; (4) seeing gestures seems to help L2 comprehension for beginning level learners and vocabulary learning, but not the acquisition of L2 phonology; (5) corrective feedback can include non-verbal features and when the feedback, notably recasts, is provided along with gestures, it can help learners retain their L2 development for a prolonged period; and (6) learners' response to feedback can occur gesturally.

Although the number of gestural studies in the field of SLA has been increasing, the field needs more studies to fully understand the impact of teachers' and students' gestures on L2 development. For instance, it has been reported that gestures are not helpful when used as a part of the L2 pronunciation instruction; however, none of the studies included actual L2 learners. Thus, further studies need to recruit L2 learners who are phonologically ready to be taught the problematic phonological contrasts. In addition, as mentioned earlier, there has not been a study which examined the effectiveness of gestures for teaching grammatical structures. Some observational studies have shown that the instructors indeed use gestures and other non-verbal cues when teaching tense and aspect (e.g., Hudson, 2011). Intervention studies with gesture and non-gesture conditions could help determine if the presence of gestures facilitates learners' L2 development.

Specifically with regards to corrective feedback, the field could benefit from both descriptive and intervention studies. For instance, so far very few studies have identified to what extent gestures are used when providing corrective feedback. It would be informative to identify if there are significant differences in frequency and characteristics of gestures across linguistic targets, proficiency levels, different target languages, and different regions. As for the intervention studies, so far there has only been one study which examined the effectiveness of gestures when used along with verbal corrective feedback. The possible topics for further studies include the contrast of effectiveness across different proficiency levels, the effectiveness and learners' interpretation of gesture-only feedback, and whether or not learners' production of the instructor's gestures leads to better L2 development.

Pedagogical Implications

Due to the limited number of studies, it is premature to argue that the use of gestures in a classroom is always helpful. Yet, as for the instructor's gestures with pedagogical purposes, several intervention studies have reported that seeing and repeating the matching gestures of newly introduced vocabulary items can help L2 vocabulary development. This is certainly applicable in a classroom context, especially when teaching vocabulary items related to concrete objects and actions. Furthermore, studies reported that lower-level students benefited from seeing a speaker's facial expressions and gestures in L2 comprehension. These results suggest the potential value of the active incorporation of gestures and other visual cues in a language classroom.

In terms of the use of gestures during corrective feedback, language educators may find it useful to incorporate gestures, especially when providing implicit forms of feedback such as recasts. Even when the linguistic targets are not mentioned verbally during feedback, linguistic targets can be marked implicitly via gestures, which will allow learners to be aware of the source of error without being corrected explicitly in front of the class. Also, because the instructor does not necessarily need to explain the error verbally, gesture-incorporated feedback could potentially save time in class. In addition, as the studies on vocabulary learning have collectively shown, seeing gestures appears to promote long-term retention of knowledge. Thus, learners may benefit from the gestural corrective feedback compared to when it was given verbally only. In these cases, it becomes important that the learners are aware of the meaning of gestures. Thus, it may be necessary to incorporate gestures which have been frequently used in the classroom or to explicitly tell the meaning of the gestures in advance.

Related to corrective feedback, language educators may also benefit from observing learners' gestures during and following feedback. Even if learners do not verbalize their thoughts, their gestures and other non-verbal behavior may signal what they have noticed through feedback. For example, in a situation where a student forgets to use past tense, the instructor may provide corrective feedback with a 'point-back' gesture to indicate the lack of past tense. Following this feedback, a learner may remain silent but repeat the point-back gesture, which could indicate that the learner became aware of the source of the error. Such awareness is a crucial initial step for L2 development, even if the learner is unable to or unwilling to verbally produce the correct utterance.

In summary, it is somewhat surprising that there has not been more research investigating non-verbal feedback even though there has been considerable research on corrective feedback and L2 gestures respectively. It is hoped that the current review will be an impetus for increasing our understanding of the role of gestures, either alone or accompanying verbal feedback, during focus on form in meaning-focused interaction.

References

Adams, T. W. (1998). *Gesture in foreigner talk*. Unpublished doctoral dissertation, University of Pennsylvania, Philadelphia, US.

Alibali, M., Flevares, L., & Goldin-Meadow, S. (1997). Assessing knowledge conveyed in gesture: Do teachers have the upper hand? *Journal of Educational Psychology, 89*, 183–194.

Allen, L. Q. (1995). The effects of emblematic features on the development and access of mental representations of French expressions. *The Modern Language Journal, 79*, 521–529.

Allen, L. Q. (2000). Form-meaning connections and the French causative. *Studies in Second Language Acquisition, 22*, 69–84.

Brown, D. (2016). The type and linguistic foci of oral corrective feedback in the L2 classroom: A meta-analysis. *Language Teaching Research, 20*, 436–458.

Church, R. B., Ayman-Nolley, S., & Mahootian, S. (2004). The role of gesture in bilingual education: Does gesture enhance learning? *International Journal of Bilingual Education and Bilingualism, 7,* 303–319.

Cook, S. W., Yip, T. K., & Goldin-Meadow, S. (2010). Gesturing makes memories that last. *Journal of Memory and Language, 63,* 465–475.

Crowder, E. M. (1996). Gestures at work in sense—making science talk. *The Journal of the Learning Sciences, 5,* 173–208.

Dahl, T. I., & Ludvigsen, S. (2014). How I see what you're saying: The role of gestures in native and foreign language listening comprehension. *The Modern Language Journal, 98,* 813–833.

Davies, M. (2006). Paralinguistic focus on form. *TESOL Quarterly, 40*(4), 841–855.

Ellis, R., Loewen, S., & Erlam, R. (2006). Implicit and explicit corrective feedback and the acquisition of L2 grammar. *Studies in Second Language Acquisition, 28,* 339–368.

Faraco, M., & Kida, T. (2008). Gesture and the negotiation of meaning in a second language classroom. In S. McCafferty & G. Stam (Eds.), *Gesture: Second language acquisition and classroom research* (pp. 280–297). New York: Routledge.

Flevares, L. M., & Perry, M. (2001). How many do you see? The use of nonspoken representations in first-grade mathematics lessons. *Journal of Educational Psychology, 93,* 330–345.

Goo, J., & Mackey, A. (2013). The case against the case against recasts. *Studies in Second Language Acquisition, 35,* 127–165.

Goldin-Meadow, S., Cook, S. W., & Mitchell, Z. A. (2009). Gesturing gives children new ideas about math. *Psychological Science, 20,* 267–272.

Goldin-Meadow, S., & Sandhofer, C. M. (1999). Gesture conveys substantive information to ordinary listeners. *Developmental Science, 2,* 67–74.

Goldin-Meadow, S., & Singer, M. A. (2003). From children's hands to adults' ears: Gesture's role in the learning process. *Developmental Psychology, 39,* 509–520.

Hall, J. A., Coats, E. J., & Labeau, L. S. (2005). Nonverbal behavior and the vertical dimension of social relations: A meta-analysis. *Psychological Bulletin, 131,* 898–924.

Hirata, Y., & Kelly, S. D. (2010). Effects of lips and hands on auditory learning of second-language speech sounds. *Journal of Speech, Language, and Hearing Research, 53,* 298–310.

Hirata, Y., Kelly, S. D., Huang, J., & Manansala, M. (2014). Effects of hand gestures on auditory learning of second-language vowel length contrasts. *Journal of Speech, Language, and Hearing Research, 57,* 2090–2101.

Hudson, N. (2011). *Teacher gesture in a post-secondary English as a second language classroom: A sociocultural approach.* Unpublished doctoral dissertation, University of Nevada, Las Vegas, US.

Inceoglu, S. (2015). Teacher gesture and lexical focus on form in a foreign language classroom. *Canadian Modern Language Review, 71,* 130–154.

Jungheim, N. O. (2001). The unspoken element of communicative competence: Evaluating language learners' nonverbal behavior. In T. Hudson & J.D. Brown (Eds.), *A focus on language test development* (pp. 1–34). Honolulu, HI: University of Hawaii at Manoa.

Kelly, S. D., Hirata, Y., Manansala, M., & Huang, J. (2014). Exploring the role of hand gestures in learning novel phoneme contrasts and vocabulary in a second language. *Frontiers in Psychology, 5,* 180–210.

Kelly, S. D., & Lee, A. L. (2012). When actions speak too much louder than words: Hand gestures disrupt word learning when phonetic demands are high. *Language and Cognitive Processes, 27,* 793–807.

Lazaraton, A. (2004). Gesture and speech in the vocabulary explanations of one ESL teacher: A microanalytic inquiry. *Language Learning, 54*, 79–117.

Li, S. (2010). The effectiveness of corrective feedback in SLA: A meta-analysis. *Language Learning, 60*, 309–365.

Loewen, S. (2004). Uptake in incidental focus on form in meaning-focused ESL lessons. *Language Learning, 54*(1), 153–187.

Loewen, S., & Philp, J. (2006). Recasts in the adult English L2 classroom: Characteristics, explicitness, and effectiveness. *Modern Language Journal, 90*, 536–556.

Lyster, R., & Ranta, L. (1997). Corrective feedback and learner uptake: Negotiation of form in communicative classrooms. *Studies in Second Language Acquisition, 19*, 37–66.

Lyster, R., & Ranta, L. (2013). Counterpoint piece: The case for variety in corrective feedback research. *Studies in Second Language Acquisition, 35*(1), 167–184.

Lyster, R., & Saito, K. (2010). Oral feedback in classroom SLA: A meta-analysis. *Studies in Second Language Acquisition, 32*, 265–302.

Lyster, R., Saito, K., & Sato, M. (2013). Oral corrective feedback in second language classrooms. *Language Teaching, 46*, 1–40.

Macedonia, M., & Klimesch, W. (2014). Long-term effects of gestures on memory for foreign language words trained in the classroom. *Mind, Brain, and Education, 8*, 74–88.

McCafferty, S. G., & Rosborough, A. (2014). Gesture as a private form of communication during lessons in an ESL-designated elementary classroom: A sociocultural perspective. *TESOL Journal, 5*, 225–246.

Macedonia, M., Müller, K., & Friederici, A. D. (2011). The impact of iconic gestures on foreign language word learning and its neural substrate. *Human Brain Mapping, 32*, 982–998.

McNeill, D. (1992). *Hand and mind: What gestures reveal about thought.* Chicago, IL: University of Chicago Press.

Nakatsukasa, K. (2016). Efficacy of recasts and gesture on the acquisition of locative prepositions. *Studies in Second Language Acquisition, 38*, 771–799.

Perry, M., Birch, D., & Singleton, J. (1995). Constructing shared understanding: The role of nonverbal input in learning contexts. *Contemporary Legal Issues, 6*, 213–235.

Roth, W. (2001). Gestures: Their role in teaching and learning. *Review of Educational Research, 71*, 365–392.

Roth, W., & Lawless, D. V. (2002a). Signs, deixis, and the emergence of scientific explanations. *Semiotica, 138*, 95–130.

Roth, W., & Lawless, D. V. (2002b). When up is down and down is up: Body orientation, proximity, and gestures as resources. *Language in Society, 31*, 1–28.

Russell, J., & Spada, N. (2006). The effectiveness of corrective feedback for the acquisition of L2 grammar: A meta-analysis of the research. In J. Norris & L. Ortega (Eds.), *Synthesizing research on language learning and teaching* (pp. 133–164). Philadelphia: John Benjamins.

Sime, D. (2006). What do learners make of teachers' gestures in the language classroom? *International Review of Applied Linguistics, 44*, 211–230.

Smotrova, T. (2014). *Instructional functions of speech and gesture in the L2 classroom.* Doctoral dissertation, Pennsylvania State University, US.

Smotrova, T., & Lantolf, J. P. (2013). The function of gesture in lexically focused L2 instructional conversations. *The Modern Language Journal, 97*, 397–416.

Sueyoshi, A., & Hardison, D. M. (2005). The role of gestures and facial cues in second language listening comprehension. *Language Learning, 55*, 661–699.

Tellier, M. (2006). *L'impact du geste pédagogique sur l'enseignement/apprentissage des langues étrangères: Etude sur des enfants de 5 ans.* Unpublished doctoral dissertation, Université Paris-Diderot Paris VII, Paris, France.

Tellier, M. (2008). The effect of gestures on second language memorisation by young children. *Gesture, 8,* 219–235.

Wang, W. (2009). *The noticing and effect of teacher feedback in ESL classrooms.* Unpublished doctoral dissertation, Michigan State University, US.

Wang, W., & Loewen, S. (2016). Nonverbal behavior and corrective feedback in nine ESL university-level classrooms. *Language Teaching Research, 20,* 459–478.

Zhao, J. (2007). *Metaphors and gestures for abstract concepts in academic English writing.* Unpublished doctoral dissertation, University of Arizona, US.

CONCLUSION, REFLECTIONS, AND FINAL REMARKS

Hossein Nassaji and Eva Kartchava

The goal of this edited volume has been to provide an in-depth analysis and discussion of the role of corrective feedback in second language (L2) acquisition (SLA) and instruction. The overall aims were not only to synthesize current knowledge on such fundamental feedback areas as oral, written, and computer-mediated feedback, but also to examine the implications of this knowledge for the various contexts where L2 is the focus. The focus has been on recent advancements in these domains as well as a number of other new topics such as the role of feedback timing, peer feedback, and the contributions of non-verbal feedback. Taken together, the 11 chapters confirm the positive role for corrective feedback reported in the literature (e.g., Li, 2010; Lyster & Saito, 2010; Mackey & Goo, 2007; Nassaji, 2015, 2016; Russell & Spada, 2006). However, they also add valuable insights in a number of other areas, including how contexts, individual variables, and the various conditions under which corrective feedback is provided can influence feedback effectiveness. Individually, the chapters also highlight notable implications for L2 teaching and outline many issues for future research. In what follows, we examine some of the key themes emphasized across chapters and discuss a number of issues that can be addressed more systematically in future research and also in other books on corrective feedback.

The Main Themes Running Through the Chapters

The various articles in this volume have raised many important issues that need to be considered when examining the use of feedback in various contexts and have also offered many insights into how and when feedback should be provided to assist L2 development. Among the insights gained from the chapters, in this summary, we highlight the following: (a) the role and importance of feedback explicitness and noticing; (b) the need to examine long-term effects of feedback; (c) new insights and opportunities for learner–learner feedback in oral, written, and computer-mediated contexts; (d) the need for feedback training; (e) the importance of evaluating the advice to teachers in light of research; (f) insights into differences and similarities between computer-mediated and face-to-face interactions; and (g) the view of feedback as a complex phenomenon. Several other issues such as those related to feedback timing, feedback negotiation, and the role of non-verbal feedback addressed in the later chapters are also discussed and commented on.

The Role and Importance of Feedback Explicitness and Noticing

One of the key themes running through several chapters is the role of feedback explicitness and learners' noticing in the effectiveness of feedback. Although there is significant variation in the results of studies comparing implicit and explicit feedback, several chapters in the book have supported the idea that learners need to notice the corrective force of the feedback in order to benefit from the feedback. Noticing has been identified as a necessary condition for language acquisition by many current SLA theories. It is a process that turns input into intake, which is subsequently integrated into the learners' developing system (Gass & Selinker, 2008). Reviewing research on oral feedback in the opening chapter, Ellis highlights this notion and also argues for the role that feedback explicitness plays in noticing feedback. He concludes that "[l]earners are more likely to notice a correction if the strategy is explicit in nature" (p. 10), although noticing may also take place when feedback is implicit. Heift & Hegelheimer (Chapter 4) make a similar observation. They report on a number of studies that investigated the impact of feedback in Computer-Assisted Language Learning (CALL) programs such as Automatic Writing Evaluation (AWE) systems and conclude that "this line of research has shown that students generally benefit from explicit, metalinguistic feedback because they subsequently perform better on particular target language structures and/or because students' grammatical awareness is subsequently raised" (p. 56). Li's analysis of research on teachers' and learners' beliefs (Chapter 10) showed strong learner preference for explicit rather than implicit feedback. The author also found that "learners who were more enthusiastic about feedback did benefit more from feedback when the corrective intention was salient" (p. 155). Moreover, these learners were more perceptive to the corrective force of the feedback.

Pedagogically, the above insights emphasize the need to use feedback in ways that facilitate learners' noticing and recognizing the function of the feedback. Since learners' ability to notice is also mediated by learners' preferences for a particular feedback strategy, teachers should also consider varying corrective feedback types and modalities when addressing learner errors. One way to enhance noticing is to use feedback more explicitly. Of course, when feedback becomes very explicit (through, for example, metalinguistic information), it may encourage more the development of explicit knowledge (Ellis, 2005). However, it has been shown that explicit feedback may also facilitate the development of implicit knowledge (e.g., Ellis, Loewen, & Erlam, 2006).

The Need to Examine Long-term Effects of Feedback

A number of chapters in the book have stressed the need to examine long-term effects of feedback. Although some studies on oral, written, and computer-mediated feedback have revealed some delayed effects, these effects have often been shown for a short delay after the feedback. Studies reporting longer-term effects are very limited. Reviewing research on written feedback in Chapter 9, Bitchener pointed out that most studies in this area have demonstrated temporary effects or retention over one or two weeks, although there are studies showing more durable effects as well. Ellis (Chapter 1) also made a similar observation with regard to the role of oral feedback and thus called for investigation into the effect of such feedback on acquisition over time. In examining the effects of feedback generated through computer-assisted programs such as tutorial CALL and auto-mated AWE, Heift & Hegelheimer (Chapter 4) conclude that although previous research in this area has provided some insight into the effectiveness of such tools, "there is a scarcity of research evidence, especially with regards to whether automated AWE feedback results in accuracy development and retention over time" (p. 60). Finally, examining peer feedback in L2 writing, Tigchelaar & Polio (Chapter 7) argue that despite the effectiveness of such feedback, we do not yet know whether the feedback has any long-term effects.

In short, although positive effects have been shown for feedback in various contexts, since these effects have often been examined after a short interval, there is a need to examine whether feedback has more enduring effects. To this end, as highlighted by several authors in this volume and elsewhere, it is essential to conduct longitudinal studies, which Ellis (Chapter 1) considered currently lacking in the literature.

New Insights and Opportunities for Learner–Learner Feedback in Oral, Written, and Computer-Mediated Contexts

Much research on corrective feedback has focused on teacher feedback. However, a number of recent studies have also focused on whether or not learners are able to provide each other with peer feedback. Three chapters in this book have addressed this issue in different contexts, including oral, written and computer-mediated settings. They have provided a number of insights. First, they conclude that learners are indeed able to supply corrective information and that such feedback may be beneficial, although the appropriate focus and the amount of peer feedback needed for L2 development remains unknown. With a focus on oral feedback, Sato (Chapter 2), for example, underscores this point, noting a number of cognitive and affective benefits of peer feedback. On the cognitive level, he argues, the benefits of peer feedback are twofold. First, compared to teacher–learner communication, interaction with a peer allows for more exposure to and production of modified output that is self- or other-initiated. Second, peer feedback promotes added opportunities for learners to receive and provide feedback, which encourages them to monitor their own L2 production and that of a classmate and to detect errors within it. This process of receiving and providing correction brings about important interlanguage changes. However, for learner feedback to be effective, it should also meet certain criteria. As Sato points out, for the cognitive benefits of peer feedback to occur, affective and social dynamics between learners must be considered. This is because peer feedback is most effective when learners view correction positively, trust each other's linguistic knowledge, and are comfortable with correcting and being corrected by a peer. Tigchelaar & Polio make a similar point and review studies that have shown that learners may not have confidence or understand the feedback they receive from their peers.

As for opportunities for peer feedback, in addition to peer editing, both Tigchelaar & Polio and Storch show how collaborative writing (i.e., co-creation of a text by two or more writers) promotes favorable conditions for peer feedback (see also Tian & Nassaji, 2016). According to Tigchelaar & Polio, collaborative writing may even yield more peer feedback than individual writing because in constructing a text together, learners negotiate the language they need to create the text. Asking learners to provide feedback on a peer's essay, on the other hand, can resemble evaluation of the peer's writing ability and therefore may not lead to a lot of constructive feedback. With a focus on peer feedback in computer-mediated collaborative writing through online tools such as wikis and Google Docs, Storch provides a detailed discussion of the advantages that such activities bring about in terms of peer feedback. These include increased opportunities not only for receiving and providing peer feedback, but also for negotiating the feedback through collaboration (see Nassaji, this volume).

The above insights suggest that teachers need to incorporate peer feedback in their classrooms as much as possible. Furthermore, since peer feedback can also be generated through computer-mediated platforms, teachers should embrace technology for supporting peer feedback inside and outside the classroom. However, to ensure positive outcomes of peer feedback, there is a need to create a supportive environment where errors are welcomed, learners are shown how to provide correction, and teachers are available to offer ongoing assistance. The trust that develops during peer feedback sessions can also impact learners' perceptions of feedback. This can, as shown by Li, also have a positive effect on how much learners learn from feedback.

The Need for Feedback Training to Enhance the Effectiveness of Feedback

One issue that has been stressed in multiple chapters of this book is the role and effects of feedback training. When teachers provide feedback, they need to know what type of feedback is more effective and when. Similarly, when learners receive feedback, whether written or oral, from the teacher or peers, they need to be able to correctly recognize the intention of the feedback. Sato and Tigchelaar & Polio highlight the role of training in oral and written peer feedback, respectively, emphasizing that learners need to be trained on both how to provide and how to interpret peer feedback. Tigchelaar & Polio also note that for written peer feedback, students should receive clear instructions, including perhaps editing guidelines and/or rubrics to provide feedback, although they believe that the facilitative role of these resources still needs to be empirically investigated. In addition, both Sato and Tigchelaar & Polio draw our attention to the need to train learners to develop trust in each other's feedback. When a peer provides corrective feedback, the peer who receives the correction may ignore it or not take it seriously if he or she does not have enough confidence in the feedback. In this case, training to provide and receive feedback might be needed and, as studies show, is very helpful. Li's review of research on the effects of training on teachers' and learners' attitudes and beliefs also shows positive effects for feedback training. It shows, for example, how training can change teachers' and students' negative attitudes about feedback so that it can lead to positive effects.

Insights into the Differences and Similarities between Computer-Mediated and Face-to-Face Interaction

Discussing the differences and similarities between feedback in computer-mediated and face-to-face (FTF) interaction is another significant theme highlighted in this volume. The three chapters devoted to this topic (Storch; Ziegler & Mackey; Heift & Hegelheimer) all support the notion that corrective feedback does occur in computer-mediated contexts. However, they also note that the amount and the effectiveness of feedback may differ in the two settings. Reviewing research on feedback using computer-assisted collaborative writing tools, Storch, for example, concludes that learners are unlikely to focus on form when they write collaboratively unless teachers encourage this practice. Ziegler & Mackey discuss feedback in FTF versus synchronous computer-mediated communication (SCMC) environments and note many similarities in the amount, type, and patterns of interaction in the two contexts. However, they also point to certain differences, some of which relate to the added advantages of SCMC. These include enhanced opportunities for noticing and reviewing input and output, as well as the longer processing time provided due to the text-based nature of the exchanges. Because of increased opportunities for noticing, they argue that SCMC "may be *more* facilitative of noticing certain target forms than FTF interaction" (p. 83). Examining research on the effectiveness of feedback in two CALL environments—Tutorial CALL and AWE, Heift & Hegelheimer argue that, like in FTF interaction, feedback can also be provided in these computer-mediated contexts. However, they draw our attention to the mixed results from empirical research regarding the effectiveness of such tools in promoting appropriate feedback for the development of L2 writing skills.

The Importance of Evaluating the Advice given to Teachers in Light of Research

The importance of examining the validity of the advice often given to teachers on how and when to correct learner errors is another issue emphasized in some of the chapters. Ellis particularly highlights this theme in his chapter on oral feedback. He presents an analysis of the advice given to teachers in mainstream teacher guides about whether, when, who, and how to provide feedback and concludes that while certain suggestions are in line with empirical findings (such as the usefulness of feedback for L2 development, being selective when targeting errors, and using a variety of feedback techniques), others are often based on the experiences of the authors rather than research. Taking a similar approach, Tigchelaar & Polio analyze the advice given to teachers regarding peer feedback in writing and conclude that these recommendations are not always supported by research. They note that while some suggestions given in textbooks, such as the priority of correcting global errors versus local errors or focusing on only a few errors at a time, might make sense theoretically, there is little evidence to ascertain which procedure is more effective. They argue, for example, that there is no evidence to show that focused peer feedback will be more effective than unfocused feedback.

Feedback as a Complex Phenomenon

Almost all chapters in the book take the view that feedback is a complex phenomenon, emphasizing the notion that a wide range of factors mediate the effectiveness of feedback. Ellis reminds us of the role of a number of such factors, including the type of feedback, the context of feedback, the nature of the target structure, and the various individual learner differences. Both Storch and Bitchener have, too, stressed the role of these mediating factors. Storch also adds the impact of careful task design as well as group size and composition as other important factors mediating the effect of peer feedback in collaborative writing tasks. Bitchener, in his chapter on written errors, provides an excellent analysis of why, despite the general beliefs about the effectiveness of written feedback, some learners fail to benefit from it. He concludes that this is because of the complexity of the feedback and the interaction of the feedback effects, with many mediating factors, including both internal (i.e., cognitive and affective individual differences) and external (i.e., learning context and social dynamics of the classroom) factors.

Attention to the complexity of feedback and the various mediating factors, emphasized by the authors in this volume and other places (see, e.g., Nassaji, 2015 for a comprehensive review), is important both pedagogically and empirically. Pedagogically, it helps teachers to lower their expectations when it comes to the effectiveness of feedback and thus, not get disappointed when they do not observe favorable results. Empirically, being mindful of and considering the multitude of factors that can influence feedback effectiveness can help researchers to become more careful when designing their studies and also when interpreting the results.

Other Important Issues

A number of other important topics have also been discussed in this book. These include the timing of feedback, the role of oral negotiation in response to written errors, and the use and effectiveness of non-verbal feedback. Quinn & Nakata provide a comprehensive analysis of the role of feedback timing and how it affects L2 learning. An important highlight of their chapter is that while theoretical distinctions have been made between the effect of immediate and delayed feedback, current research has not yet been able to find a significant difference between the two. Thus, they point out that both immediate and delayed correction can contribute to effective language learning. This point is echoed by Ellis, who notes that there is currently no evidence to suggest that delayed feedback is not effective. Teachers are then encouraged to provide both immediate and delayed feedback or, alternatively, include "hybrid" patterns of the two methods to ensure consistent accuracy focus. Nassaji explores the use and effectiveness of oral negotiation in addressing written errors. He argues that negotiation coupled with corrective feedback (i.e., negotiated feedback) can enhance accuracy of learners' writing. He reviews several studies that have shown negotiation to be helpful because it allows students to understand the feedback and teachers to recognize the reasons for the error. Teachers are, then, encouraged to engage learners in the feedback process and make use of various negotiation methods (e.g., oral conferencing) that facilitate the interpretation and incorporation of the feedback. Finally, Nakatsukasa & Loewen deal with the little-researched area of non-verbal feedback and its role in L2 learning. The authors argue that gestures, a non-verbal behavioral element, can assist classroom interaction in general and augment corrective feedback provision in particular. Based on current evidence, teachers are encouraged to use gestures when providing verbal feedback. This is because gestures can serve as a face-saving device that signals the source of error to individual learners without calling the attention of the whole class to the problem. They can also bring to the forefront the corrective intent of implicit feedback types, thus making them more noticeable. Additionally, the use of gestures can save classroom time and teacher's effort as they do not need to be explained verbally.

Final Remarks and Further Issues to Consider

This collection is a concerted attempt to bring together the leading researchers and thinkers in the area of L2 acquisition to not only share the knowledge accumulated over the years regarding the role of corrective feedback in the field of language teaching and learning, but to also provide practitioners with solid advice for the classroom and to identify areas for researchers to consider further for future research and discussion of corrective feedback. As noted, the book covers a wide range of feedback areas ranging from oral, written, and computer-mediated feedback to teacher and peer feedback, as well as various processes involved in such feedback, including noticing, negotiation, timing, and explicitness. While the book addresses all these topics, this is by no means an exhaustive list of potential areas of inquiry. Many of the issues addressed are also worthy of further investigation and discussion.

For example, while the results available today confirm that, overall, exposure to, and in the case of peer feedback, provision of feedback can facilitate L2 acquisition, more research is needed to understand the role of various learner-related factors and how they can influence the effectiveness of feedback. This is important in light of the research that has repeatedly demonstrated the role of the learner and his or her contributions to the learning process. While the idea of learners' beliefs and preferences for feedback has emerged as important in this volume and elsewhere, there is still much that we do not know. That is, although many studies have surveyed students' and teachers' opinions, it is not clear what the actual relationship between learners' attitudes and the effect of feedback is, and how the role of learners' attitudes and preferences interact with that of other individual learner differences.

Sato, Tigchelaar & Polio, and Storch discussed intensively the issue of peer feedback in oral, written, and computer-mediated contexts and the need for training. However, despite ample research in these areas many questions still remain, some of which include the effects of training on the efficacy of peer feedback, how training works and how it should be provided to maximize its impact, how best to organize collaborative writing sessions to encourage peer feedback, the impact of context, affective factors, social dynamics (as noted by Sato), and the roles learners assume as providers and receivers of correction on the nature of peer feedback and its effectiveness (as noted by Tigchelaar & Polio). To ascertain qualitative differences between teacher and peer feedback, methodologically sound comparisons are also needed.

Further investigations into the role that technology plays in the provision and effectiveness of feedback are also needed. As noted by Ziegler & Mackey, Storch, and Heift & Hegelheimer, who examined the current state of research in different computer-assisted contexts, there is still a great deal that we do not know in each area. Ziegler & Mackey pointed out that current research could put teachers' worries about the use of technology at ease, as it shows the facilitative role of the computer to provide negotiation opportunities similar to those in FTF settings. However, while this is reassuring, how these effects interact with the various mediating factors is not yet clear and therefore, an investigation of these issues and their complexity merits further attention and discussion. Moreover, although research has started to examine the use of a range of technological resources in learning in general, including various web-enhanced resources, mobile-assisted learning and the different audio and video-based platforms, there is much less research on how feedback works in these contexts and how its effects compare with those in traditional contexts, or when these technologies are integrated with various classroom tools.

Last but not least, as reviewed by Nakatsukasa & Loewen, research has demonstrated an important role for non-verbal feedback and, in particular, gestures that accompany verbal feedback. Yet, this is a very under-explored area of research and, as the authors point out, more descriptive and interventional research is needed to understand the role and effectiveness of non-verbal feedback in bringing about language learning. Future studies should focus not only on the different types of non-verbal cues, but also on how learners respond to such feedback. Non-verbal feedback can also be examined in different instructional contexts as well as across different proficiency levels, target languages, and linguistic targets.

In sum, despite the many issues that still need to be explored, we hope that this volume fills in some of the gaps in our knowledge in the field of L2 corrective feedback. We also hope that it serves as impetus for more research and discussion into how corrective feedback is used and contributes to L2 acquisition in various areas and contexts.

References

Ellis, R. (2005). Measuring implicit and explicit knowledge of a second language—a psychometric study. *Studies in Second Language Acquisition*, *27*, 141–172.

Ellis, R., Loewen, S., & Erlam, R. (2006). Implicit and explicit corrective feedback and the acquisition of L2 grammar. *Studies in Second Language Acquisition*, *28*, 339–369.

Gass, S., & Selinker, L. (2008). *Second language acquisition: An introductory course.* (3rd ed.). New York: Taylor & Francis.

Li, S. (2010). The effectiveness of corrective feedback in SLA: A meta-analysis. *Language Learning*, *60*, 309–365.

Lyster, R., & Saito, K. (2010). Oral feedback in classroom SLA: A meta-analysis. *Studies in Second Language Acquisition*, *32*, 265–302.

Mackey, A., & Goo, J. (2007). Interaction research in SLA: A meta-analysis and research synthesis. In A. Mackey (Ed.), *Conversational interaction in second language acquisition: A collection of empirical studies* (pp. 407–452). Oxford: Oxford University Press.

Nassaji, H. (2015). *The interactional feedback dimension in instructed second language learning.* London: Bloomsbury Publishing.

Nassaji, H. (2016). Anniversary article: Interactional feedback in second language teaching and learning: A synthesis and analysis of current research. *Language Teaching Research*, *20*, 535–562.

Russell, J., & Spada, N. (2006). The effectiveness of corrective feedback for second language acquisition: A meta-analysis of the research. In J. Norris & L. Ortega (Eds.), *Synthesizing research on language learning and teaching* (pp. 131–164). Amsterdam: Benjamins.

Tian, J., & Nassaji, H. (2016). Collaborative writing approaches in practice: Effects of peer review and co-writing on Chinese L2 performance. Conference of the American Association for Applied Linguistics (AAAL), Orlando, Florida, USA, April 2016.

LIST OF CONTRIBUTORS

John Bitchener, Auckland University of Technology, New Zealand

Rod Ellis, Curtin University, Australia

Volker Hegelheimer, Iowa State University, USA

Trude Heift, Simon Fraser University, Canada

Eva Kartchava, Carleton University, Canada

Shaofeng Li, The University of Auckland, New Zealand

Shawn Loewen, Michigan State University, USA

Alison Mackey, Georgetown University, USA

Tatsuya Nakata, Kansai University, Japan

Kimi Nakatsukasa, Texas Tech University, USA

Hossein Nassaji, University of Victoria, Canada

Charlene Polio, Michigan State University, USA

Masatoshi Sato, Universidad Andrés Bello, Chile

Neomy Storch, The University of Melbourne, Australia

Magda Tigchelaar, Michigan State University, USA

Paul Gregory Quinn, University of Toronto, Canada

Nicole Ziegler, University of Hawaii at Manoa, USA

INDEX